Socio-Economic
Review 2012

Socio-Economic Review 2012

SHAPING IRELAND'S FUTURE

Securing Economic Development, Social Equity and Sustainability

Seán Healy, Sandra Mallon, Michelle Murphy
and Brigid Reynolds

Social Justice Ireland

Social Justice Ireland
Working to build a just society

ISBN No. 978-1-907501-06-7

First Published April 2012

Published by
Social Justice Ireland
Arena House
Arena Road
Sandyford
Dublin 18

www.socialjustice.ie

Tel: 01- 2130724

e-mail: secretary@socialjustice.ie

TABLE OF CONTENTS

INTRODUCTION

A range of assumptions, many of which have proved to be either inaccurate or simply wrong, have underpinned Irish economic and social policy in recent years. These have resulted in some very damaging decisions being made.

Regrettably, policy is still being based on some of these false assumptions. Until they are successfully challenged the consequence will be yet further damage to Irish society.

Two of the most notable decisions were the provision of a guarantee on all Irish bank deposits and the subsequent absorption of bank debts into the State's sovereign debt.

As a result of these and other related decisions, the Irish economy was in a perilous and ultimately unsustainable position. State expenditure far outstripped revenue and both sovereign and personal debt levels were rapidly rising.

To resolve this situation Ireland's Government negotiated a financial rescue package with the EU/ECB/IMF 'troika'. This, in turn, resulted in a combination of huge cuts in exchequer spending and significant increases in taxation.

The net result of all this is that many of the important components of the basic fabric of Irish society, including the provision of healthcare, education and the range of supports needed by the poor and disadvantaged, are under increasing threat.

It is essential that Ireland learn from these mistakes if yet more damaging decisions are to be avoided in the years immediately ahead. This Socio-Economic Review 2012 seeks to address these issues and to inform the discussion on the way ahead.

Because of the sheer scale of the current crises economic and social recovery will take many years. That will be influenced by international factors, largely outside our control and national factors, many of which we can influence directly. The decisions we make in the months and years ahead, therefore, will play a huge role in determining the speed of our recovery.

Of arguably even greater importance, however, is the way in which these decisions will determine the nature of that recovery. At *Social Justice Ireland* we are convinced

---

that in our quest for recovery we need to address one simple but vital question: Where does Ireland, and Irish society, want to be in 10 years time?

To find the answer to this three further questions need to be asked and answered:
1. What precisely is the current situation and what are the key factors which brought us to this point?
2. What vision of Ireland's future should be guiding policy decision making?
3. What needs to be given priority in order to achieve that vision?

Where are we now and how did we get here?

In the period up to 2000 Ireland achieved well-grounded economic growth and significant improvements in productivity. In about 2001, however, there was a growing belief in construction as the engine of future prosperity. This was accompanied by a false underlying assumption that growth, from whatever source, was good and should be supported. Spurred on by property price inflation, investment in the construction of houses reached reckless proportions.

Vast amounts of money were effectively gambled in Ireland by banks and other financial institutions. The gamblers included financiers from the UK, France, Germany and even further afield, as well as our own domestic ones.

The availability of this finance combined with very poor financial regulation in Ireland, fuelled the property price bubble. When that burst much of the huge potential losses incurred by private banks and bondholders were transferred to the Irish people. *Social Justice Ireland* has always maintained that while Ireland was partly to blame for such losses incurred, and should carry its fair share of the cost, it is profoundly unjust and immoral that Irish people are forced to carry the full burden of this gambling debt.

The situation that produced the current series of crises was exacerbated by major mistakes in many other areas. The tax-base was narrowed and tax equity was not promoted. There was a failure to adequately address infrastructure deficiencies in such areas as broadband, primary health care, water, energy and waste. There was a failure to tackle high local authority charges on business or to promote competition in sheltered sectors of the economy, such as the professions. Nor were the high cost of living and the costs of doing business in Ireland addressed.

Today poverty in Ireland is increasing. Employment is static while unemployment is extremely high. Long-term unemployment has reached record levels. Significant deficiencies are emerging in healthcare and education. Social housing waiting lists have grown dramatically and are not being adequately addressed.

Small and medium enterprises are experiencing great difficulty in obtaining credit for working capital and investment purposes. Much of rural Ireland is struggling for survival despite some modest improvement in the agricultural sector even though agriculture has been growing. Young people are experiencing ever greater difficulties with child poverty and youth unemployment well above the national adult average levels. Inequality is growing rapidly in what already was a deeply unequal society.

Yet at the same time Ireland's ability to address these problems has been hugely inhibited by the sharp rise in sovereign debt, itself due in no small part to the transfer of bank debt to the Exchequer.

Despite achieving all the financial targets set by the EU/ECB/IMF 'troika', Ireland has yet to enjoy the benefits that were supposed to follow, such as increases in employment for example. Indeed, if anything the situation has got worse following the most unfair Budget in years in 2012. This imposed an inequitable burden on the poor and other particularly vulnerable people.

A clear future vision ....

As Ireland struggles to escape from this terrible situation, it needs to adopt a guiding vision that charts the long-term direction and shape of Irish society. *Social Justice Ireland* believes this should be centred on the core values of:
- Human dignity
- Sustainability
- Equality and human rights
- The common good.

These values must be at the core of the vision for a nation in which all men, women and children:
- have what they require to live life with dignity, including sufficient income,
- have access to the services they need and
- are actively included in a genuinely participatory society.

Sustainability is a central motif for economic, social and environmental policy development. It is implicit in this that economic development, social development and environmental protection are complementary and interdependent – three sides of the same reality.

Balanced regional and global development should also be at the heart of the vision of Ireland's future, along with the concepts of equality and a rights-based approach to the organisation of society.

The objective of sustainable international economic competitiveness will be a necessary component, along with the constant policy objective of ensuring that decisions are made in the interests of the common good, rather than to unfairly advantage individuals and vested interests over others.

... and the priorities needed to realise it

What should Ireland's policy priorities be if it is to move from its present situation towards this vision of its future?

Firstly, it is crucial that Ireland's debt burden be reduced. When Ireland took on the debts of the banks it was protecting the financial institutions of Europe. These debts should now be shared in a just manner.

Secondly, Ireland's total tax take should rise but in a manner that makes the tax system fairer and more equitable. Linked to this is a third priority, a reversal in the ratio of tax increases to expenditure cuts in the Government's annual budget. Taxes should increase by €2 for every €1 in expenditure cuts.

Fourthly, Government should launch a major investment programme focused on creating employment. It should prioritise initiatives that strengthen social infrastructure such as the school building programme and the social housing programme. *Social Justice Ireland* is one of a number of groups that have developed proposals on how such an initiative could be funded[1].

Fifthly, a constant focus is needed on ensuring Ireland's economy is internationally competitive. Already unit labour costs have fallen relative to our EU counterparts and this trend looks set to continue in 2012. However, there is far more to competitiveness than just labour costs. As Ireland recovers attention will need to be given to the other key areas of competitiveness, including infrastructure, technological connectivity, public sector efficiency, innovation, education/skills and the cost of doing business and living in Ireland.

---

[1] The most recent version of these are contained in *Policy Briefing* on Budget Choices for 2012

A range of other priorities are identified throughout this review. They range from integrating the tax and welfare systems to focusing economic growth on increasing per capita national income; from ensuring all initiatives taken are sustainable economically, environmentally and socially to tackling inequality; from developing a 'shared responsibility' approach to democratic decision-making, involving all stakeholders, to ensuring that all policy development is evidence-based and outcome-focused. All policy initiatives should be focused on moving Ireland towards its guiding vision and this should be clear and transparent.

Today, Ireland faces substantial challenges and choices as it responds to the current crisis, acknowledges the national policy failures of recent years and plans for the years to come. The future that emerges will result from the decisions taken now. Some of the choices to be made will be difficult, so Ireland needs to achieve a real consensus behind a logical and coherent agenda for shaping Ireland's future. That is what the remainder of this review is all about.

2. IRELAND TODAY – A NARRATIVE

In this chapter we set the scene for this *Socio-Economic Review*. We outline what happened over recent decades to bring Ireland to where it is today, where exactly Ireland finds itself now, where Ireland should go into the future and what it needs to do to get there. The remainder of this review will address key policy areas, present a detailed analysis and highlight the key policy initiatives that are required if Ireland is to emerge from the current series of crises.

Given the space constraints, it has not been possible in this review to address every issue that should be tackled or to present extensive detail in respect of every policy area. Our focus in this chapter is on the broad socio-economic reality that has emerged. We do not accept many of the assumptions that have informed much of the commentary in public and policy-making arenas in recent times. The analysis of the past that seems to have underpinned decision-making is flawed and inaccurate. While some of the policy decisions that have been adopted did move in the right direction, many initiatives since the current crisis emerged:

- have been deeply flawed and are producing growing inequality;
- are built on a vision of the future that is unsustainable;
- fail to put human dignity and the common good at the core of the policy-making process; and
- appear to be guided by a questionable vision of Ireland's future.

The scale and severity of the crises Ireland is currently facing raise obvious questions about how they came about. This chapter provides a commentary on the background to these events. It also addresses questions about how Ireland can recover from these crises and, more importantly, how we can shape a future Ireland that cares for the well-being of its entire people and protects the environment.

The chapter is structured in four parts:

2.1 How Ireland got here: the background to the crises
2.2 Ireland in 2012: the context
2.3 The need for vision: where is Irish society going?
2.4 Priorities for a New Ireland

2.1 How Ireland got here: the background to the crises

There are both international and national roots to the current crises. This understanding has not always been recognised or acknowledged. Both dimensions are significant.

2.1.1 The international background

The origin of the international financial crisis can be traced back to the decisions taken by Ronald Reagan and Margaret Thatcher when they led their respective governments in the early 1980s. The rapid economic growth of the preceding decades had been driven by the reconstruction of Europe and East Asia following devastation by war. In that period the world's economies were regulated through strong state controls over market activity and strong state intervention to minimise inflation and recession, using such instruments as monetary policy, for example. These were accompanied by relatively high wages which were seen as essential to stimulate and maintain demand for what was being produced. It was the era of the Keynesian state.

However, as the reconstruction of Germany and Japan reached completion and the capacity of other economies such as Brazil, Taiwan and South Korea also began to grow a new problem emerged. The world's capacity for economic growth was increasing dramatically, leading to the emerging problem of over-production. As production capacity exceeded demand two kinds of responses were encouraged. The first was the creation of intense competition between the various producers and the second was to stimulate demand for products and services. The former led to a process of driving down costs which in turn led to reduction in many people's wages. This had the effect of increasing inequality, both within countries and between countries. It had the added effect of driving down demand because people could not afford the products being produced which, in turn, led to the erosion of profitability among companies. The huge increases in the price of oil in 1973 and 1979 also had a negative effect on this situation.

Since the late 1970s capitalism has tried three approaches to solving the problem of overproduction – neoliberal restructuring, globalisation and financialisation. The first of these was the route chosen by Reagan and Thatcher. This has been followed by globalisation and in turn by financialisation. The problems produced by financialisation are the immediate cause of the crisis in the financial system in recent years.

Neo-Liberal Restructuring: Reagan and Thatcher agreed that the way to save capitalism was to promote capital accumulation. They did this by:

- removing state constraints on the growth, use and flow of capital and wealth; and
- redistributing income from the poor and middle classes to the rich on the understanding that the rich would then be motivated to reinvest their new profits and reignite economic growth.

This theory proved fallacious. Global growth, which had averaged 3.5 per cent a year in the 1960s and 2.4 per cent in the 1970s, when state interventionist policies were the accepted norm, only averaged 1.4 per cent in the 1980s and 1.1 per cent in the 1990s. This neo-liberal approach redistributed income to the rich and seriously damaged the incomes of the poor and the middle classes. But it failed to increase the demand for products on the scale required because those whose incomes were being reduced did not have the resources to spend and the rich did not reinvest as much of their new gains as had been expected.

Globalisation: The second approach used to try to save capitalism was globalisation. Great effort has gone into the creation of a global market. Countries that had been outside the market or had been non-capitalist were integrated into the global market. This was accompanied by trade liberalisation, the removal of barriers to the mobility of global capital and the abolition of barriers to foreign investment. This was seen as the solution to overproduction. China was the largest non-capitalist country to move into this system. This process, however, exacerbated the problem of overproduction. Growth in world consumption was surpassed by even greater growth in production capacity. Paradoxically, much of the production capacity growth occurred in the countries that had been targeted as sources of potential increased consumption. The profits of major corporations did not grow as fast as they had in preceding decades. In the 1960s the annual profit margin of the Fortune 500 companies was 7.15 per cent. This declined to 5.3 per cent in the 1980s and 2.29 per cent in the 1990s. Profit margins continued to fall in the early years of this century.

Financialisation: To increase profitability the capitalist world turned to 'financialisation'. In the past the financial sector had made the funds of savers available to entrepreneurs to finance their production capacity. Confronted with the continued reality of overproduction, the financial world began to invest surplus funds into the financial world itself and into property. A range of new financial 'products' were created that could be traded. Interest rates were lowered to facilitate this process.

The increasing resources available for purchasing property led to huge price increases. Mortgage companies became more aggressive in marketing their products, lending less prudently and over greater periods of time. They introduced such innovations as 100 per cent loans, 'interest only' mortgages and 40-year term mortgages. House prices soared at the same time as prudential standards fell. Many of these mortgages were enthusiastically advanced to people who could not afford to repay on the agreed terms. These were to become the category of loans known as 'subprime' mortgages.

A further problem was created when these mortgages were included with other assets in new derivative products called 'collateralised debt obligations' (CDOs). These products were sold to banks and financial institutions who were not fully aware of the underlying "quality" of the individual loans within the CDOs. As interest rates rose, however, it became apparent that many of these products were not worth their face value. The total value of these products is not known but has been estimated to run into trillions of dollars. Companies such as Lehman Brothers, Merrill Lynch, Fannie Mae, Freddie Mac and Bear Stearns in the USA and others across the world were simply overwhelmed as their reserves could not meet the losses being faced. Some collapsed and others were bought out. The major international insurance company American International Group (AIG) was brought down by its huge exposure in the area of 'credit default swaps'. These are another type of financial product that make it possible for investors to bet on the possibility that companies will default on repaying loans. Well known investor George Soros has estimated that €45 trillion are invested in a market on these swaps – a market that is totally unregulated. The seriousness of this situation was exacerbated by the broad adoption of a policy of "light-touch" regulation of financial markets.

What we have witnessed over the past few years is the collapse of financialisation – the third strategy to rescue capitalism from its core problem of overproduction.

Socialising debt, austerity and structural reform: As financialisation collapsed it became clear that much of the world's financial system was in a precarious state. Banks, financial institutions and others had taken huge risks in their investing. In many cases these investments were reckless and there was little, if any, possibility of their being recouped. In some countries, such as Ireland, this reality was acknowledged. In other countries, such as Germany and France, there was a total denial of their banks being in any way either at risk or at fault. Institutions such as the European Central Bank were adamant that no bank should be allowed to default. The alternative, they believed, would be serious 'contagion' and the possible failure of other banks. Countries such as Ireland were pressed by some international institutions to 'socialise' their debt by agreeing that government would take full responsibility to repay all the debts accumulated by private banks. In practice this would move responsibility for repaying these debts from the banks to the State. Those who had gambled their money and lost would, as a result, be repaid in full. The repayments would be funded by increased taxes and cuts in public expenditure. In practice, this would mean a programme of austerity would have to be imposed. Poor and vulnerable people and ordinary taxpayers would pay for debts they had no hand, act or part in accumulating. There is something profoundly unjust, unfair and immoral about this approach. Yet it was insisted upon, particularly by German and French political leaders.

Following the socialising of debt and the imposition of "austerity measures" came 'structural reform'. This involves the introduction of measures to ensure that national budgets are balanced and economic growth promoted. Before the crisis of recent years economies were growing and credit was readily available. The middle classes were able to share the benefits of economic growth by borrowing heavily. At the same time poor people could be protected through generous social spending.

Now, however, credit has become extremely difficult to obtain and there is growing pressure on social welfare budgets. Hence the promotion of 'structural reform'. This includes a range of proposals, including a raising of the retirement age, reducing the size of the public sector, privatisation of services and reductions in welfare rates, salaries and other entitlements. A recent 'Shadow Report' on the Europe 2020 Strategy produced by Caritas Europa, which drew on the experiences of 16 EU countries, concluded that austerity measures such as these, which are being pursued in many countries, "will result in the erosion of social services and will lead to the further exclusion of people who already find themselves on the margins of society. This is in direct contradiction to the inclusive growth focus of the Europe 2020 Strategy." (Caritas Europa 2011)

To support this new approach, on January 30, 2012 the European Council finalised a new 'Treaty *on Stability, Coordination and Governance in the Economic and Monetary Union'*. Only the UK and Hungary indicated their unwillingness to sign this treaty. Introducing strict new limits on public debt and budget deficits, it heralds a fundamental change in the way all participating governments will organise their national budgets. It appears there will be intrusive external oversight by the European Commission in the internal affairs of each country, which will have far less discretion over fiscal policy than heretofore as a result. There will also be heavy penalties for any breaches in the terms of the treaty. Each country will have a permanent "debt-brake", a binding "deficit-brake" and an automatic corrective mechanism to reverse any slippage. Countries that do not ratify this treaty will have no further right to aid from the permanent bailout fund of the European Stability Mechanism. This treaty, therefore, will severely restrict all elected governments' room for manoeuvre. The implication is that the rest of Europe is being required to re-model itself in Germany's image. Yet the justification for such a move is far from proven, even in economic terms.

Of great significance is that this treaty, which is seen as the final critical step in the process of socialising debt, prioritising austerity and securing structural reform in the EU, would have made no difference to Ireland in the decade prior to the 2008 crash. It would not have forced either the Government or the banks to do anything differently. So, while presented as a solution to Europe's present predicaments, it fails to address the very causes of these predicaments. It also ignores social context, containing no reference to social policy, poverty, inequality or social inclusion. Its development has also ignored much of the carefully-constructed European democratic architecture which was put in place to maintain balance between competing countries and interests in the EU. We return to this issue in chapter 11.

The structural reform approach overlooks the fact that globalisation in its present form contributes to inequality in the 'developed' world by creating a global labour pool that holds down wages and boosting corporate profits at the same time. This is a recipe for increasing inequality and widening gaps between the poor and the better off in society. The current approach of socialising debt, austerity budgets and structural reform will copper-fasten growing inequality and deepening division. It is just as likely to fail as previous approaches to rescuing capitalism's problems. Much more radical solutions are required if the world's current broken economic development model is to be replaced by one which produces a fairer and more just solution.

These recent experiences give rise to a number of important questions:

- What is needed to ensure effective and efficient regulation at both national and international level of the world's financial systems and how can the current situation of moral hazard be eliminated?
- Recognising that there is a fundamental flaw in capitalism, how is this to be addressed?
- What needs to be done to ensure that economic development and social development are given equal priority in countries across the world?
- How is the environment to be protected and sustainability secured?

2.1.2 The Irish background

Because Ireland is a small open economy, international recession is bound to have implications for this country's economic growth, jobs and trade. Consequently, the severity of the recent international recession would of itself have had serious implications for Ireland and ensured that this country experienced some degree of recession. However, the recession experienced since 2008 has been far more severe and protracted than it might have been otherwise due to an array of national policies and decisions over recent decades. Ireland may have been unfortunate to have experienced national and international recession at the same time but it was headed for a substantial economic slowdown notwithstanding international developments.

By the mid-1970s Ireland was well positioned for strong economic growth. It had just joined the European Union, was pursuing well-focused industrial policies, had low corporate tax rates, was beginning to reap the benefits of strong investment in education since the mid-1960s, had a favourable geographic location for European markets and an English speaking labour force. However, poor fiscal and monetary policy between 1977 and 1986 failed to provide the stability required to realise this potential. . Eventually, Government did begin to pursue appropriate policies and from 1987 onwards Social Partnership provided the framework to secure the stability required.

Since the late 1980s Ireland's population changed its relationship to employment. This change provided a stimulus to economic growth in three ways.[2]

---

[2] We explore these trends in more detail in chapter 5 of this review.

Firstly, the proportion of Ireland's population that was employed converged with the levels experienced elsewhere in Europe and the OECD. In 1989 only 31 per cent of Ireland's population was in employment. This proportion climbed to over 45 per cent by the end of the following decade. Secondly, the proportion of the labour force that was employed grew dramatically in the decade and a half from the early 1990s while the proportion unemployed fell dramatically after a period of jobless growth in the early 1990s. Thirdly, the labour force itself grew dramatically, increasing by over 900,000 during the 1990s. A key change in all of this was the increase in female participation in the labour force. Between 1990 and 2000 the number of females in the Irish labour force increased by almost 250,000 and the female labour force participation rate rose from 44 per cent to 56 per cent (OECD Labour Force Database, 2010).

This labour force driven growth was complemented by a very strong growth in productivity, as measured by average output, during the 1990s. Productivity growth helped Ireland become richer. However, as Ireland grew richer its productivity levels drew closer to those of world-leading countries and the underlying pace of such growth slowed. Subsequent growth in the later years of the 'Celtic Tiger' was driven by a combination of population growth and reckless over-investment in a property rather than productivity or an increased employment ratio. This population growth, and the consequent increase in labour supply and economic activity, was supported by a huge increase in immigration and it was unlikely that it would be sustainable over a long period. By 2000/2001 Ireland had lost focus on productivity growth as the key to improving living standards and focussed simply on economic growth.

Two false conclusions

In effect, Ireland had reached two false conclusions – one with regard to growth and the other to taxation. Government became fixated with economic growth. It became convinced that economic growth was good in itself and that the higher the rate of economic growth, therefore, the better it would be for Ireland. It followed that whatever supported economic growth was to be facilitated and whatever restricted economic growth was to be resisted. Consequently, Ireland followed a very questionable pathway, putting considerable faith in the ability of a highly incentivised property and construction sector to maintain the high growth levels enjoyed in previous years.

For several years, commencing in 2000/2001, growth in housing activity masked Ireland's deteriorating 'fundamentals'.[3] As Ireland's per-capita income grew, so too

---

[3] We examine Housing and Accommodation issues in more detail in chapter 7 of this review.

did the demand for housing. As we detail in chapter 7 of this review, Ireland's housing construction rose from 19,000 completions in 1990 to a peak of over 93,000 completions in 2006. While there were 48,413 households on local authority waiting lists for social housing in 2002, this level of housing construction was unsustainable. Most of the new construction was for private housing. Of the 57,695 houses completed in 2002, 51,932 were private housing. Of the 93,419 completed in 2006, 88,211 were private housing. Overall, the number of houses in Ireland rose from 1.2 million homes in 1991 to 1.4 million in 2000 and then exploded to 1.9 million in 2008. By 2007, construction accounted for 13.3 per cent of all employment, the highest share in the OECD (OECD, 2010).

This level of construction was encouraged and supported by many factors. Three key ones were:

- Very low interest rates. These were dictated by the large EU economies which, unlike Ireland, were experiencing very low growth rates. Interest rates were reduced to very low levels to encourage investment in those countries. The same rates applied in Ireland, however, which was at the opposite end of the economic cycle.
- Large tax incentives for construction provided by the Irish Government.
- Unsustainable house price inflation and profiteering.

The results of this housing boom were catastrophic for Ireland.

During this period Ireland had reached a second false conclusion, this time on taxation.[4] It had come to believe that low taxation was good in itself, and that reducing tax rates would lead inevitably to an increase in tax-take. The theory was that "giving people back their own money", through reducing taxes, was far better than investing that money in developing and improving infrastructure and services. The result of these beliefs was that by the end of the Celtic Tiger years Ireland had one of the lowest total tax-takes in the EU. At the same time, while there had been some improvements in areas such as housing, public transport and social welfare during those years, many aspects of Ireland's infrastructure and social services remained far below EU-average levels. A strong assumption persisted that infrastructure and social services could be improved to EU-average levels at the same time as having one of the lowest total tax-takes in the EU. This belief endured despite the very strong efforts of some policy analysts to convince Government and policy-makers otherwise.

---

[4] We review these issues in greater detail in chapter 4 of this review.

By 2007 Ireland had 'run out of road', with no scope for any further substantial improvement in the population/labour force/employment situation. The labour market had become over-heated and was relying on inward migration to sustain supply. At the same time, productivity was weakening, the tax-base was narrowing and the economy and the total tax-take were over-reliant on a housing construction and property sector that had already over-expanded. Even with a serious slowdown inevitable, the General Election of 2007 was still ought on the generally accepted assumption that growth would average 4.5 per cent per year over the 2007-2012 period. All political parties, with just one exception, drew up their manifestos on this basis. Those who challenged this assumption of continued growth were rejected, often with derision.

Eight false assumptions
Overall, Ireland's policy-making during this period was underpinned by a series of false assumptions and conclusions. These included:

- Economic growth was good in itself and the higher the rate of economic growth the better it would be for Ireland.
- Everyone would enjoy the benefits of economic growth, which would trickle down automatically.
- Infrastructure and social services at an EU-average level could be delivered with one of the lowest total tax-takes in the EU.
- The growing inequality and the widening gaps between the better-off and the poor that followed from this approach to policy-development were not important because everyone was gaining something.
- Low taxation was good.
- Reducing tax rates would lead inevitably to an increase in tax-take.
- "Giving people back their own money", through reducing taxes, was far better than investing that money in developing and improving infrastructure and services. The sum of Irish people's individual decisions would produce far better results for Ireland than allowing Government to decide how best to use the money.
- Ireland had a great deal to teach the rest of the world, particularly about how it could reach full employment, generate huge economic growth and provide for all the society's needs while having one of the lowest total tax-takes in the Western world.

Eight policy failures
Arising from this series of false policy conclusions and false assumptions, there were many resulting policy failures. Among these were:

- Failure to take action to broaden the tax base by, for example:
  - introducing a property tax;
  - removing existing tax exemptions which have no demonstrated benefit-cost advantage;
  - introducing user service charges.
- Failure to promote tax equity by, for example, introducing Refundable Tax Credits.
- Failure to overcome infrastructure deficiencies, such as broadband, public transport, primary health care, water, energy and waste.
- Failure to adequately address high energy costs.
- Failure to address high local authority charges on business.
- Failure to promote competition in sheltered sectors of the economy, such as professions.
- Failure to appropriately regulate the banking and financial services sector.
- Failure to manage the growth of personnel numbers in the public service.

2.2 Ireland in 2012: the context

In this section we analyse where Ireland stands today. We assess various dimensions of the current crisis and subsequently explore the present context in economic, social, political and cultural terms.

2.2.1 Ireland's five-part crisis

Today, Ireland remains in crisis. At the outset of this period the National Economic and Social Council (NESC, 2009) summarised this crisis as having five closely related dimensions, summarised below.

A banking crisis in which the taxpayer is taking responsibility for rescuing all the major banks and financial institutions from the consequences of the dishonesty and incompetence of individuals and institutions which were in charge of running and regulating our financial system. As NESC has pointed out (2009: *x*), the policy response to the banking crisis must also address:

- The need to ensure that recent policy measures provide protection to the increasing number of households with mortgage arrears;
- The need to ensure that recent government action prompts a renewed flow of credit to businesses in Ireland;

- The need to convince Irish society as a whole, and particularly groups making visible sacrifices, that those who led Irish financial institutions into their current reliance on the state, and who were major beneficiaries of the boom, are being held accountable and are bearing their share of the adjustment burden;
- The need to persuade our EU partners, other international institutions and participants in the global financial market that a new regulatory regime and governance culture is being created in Ireland.

Social Justice Ireland proposes a fifth policy response to the four identified by NESC:

- The need to ensure those international institutions (e.g. foreign banks and financial institutions, bond holders etc.) who contributed to causing the problems in Ireland take their share of the responsibility and contribute to its solution.

A Public Finance Crisis because we are borrowing far more than we are collecting in taxes. To bring Ireland back into line with our EU/IMF commitments, major budgetary adjustments have been required and will be required over the next few years. We discuss the nature of these changes later in this chapter. However, as the NESC has noted, these fiscal adjustments need to be considered and implemented not just with regard to how they address the gap between taxes and spending but also with regard to the impact these adjustments may have on the other dimensions of Ireland's challenges: the economic crisis, the social crisis and the country's reputation (2009: x).

An Economic Crisis because we have lost many jobs and, throughout much of the last decade, fundamentally undermined our competitiveness. The speed, depth and nature of Ireland's economic decline demands a policy response which collectively addresses what NESC describes as "a difficult set of overlapping and competing objectives and factors" (NESC: xi). These include:

- the employment situation - particularly the threat of further unemployment and, in particular, large levels of long-term unemployment;
- Ireland's loss of competitiveness over the past decade;
- the pressures on certain enterprises created by the devaluation of sterling;
- the evolution of prices, including policy instruments that influence input costs to business, professional fees and rents;
- the level of domestic demand;
- the state of the public finances, which are directly affected by public sector pay developments and indirectly influenced by wider unemployment, economic and income developments;

- the burden of mortgage debt, particularly on those who become unemployed; and social solidarity, encompassing the whole of Irish society, not just those whose incomes are determined through collective bargaining. The nature of this economic crisis is described in greater detail later in this section.

A Social Crisis because our social services and social infrastructure are being eroded, unemployment has dramatically increased, incomes are falling, debt levels are rising and the prospect of a sustained period of high long-term unemployment levels now seems unavoidable. While the economic crisis, and in particular the collapse of private construction, provides some opportunities to address the social housing deficit (see chapter 7), policy makers need to be keenly aware that their responses to the other crises should not further undermine the vulnerable in Irish society and the social services and infrastructure on which they depend. The nature of this social crisis as described in greater detail later in this chapter.

A Reputational Crisis because our reputation around the world has been damaged for several reasons (NESC, 2009: *xii*):
- The perception that, along with a number of other countries, Ireland has,, had a lax and ineffective system of regulation of the financial sector;
- The perception that Ireland's response to the banking crisis may not include sufficient change in governance and personnel;
- The uncertainty about Ireland's willingness to participate in major developments in the EU. This crisis is compounded by the perception that Ireland's public finances are vulnerable to default because of a combination of low growth, contingent liabilities to the banking system and the increasing ratio of debt to GDP.

2.2.2 The economic context
The dramatic and sudden turnaround in Ireland's economic experiences since 2007 needs to be considered in the context of its economic growth and expansion throughout the last decade. Clearly, as indicated earlier, there have been a number of major policy failures behind some of this growth – for example, the excessive fuelling of the construction industry and an unregulated banking sector. However, as table 2.1 shows, Ireland's Gross Domestic Product (GDP) and Gross National Income (GNI) have increased significantly since 1997.[5] The final column of the

---

[5] GDP is calculated as the value of all economic activity that occurs in Ireland. GNI is calculated as GDP minus the net outflow of income from Ireland (mainly involving foreign multinationals repatriating profits), minus EU taxes and plus EU subsidies (for further information see CSO, 2008:76).

table tracks the per-capita value of GNI over the last decade. In the early years of that decade it increased in real-terms (after taking account of price changes) by over 30 per cent.[6] However, the current economic slowdown has brought per capita income levels back below the levels experienced in the early years of this century.

Table 2.1: Ireland's National Income, 1997-2010			
Year	GDP (€b)	GNI (€b)	GNI per capita €*
1997	68.6	61.4 n/a	
1998	79.3	70.4	n/a
1999	91.4	78.8	n/a
2000	105.9	1.4	n/a
2001	118.1	100.0	30,488
2002	131.3	109.2	30,720
2003	141.0	120.7	31,711
2004	150.6	129.1	32,470
2005	163.5	141.0	33,433
2006	178.3	156.3	34,676
2007	189.9	164.6	35,061
2008	180.0	156.0	33,475
2009	160.6	133.6	29,958
2010	156.0	129.3	29,959

Source: CSO, 2011:17 and CSO online database
Note: * Gross National Income per capita at constant 2009 prices;

The speed and severity of Ireland's economic decline is also visible in chart 2.1. It shows the strength of economic growth between 1995 and 2006 (a period in which most developed world countries experienced 2-3 per cent growth per annum) and the rapid decrease between 2007 and 2010. While the nature, timing and pace of the recovery remain unclear, all agree that there is likely to be a return to small positive annual GDP growth rates from 2011.

---

[6] We examine the distribution of this income, which was far from even, in chapter 3.

Chart 2.1: Ireland's GDP Growth, 1995-2015 (%)

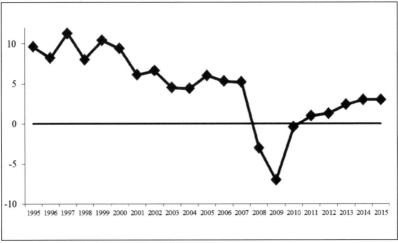

Source: OECD Factbook 2008, CSO (2011) and Department of Finance (2012).

The sharp decrease in the rate of house building after 2007 was a significant component in the decline in GDP growth rates. Between 1995 and 2006 the number of units completed soared from just 30,000 units in 1995 to a peak of 93,419. But completions plummeted to 23,000 units in 2006 and approximately 10,480 units in 2011 (Department of Environment, Heritage and Local Government, 2009; AIB, 2011). The property bubble also produced over-priced housing, the product of foolish lending irrational borrowing and unrealistic profit expectations.[7] The legacy of this policy disaster was empty housing units, many of them in inappropriate locations, negative equity and high numbers of unemployed construction workers.

Similarly, the scale of the international recession had an impact on the level of exports, which fell by almost 3 per cent in 2009. During that period as production declined both the number of workers and hours worked per worker also fell. Exports have subsequently increased, growing by 6 per cent in 2010 and 4.6 per cent in 2011.

---

[7] See Drudy and Collins (2011) who discuss this further.

The combined effect of these changes on the public finances has been dramatic.. Over the decade to 2008 the state had become heavily dependent on tax revenue derived from construction related activities, including stamp duty, building related VAT, PRSI and income taxes. Table 2.2 shows that as the economy turned these revenues rapidly declined. Overall, total tax receipts fell from over €59 billion in 2007 to €43.3 billion in 2010.[8] Comparative figures for 2011 were not available when this review was prepared. However, the Government's income from taxation rose by about 8% in 2011 due to the introduction of the Universal Social Charge and receipts from the temporary levy on private pension funds introduced during 2011. (Department of Finance, 2011: D6)

Table 2.2: The changing nature of Ireland's tax revenue (€m)				
	2007	2008	2009	2010
Taxes on income and wealth				
Income tax (including sur tax)	13563	13148	11684	11237
Corporation tax	6393	5071	3889	3944
Motor tax - Estimated portion paid by households etc.	526	583	582	563
Other taxes (	5	6	5	8
Fees under the Petroleum and Minerals Development Acts (	5	10	2	3
Training and Employment Levy	411	414	373	309
Social Insurance contribution	9053	9259	8924	8709
Total taxes on income and wealth	**29957**	**28491**	**25458**	**24773**
Taxes on capital				
Capital gains tax	3097	1424	545	345
Capital acquisitions tax	391	343	256	237
Total taxes on capital	**3488**	**1767**	**801**	**582**
Taxes on expenditure				
Custom duties (€ml)	30	21	11	23
Excise duties including VRT	5993	5547	4909	4820
Value added tax	14057	12842	10175	9609

---

[8] In these calculations we have included items such as social insurance contributions that do not appear in the usual Budget calculations on taxation.

Rates	1267	1353	1467	1413
Motor tax - Estimated portion paid				
by businesses	431	477	476	461
Stamps (excluding fee stamps)	3244	1763	1003	962
Other fees	171	219	201	259
Total taxes on expenditure	**25193**	**22223**	**18243**	**17547**
EU Taxes	**519**	**484**	**359**	**400**
Total Taxation (i.e. sum of the rows				
in bold above)	**59157**	**52964**	**44861**	**43301**

Source: CSO Statistical Data Bank, National Income and Expenditure annual results, various years, selected from table N1022:T22. Details on Taxation by Statistical Indicator and Year

In the three-year period 2007-2010 taxes on capital fell by 83 per cent, on expenditure by 30 per cent and on income and wealth by 17 per cent. In money terms the biggest fall was €7.6bn in expenditure taxes compared to a fall of €5.2bn on taxes on income and wealth and €2.9bn on capital taxes.

The state continues to invest in infrastructure and other capital projects and, as in previous years, has borrowed money to make these investments. However, following the collapse in taxation revenues, since 2008 the state has been borrowing to pay its day-to-day (current account) costs. While this might be acceptable during a 'normal' down-turn, it is unsustainable in the medium to longer term. In 2009 the government borrowed over €12 billion to meet its day-to-day costs and a further €13 billion for capital investment. The latter includes contributions to fund the rescue of Anglo Irish Bank and to bail out the major banks via investment contributions from the national pensions reserve fund.

By November 2010 the scale of the exchequer deficit and the on-going, and escalating, bank bailout costs forced the state to turn to outside agencies for economic support. An agreement was reached with the IMF, the EU and the European Central Bank, to secure €85 billion in funding over the period 2010-2013. The bailout funds comprise €50 billion to facilitate state borrowing and refinancing over this period and up to €35 billion to rescue the banking system. In return for the right to borrow this money, the Irish Government signed a

Memorandum of Understanding which set out a severe austerity programme over the period to 2014.[9]

Budget 2011 commenced this programme with tax increases and spending cuts totalling €6 billion in 2011. Further tax increases and spending cuts totalling €3.8 billion were included in Budget 2012. Budget 2012 also projected that in 2012 the Government will need to borrow over €11.2 billion to meet its day-to-day costs and €7.7 billion for capital purposes. This money is being drawn down from the bailout funds. Some of this borrowing will be used to service the banking debt incurred by the State as part of the Bank Guarantee and the Bailout Agreement.

But this is not the whole story. Budget 2012 marked the seventh fiscal adjustment to the Irish economy since the beginning of the current economic crisis in 2008. Following that Budget's increases to taxes and decreases in public expenditure, the total adjustment to date has risen to almost €24.5 billion - equivalent to 15% of GDP which has been directly removed by government from the economy. Of course, the knock-on implications of these adjustments have removed additional economic activity from the economy explaining the large overall drop in GDP since 2007.

Table 2.3 shows the cumulative impact of tax increases and expenditure cuts since the adjustment process began in July 2008. It also shows what is planned to the end of 2015. Government has indicated that it intends to remove a further €8.6 billion from the economy over three Budgets from 2013-2015. If these plans are implemented, the overall sum of the adjustments from 2008-2015 will total €33 billion - equivalent to 18% of the GDP forecast for 2015.

The implications of these large and harsh adjustments is visible in the continued extension of the adjustment plan, the sustained increases in unemployment and the lack of confidence domestically and internationally in the Irish economy's recovery.
   As spending cuts and tax increases take effect, households are spending less, investment is falling and it is only export growth (entirely driven by non-domestic demand factors) that is pulling the economy out of recession.

---

[9] The memorandum has subsequently been revised and extended to 2015 by the Government elected in 2011.

Table 2.3 Budgetary Adjustments 2008-2015 (€m)				
Adjustment Description	**Taxation** ↑	**Expenditure** ↓	**Total**	**Running Total**
Adjustment July 2008		€1,000	€1,000	**€1,000**
Budget 2009	€1,215	€747	€1,962	**€2,962**
Adjustments Feb/March 2009		€2,090	€2,090	**€5,052**
Supplementary Budget 2009	€3,621	€1,941	€5,562	**€10,614**
Budget 2010	€23	€4,051	€4,074	**€14,688**
Budget 2011	€1,409	€4,590	€5,999	**€20,687**
Budget 2012	€1,600	€2,200	€3,800	**€24,487**
Budget 2013★	€1,250	€2,250	€3,500	**€27,987**
Budget 2014★	€1,100	€2,000	€3,100	**€31,087**
Budget 2015★	€700	€1,300	€2,000	**€33,087**
Total of Adjustments	**€10,918**	**€22,169**		
% Division of Adjustments	**33.0%**	**67.0%**		

Note: ★ indicates projected adjustment from Medium Term Fiscal Review Nov. 2011

An obvious question arises regarding the sustainability of this policy approach. *Social Justice Ireland* believes that Government needs to adopt policies to stimulate the economy rather than continually run it down. Domestic demand should be given a chance to recover through policies which promote government or European Investment Bank led investment while further building domestic economic confidence through addressing the unemployment crisis via initiatives such as our Part Time Job Opportunities proposal to take 100,000 people off the dole queues (outlined in chapter 5).

Where further adjustments have to be made in the period to 2015 there is a clear need to alter the balance of adjustments towards additional taxation measures and away from reductions in public sector expenditure which is now impacting heavily on basis public service provision.

Ireland's General Government Balance (GGB) for 2012 as a percentage of GDP (the key indicator used by the European Central Bank to judge fiscal policy control) will be 8.6 per cent, down from 10.1 per cent in 2011. These figures are well above the 3 per cent limit set in the EU *Stability and Growth Pact*. The objective of Government economic, or fiscal, policy, as agreed with the EU and IMF, is to reduce the GGB deficit indicator to 3 per cent by 2015. Table 2.4 outlines the pathway signalled by the outgoing Government to achieve this; a pathway that has been endorsed by the EU and IMF.

Table 2.4: Plan to reduce the General Government Balance, 2011-2015					
	2011	**2012**	**2013**	**2014**	**2015**
GGB €m	-15,615	-13,650	-12,385	-8,505	-5,215
GGB as % GDP	-10.1	-8.6	-7.5	-5.0	-2.9

Source: Calculated from Department of Finance, Budget 2012: D18.

Achieving these targets will be very challenging given the continuing decline in domestic demand and the challenges being faced at international level by Ireland's main trading partners. The Government's projections also assume that the on-going banking crisis does not require the exchequer to further invest in the banks and that the excessive budgetary cuts in Budget 2011 and 2012 do not damage the economy so badly that it spirals further into recession, a risk we highlighted in our *Analysis and Critique of Budget 2012* (Social Justice Ireland, 2011). Given that the Government is projecting a fall in net employment in 2012 and that the growth target is unlikely to be attained, it is difficult to see how the conditions of the EU/IMF/ECB deal can be maintained in their current form. Some serious adjustment to the terms of the agreement is needed for Ireland to reach the 3 per cent of GDP threshold.

Table 2.5 presents a summary of projections for Ireland over the years 2012-2015. Most of this data is derived from the Department of Finance's Budget 2012 documentation and, where appropriate, we highlight those projections we consider unreliable given the economic and banking events that have occurred since the Budget was presented in December 2011.

Table 2.5: Ireland's Economic Position, 2012-2015

National Income

GDP in 2012 (€m)#	€159,125
GNP in 2012 (€m) #	€128,800
GDP growth in 2012#	1.3%
GNP growth in 2012#	0.7%
GDP growth 2012-2015 (average) #	2.4% per annum
GNP growth 2012-2015 (average) #	1.8% per annum

Exchequer Budgetary Position

Current Budget Balance, 2012 (€m)##	- €11,180
Net Capital Investment, 2012 (€m)	€9,495
Capital Investment paid from current resources, 2012 (€m)	Zero
Capital Investment paid from borrowing, 2012 (€m)	All
Exchequer Borrowing, 2012 (€m)	€18,860
General Government Balance (%GDP)	€13,650 (8.6%)
Current Budget Balance 2013 (€m)	- €8,660
Current Budget Balance 2014 (€m)	- €5,000
Net Capital Investment 2012-2015 (€m)	€7,700 (average)
Exchequer Borrowing 2012-2015 (€m)	€12,500 (average)
National Debt 2012 % GDP★	115%
National Debt 2015 % GDP★	115%

Inflation and the Labour Market

HICP inflation in 2012	1.8%
HICP inflation 2012-2015 (average)	1.7% per annum
Unemployment rate in 2012##	14.1%
Employment growth in 2012	-0.2%
Unemployment rate 2012-2015 (average)##	13%
Employment growth 2012-2015 (average)	0.85%

Source: Department of Finance, Budget 2012 (various tables) and separate calculations where indicated.

Notes: ★ Adjusted upwards to account for subsequent CSO revisions to GDP and borrowing to fund capital injections into the banks.
This is a Department of Finance Budget 2012 estimate and the actual number is likely to be smaller.
This is a Department of Finance Budget 2012 estimate and the actual number is likely to be larger.

A further insight into Ireland's economic standing is presented in table 2.6. Using figures highlighted in chapter 4 it outlines where Ireland stands relative to our fellow EU members on the issue of total taxation. Ireland is near the bottom of the rankings.

Table 2.6: Total tax revenue as a % of GDP, for EU-27 Countries in 2009

Country	% of GDP	+/- from average	Country	% of GDP	+/- from average
Denmark	48.1	+12.3	United Kingdom	34.9	-0.9
Sweden	46.9	+11.1	Czech Rep	34.5	-1.3
Belgium	43.5	+7.7	**Ireland GNP**	**34.3**	**-1.5**
Italy	43.1	+7.3	Malta	34.2	-1.6
Finland	43.1	+7.3	Poland	31.8	-4.0
Austria	42.7	+6.9	Portugal	31.0	-4.8
France	41.6	+5.8	Spain	30.4	-5.4
Germany	39.7	+3.9	Greece	30.3	-5.5
Hungary	39.5	+3.7	Lithuania	29.3	-6.5
Netherlands	38.2	+2.4	Bulgaria	28.9	-6.9
Slovenia	37.6	+1.8	Slovakia	28.8	-7.0
Luxembourg	37.1	+1.3	**Ireland GDP**	**28.2**	**-7.6**
Estonia	35.9	+0.1	Romania	27.0	-8.8
Cyprus	35.1	-0.7	Latvia	26.6	-9.2

Source: Eurostat (2011:50) and CSO National Income and Expenditure Accounts (2011:3)

Notes: All data is for 2009. EU-27 average is 35.8 per cent.

Of the EU-27 states, the highest tax ratios can be found in Denmark, Sweden, Belgium, Italy, Finland and Austria while the lowest appear in Latvia, Romania, Slovakia, Bulgaria, Lithuania and Ireland. Overall, Ireland possesses the third lowest tax-take at 28.2 per cent, some 7.6 per cent below the EU average. Furthermore, Ireland's overall tax take has continued to fall over the past few years with the 2009 figure representing the lowest tax-take since Eurostat began compiling records in 1995 (see chart 4.1 in chapter 4). The increase in the overall level of taxation between 2002 and 2006 can be explained by short-term increases in construction related taxation sources (in particular stamp duty and construction related VAT) rather than any underlying structural increase in taxation levels.

In the context of the figures in Table 2.6 the question needs to be asked: if we expect our economic and social infrastructure to catch up to that in the rest of Europe, how can we do this while simultaneously gathering less taxation income than it takes to run the infrastructure already in place in most of those other European countries? In reality, we will never bridge the social and economic infrastructure gaps unless we gather a larger share of our national income and invest it in building a fairer and more successful Ireland.

Social Justice Ireland believes that Ireland should increase its total tax-take to 34.9% of GDP (which would still keep Ireland as a low-tax economy as defined by Eurostat). We also believe that it will be necessary to provide additional tax revenue to cover the annual cost of servicing the banking element of Ireland's debt. A rough estimate of what the latter might require would be €2.5b extra per annum. (In making this calculation we are assuming an Anglo promissory note restructuring and we calculate the cost of servicing €70b of bank debt at an average of 3.5 per cent per annum).

Increasing the tax take to 34.9 per cent of GDP is certainly feasible and unlikely to have any significant negative impact on the economy in the long term. This proposal is explored in detail in chapter 4.

The obvious question arising from this data is which countries we should choose to benchmark against? Which countries do we wish to compare ourselves with, or to emulate, in terms of public services, pensions, social welfare payments and private and public wage rates? Are Latvia, Lithuania, Romania, Slovakia and Bulgaria to be our new benchmark countries?

2.2.3 The Social Context
Ireland's social context is addressed throughout this review. This section provides a brief overview.

The ramifications for Ireland's citizens of the recent economic turmoil have been severe. Most notably, one of the great achievements of recent years has been reversed in the space of just a few months. Unemployment has returned as a widespread phenomenon.[10] In late 2006, 90,300 people were recorded as unemployed by the CSO's quarterly national household survey (QNHS),. This figure represented 4.2

---

[10] The data cited in this section comes from the CSO's QNHS, the official measure of employment and unemployment. We analyse the live register figures in Chapter 5.

per cent of the labour force. Five years later, the number of people unemployed had more than tripled to 314,000, equal to approximately 14.2 per cent of the labour force. In a relatively short period Ireland returned to levels of unemployment not experienced since the mid-1980s. Behind each of these figures are people and families — the society-wide impact of these increases cannot be over-estimated.

The scale of this unemployment crisis, and the simultaneous collapse in employment opportunities, has resulted in many people becoming stranded in unemployment. Consequently long-term unemployment, defined as those unemployed for more than one year, has rapidly increased. By late 2011, 177,200 people were recorded as long-term unemployed, a rate equal to 8.4 per cent of the entire labour force, and the figure looks set to climb towards 200,000 during 2012. It is of considerable concern that a large proportion of the newly long-term unemployed possess skills for which there is likely to be limited demand over the next few years. In particular, large numbers of males who formerly worked in the construction sector have joined this group and they will require significant assistance and retraining before many of them can return to employment.[11]

Another of the social ghosts of the 1980s and 1990s has also returned – emigration. The preliminary estimates from the CSO Population and Migration Estimates, April 2011 suggest that net migration is running at over 34,000 a year in 2010 and 2011. (CSO, 2011: 2) Preliminary estimates suggest total emigration in 2011 was over 76,000 of which more than 40,000 were Irish - a sharp increase from 27,700 to 40,200 over the 12 months to April 2011. The ESRI in its Quarterly Economic Commentary Outward states that this level of emigration is expected to reduce the total numbers unemployed. (ESRI: 2012: 28) As Ireland's employment is not expected to grow until domestic demand increases substantially and the international economy recovers, it is expected that emigration will remain at these high levels with a large outflow of young and skilled Irish-born people for a number of years to come.

The collapse in tax revenues has forced the government into six challenging budgets and a series of spending cutbacks in 2008, twice in 2009, 2010, 2011 and in 2012. Throughout this review we highlight and critique many of the cuts in social spending, including the unacceptable cut in many social welfare payments delivered in the 2010 and 2011 Budgets.

---

[11] We analyse the issues of unemployment, employment and work in Chapter 5.

Cuts in both national and local social services and support initiatives are being made at a particularly difficult time, just when demand for these services is rising. All too often decisions made in times of crisis focus on short-term gains and savings with no regard for their potentially negative long-term consequences. Cutting funding for particular disability services, for example, may save money in the short term but can also imprison people with a disability in their own homes and result in increased acute hospital costs subsequently. In reality, many decisions made during the current series of crises are set to have such negative effects.

Many public services are provided by community and voluntary organisations. These have come under huge pressure in recent years as the recession has forced an ever-growing number of people to seek their help on a wide range of fronts. But, just at the very moment when the demand for their services increased, Government has reduced the funding available to many of these organisations. It is noticeable that the scale of cutbacks by Government in the funding for provision of public services by the community and voluntary sector is proportionately much larger than for public services provided directly by the public sector. There has been no adequate explanation for this inequitable disparity.

The impact of these cuts and the threats of further similar ones continue to undermine the social structures within Irish society and their ability to cope in the present circumstances.

The collective implications of these actions were well summarised by Magdalena Sepulveda, the UN independent expert on Human Rights and Extreme Poverty, who visited Ireland following an invitation from Government in January 2011.[12] She stated in her report that "the current economic and financial crisis poses a disproportionate threat to those who did not benefit much from the Irish economic boom and is a serious threat to the milestones achieved in social protection". This is further reflected in the experience of the Society of St Vincent de Paul which reported that throughout the last few years calls for its assistance dramatically increased. Many of these came from 'first-timers' struggling to cope with the impact of the current crisis. In some cases very vulnerable people have resorted to money-lenders as a last resort, making their long-term situation worse in the process.

The most recent study on poverty produced by the CSO (CSO, 2011) shows there was an increase in poverty and in income inequality between 2009 and 2010. It

---

[12] Social Justice Ireland held a detailed meeting with the UN delegation in January 2011.

found that 15.8 per cent of the population are at risk of poverty – up from 14.1 per cent the previous year. The disposable income of the highest income quintile was 5.5 times the income of those in the lowest income quintile – up from 4.3 times the year earlier. This reverses the downward trends evident since 2005.

A special CSO Quarterly National Household Survey module on the impacts of the recession on households was published in February 2012 and showed that 0 per cent of households headed by a person who is unemployed had borrowed money from family or friends to pay for basic goods and services. In addition, half of such households had missed paying household bills and more than one quarter had missed loan repayments. Two thirds of households headed by a person with a job and two thirds of those headed by an unemployed person had reduced the amount they saved. However, households headed by an unemployed person were far more likely to have spent some or all of their savings. Almost 64 per cent of these households had spent savings to pay for basic goods and services in the two years prior to the survey, compared with 46 per cent of households headed by a person who was employed.

In addition to the economic and social problems discussed above, an alarming number of people, of all ages, have literacy difficulties. We still have schools with leaking roofs and 'temporary' portacabins and a two-tier health system through which the availability of many services is related to income rather than need. Clearly, Ireland in 2012 is in social crisis.

2.2.4 The political context

The 2011 General Election produced a new government with a large majority and a mandate to address the broad economic and social problems outlined above. The *Programme for Government* covers a wide range of issues at different levels and we have published a review of the document on our website (www.socialjustice.ie). The programme contains very welcome commitments on some issues but is exceptionally vague on how it proposes to address others. It contains very few numbers or target dates. Furthermore, is implementation will be much dependent on the EU/IMF bailout agreement being renegotiated to reduce the overall debt burden and to provide sufficient economic stimulus to ensure a viable future. Overall, it is clear that difficult choices will need to be made in the years ahead. *Social Justice Ireland* continues to urge the Government to place protection of the vulnerable at the core of these decisions.

The issue of governance is of major importance for society at large. There is a substantial role for civil society in the huge task that Ireland currently faces. Social dialogue is a critically important component of effective decision-making in a modern democracy. Recently the process of consultation and society-wide cooperation has been undermined, even demonised, and its significant positive contributions ignored. The severity of Ireland's current situation is reminiscent of the late 1980s, a time when social dialogue was seen as the key to economic and social recovery; the lessons learnt then should be remembered now.

The Europe 2020 Strategy places an onus on the Irish government to include all stakeholders in framing, developing and delivering Ireland's National Reform Programme. This programme is intended to set out how Ireland proposes to meet its commitments towards achieving the Europe 2020 Strategy targets. By including all stakeholders and civil society, it is believed that these targets will be 'owned' and that all will work for their achievement. *Social Justice Ireland* believes this is a sensible and desirable approach.

Much work has been done in recent years by the Council of Europe on how such an approach might be formalised and benefit all concerned. From that has come a new Charter on Shared Social Responsibilities, which was approved by the Council of Europe in late 2011. This charter argues that having a well-defined deliberative process can ensure, among other things, that individual preferences are reconciled with widespread priorities in the field of social, environmental and intergenerational justice. It can also reduce the "imbalances of power between stakeholders and neutralise its impact on the construction of knowledge and on decision-making" (Council of European Union, 2011: 24).

It is apparent to *Social Justice Ireland* that in the on-going framing, development and implementation of policy in areas such as the National Reform Programme there is a need for Government to move towards a deliberative approach. In a deliberative process all stakeholders would address the evidence together, independent of the traditional power-differentials between the stakeholders. The evidence would be presented and discussed with a view to providing the most accurate 'reading' of the issues being addressed.

Stakeholders would collaboratively identify the:
- current situation and how it emerged;
- most desirable future that could be achieved; and the
- means by which to move towards such a future.

Were this process evidence-based it would go some way towards ensuring that the most appropriate manner in which to address issues would be identified and agreed. Such an approach requires a high level of accountability from stakeholders and encourages them to take responsibility for decisions and the subsequent implementation of the actions required.

Social Justice Ireland believes governance along these lines can be developed in Ireland. Such engagement would reflect the value of social dialogue and the need for good governance characterised by transparency, accountability and inclusion.

2.2.5 The cultural context (assumptions, values and attitudes)

At times of crisis strategic thinking and planning are often set- side. This has been quite obvious in Ireland since the current crisis began. Its most visible manifestation has been the widespread acceptance of a series of largely unchallenged assumptions that are not valid, as already outlined in this report. These include:

- that the economy should have priority over all else;
- that preventing all the major banks from collapse is the major economic priority; and
- that cuts in public expenditure are the key solution.

These assumptions fail to grasp the fact that economic development and social development are two sides of the one coin. Economic development is required to provide resources for social development. On the other hand, social development is essential if economic development is to be successful. There can be no lasting economic development of substance without the provision of social services and infrastructure. For example, it will not be possible to promote a smart, green, hi-tech economy without having an education system that ensures people are capable of taking up jobs in these areas. Similarly, infrastructure in areas such as public transport and Information and Communication Technology (ICT) are essential for a successful economy in the twenty first century. Thinking we can have economic development first and follow-up with social development later is to ignore many of the major lessons that have been learned over the past two decades.

There are other assumptions which are only half true that are repeated like mantras in policy discussion and commentary. These include:

- Everybody should make a contribution to the adjustment required; and while fairness is important, cuts are more effective than taxes increases.

Social Justice Ireland agrees everyone should make a contribution – insofar as they can. We cannot accept that some people should be driven into poverty because of the contribution that is demanded of them. To do this would be to solve one problem by creating a deeper and more long-lasting one. We reject any attempt to solve Ireland's problems by increasing inequality or by forcing the most vulnerable members of the population into a situation where they do not have the resources to live life with dignity. It is also profoundly wrong that poor people should carry a major burden while senior bond-holders, who carry a significant part of the responsibility for Ireland's implosion, make no contribution whatsoever. Nor do we believe that Ireland's socio-economic situation can be rectified fairly if we persist in prioritising expenditure cuts at the same time as retaining one of the lowest total tax-takes in the EU.

There are other values that are regularly repeated that we do accept. These include:

- getting better value for public expenditure; and reforming the public sector.

The widely quoted assumptions listed in this chapter have been adopted with limited consideration of their meaning or implications. Consequently, those that are not valid generate ill-considered policies which are met with widespread opposition and anger. As a society we lack a coherent set of guiding values and assumptions to shape the policies and actions for the decade to come.

But that is not all. Developments over the past decade and more and the response to the multi-faceted crises Ireland has been encountering have produced a situation which is dominated by individualism, anxiety and greed.

Individualism, in the sense of people being seen as isolated, self-sufficient, economic individuals, has grown dramatically in recent years. Increasingly, the individual has come to be seen as the primary unit of social reality while community connectedness is down-played

In practice, policy has done much to undermine this community dimension. Autonomy, self-sufficiency and self-reliance have increasingly been seen as virtues. This kind of individualism is seen almost exclusively in economic terms. It resonates with the 'Celtic Tiger' rhetoric of the decade before the crisis which favoured low taxation as a supposed stimulus to entrepreneurial activity. As noted above, this was based on the false premise that the combined spending and investment decisions of individuals would produce far better results for Ireland than allowing

Government to decide how best to use the money, for example through investment in infrastructure and services. This notion is demonstrably wrong. Furthermore, this focus on individualism has had another equally negative effect on Irish society, the emergence of anxiety as a constant in Ireland's core.

Anxiety accompanies the growing realisation that the individualism described above can never provide an adequate basis for either the long-term progress of society or a guarantee of the individual's well-being. The autonomous individual championed in much current economic theory becomes caught in a never satisfied quest for achievement that ultimately produces a bottomless pit of anxiety – anxiety about the markets, about performance in all spheres of activity and even about fundamental self-worth.[13] This anxiety, in turn, leads many people to experience feelings of growing insecurity, pressure and threat. The individual experiencing anxiety often responds by seeking to get more, to have more, so as to control the future. This often leads to greed. This in turn feeds into the wider society.

Greed generates what Brueggemann calls "ravenous acquisitiveness" [Brueggemann 2009) so that life becomes a passionate pursuit of every form of security and self-worth, especially through money. This may explain why people who have the most often think they do not have enough. The effective legitimisation of avariciousness amongst those already well off not surprisingly stimulates similar desires in those with less. With financial institutions suspending their own critical judgements in the quest for profits, it is not difficult to see how borrowers were also persuaded to suspend any normal sense of caution in respect of borrowing and investing. This situation was exacerbated by a culture of extremely large 'bonus' payments for some which stimulated envy and greed in others. Greed, at both corporate and individual levels, has been an important contributory factor in the recent crises not just in Ireland but worldwide.

The series of developments which produced the growth of individualism, anxiety and greed is one of the core reasons why Ireland, and much of the Western world, is where it is today. A route out of this morass is needed. That pathway should be guided by a vision of Irish society, a New Ireland.

---

[13] For further development of these points cf. Walter Brueggemann, From Anxiety and Greed to Milk and Honey, Sojourners, http://www.sojo.net/

2.3 The need for vision: where is Irish society going?

The scale of the on-going crises facing Ireland today is enormous and recovery will take many years. The nature of that recovery has both international and national aspects. While the former is out of our control, decisions regarding our national policy responses to these crises will need to be considered and taken over the next few months and years. *Social Justice Ireland* believes that these national decisions should be framed in the context of one central question: Where does Ireland, and Irish society, want to be in 10 years time?

2.3.1 A guiding vision for a New Ireland

A guiding vision that charts the future direction and shape of Irish society is needed; one that takes a long-term perspective and implements policy to achieve this. *Social Justice Ireland* believes that Ireland should be guided by the core values of:

- Human dignity
- Sustainability
- Equality and human rights
- The common good.

These values must be at the core of the vision for a nation in which all men, women and children:

- have what they require to live life with dignity, including sufficient income,
- have access to the services they need and
- are actively included in a genuinely participatory society.

Sustainability is a central motif for economic, social and environmental policy development. It is implicit in this that economic development, social development and environmental protection are complementary and interdependent – three sides of the same reality.

Balanced regional and global development should also be at the heart of the vision of Ireland's future, along with the concepts of equality and a rights-based approach to the organisation of society.

The objective of sustainable international economic competitiveness will be a necessary component, along with the constant policy objective of ensuring that decisions are made in the interests of the common good, rather than to unfairly advantage individuals and vested interests over others.

2.3.2 The Developmental Welfare State – a useful model

One useful approach that may be of help in this context is the perspective offered by NESC in its report entitled *The Developmental Welfare State* (NESC, 2005). Chart 2.2 presents the core structure of the NESC model. It proposed that every person in Ireland should have what is required to secure human dignity in three interrelated areas: (i) services, (ii) income supports and (iii) innovative measures that would secure active inclusion.

Chart 2.2: The Core Structure of the Developmental Welfare State

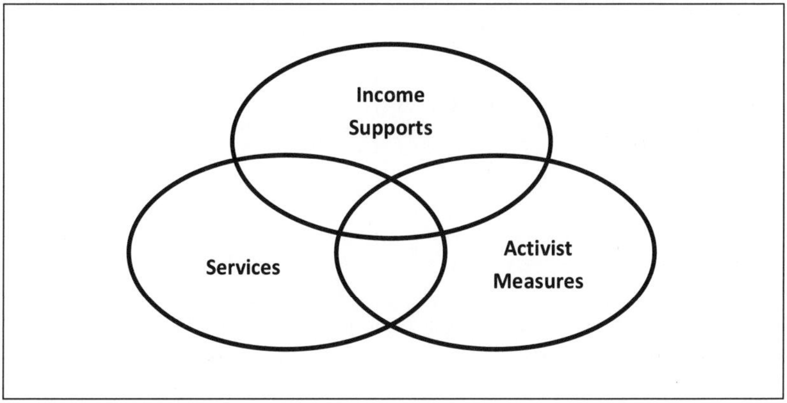

Services	Income Supports	Activist Measures
• Childcare	• Progressive child	• Social inclusion
• Education	income support	• Area-based
• Health	• Working age income	strategies
• Eldercare	for participation	• Particular community
• Housing	• Minimum pension	/group projects
• Transport	guarantee	• Emerging new needs
• Employment services	• Capped tax	• Novel approaches
• Training	expenditures	

Source: NESC (2005:144, 156)

The NESC argued that in building the developmental welfare state Irish society should take a 'life-cycle' approach to ensuring that all three dimensions were delivered. As table 2.7 shows, such an approach would focus on identifying the needs of children, young adults, people of working age, older people and people challenged in their personal autonomy, such as those in care or having a disability. The council suggested that for each group, policy should focus on securing an effective combination of income supports, services and active inclusion measures.

Table 2.7: NESC Life-cycle approach to delivering the Developmental Welfare State			
	Who?	**What?**	**How?**
0-17yrs	Integration of	Governance and	Standards and
18-29yrs	services, income	leadership	rights
30-64yrs	support and		
65+ yrs	activist measures		
People challenged in their personal autonomy			

Source: NESC (2005:147)

Successfully implementing this approach would underscore the ability of each of these groups to play a real and sustained role in Irish society and thereby play an important part in tackling social exclusion. This approach provides each sector involved with key challenges if the best options are to be taken and if the approach is to be successfully developed as a template for policy. A major part of the *Towards 2016* national agreement used this approach to social development. It identified 23 high-level goals across these age groups and interlinked areas. However, given the crisis that emerged from 2008 onwards, these goals have been ignored or overlooked by many in the policy process. *Social Justice Ireland* believes that the Developmental Welfare State model and the *Towards 2016* high level goals provide a template that could be very valuable in shaping the social aspects of the vision for Ireland we articulate here.

2.4 Twenty policy priorities for moving towards the vision

Social Justice Ireland believes that moving towards the vision outlined above would require hat Ireland:

- Reduce its debt burden.
- Address the moral hazard that protects banks.
- Raise total tax-take in a fair, equitable and sustainable manner to 34.9 per cent of GDP from the current 28.2% of GDP. Make special additional provision to cover the cost of servicing the bank element of Ireland's national debt.
- Reverse the ratio of tax increases to expenditure cuts and provide the necessary resources over time to raise Ireland's infrastructure and social services at least to the EU-average level.
- Integrate the income tax and social welfare systems to make them fit for purpose in a rapidly changing world.
- Focus economic growth on increasing per-capita national income.
- Reform the public service to ensure it maximises its capacity and delivers appropriate outcomes.
- Ensure the economy is internationally competitive.
- Address the reality of unemployment for both short-term and long-term unemployed people.
- Reduce poverty, with a particular focus on child poverty.
- Develop long-term planning and ensure all actions taken are sustainable economically, environmentally and socially.
- Tackle inequality and develop a rights-based approach to policy.
- Develop a 'shared responsibility' approach to policy development.
- Ensure that obtaining value for money is the norm in respect of public expenditure.
- Commit to reach the 23 high-level goals for various stages of the life-cycle set out in *Towards 2016*.
- Prioritise balanced local and regional development.
- Respect and support the role of the community and voluntary sectors.
- Make dialogue with social partners a central part of policy development.
- Ensure all policy development is evidence-based and outcome-focused.
- Avoid upward redistribution in the process of supporting banks, bondholders and developers; in this process minimise the exposure of the

tax-payer to the losses incurred by banks and the consequent expenditure of tax-payers money on rescuing these.

A number of these issues are explored in greater depth here. Many are also examined elsewhere throughout this review.

Reduce Ireland's debt burden

Ireland's debt burden is too large to allow it return to the bond market on a sustainable basis in the near future. Ireland is implementing the conditions of the Bailout Agreement and hitting its targets on the fiscal front. Dramatic Budget cuts and tax increases are being delivered on schedule. Borrowing targets have been reached. However Ireland's economic growth has been sluggish. GDP declined slightly in the third quarter of 2011, while GNP fell significantly by 4.2 per cent. Most economic forecasts for 2012 predict little, if any, growth – the most optimistic setting it at 1 per cent.

It is clear that Ireland will be unable to produce the employment needed to produce the growth needed to recover from the current crisis with a significant reduction in the cost of servicing its sovereign debt arising from the Bailout Agreement with the 'troika'.

But part of Ireland's current debt is not our debt. It was caused, in part at least, by the reckless gambling of German and French banks and financial institutions among others. In the decade before the crash low interest rates were being maintained because that was deemed appropriate for the German banks; but such low rates were the direct opposite of what Ireland needed.

Under major pressure from the European Central Bank (ECB) the Irish Government provided a bank guarantee in September 2008 and that has resulted in a huge burden of private bank debt being assumed by the state. Ireland was told that were it to default, even marginally, on this debt that would have devastating consequences for Europe's entire banking system To protect the banks of Europe Ireland has to bear an enormous debt burden alone. This is unjust and indefensible. This is a European problem and its solution should be shared among European nations.

The Anglo-Irish Bank promissory notes should either be written off or their redemption dates should be pushed far into the future. Either of these actions would make the situation less unjust and provide the leeway for Ireland to rescue itself from the current morass. Because of the amount involved (more than €47bn on the Anglo promissory notes and interest charges alone) a reduction in Ireland's debt burden is probably the most important action now required.

Address the moral hazard that protects banks

Moral hazard is the situation in which an individual or an institution or organisation is insulated from risk while others suffer the negative consequences of that risk. In such a situation those insulated from risk have an incentive to behave inappropriately. This is what happened to banks and financial institutions in Ireland, Germany, France and beyond in the years prior to 2008. The same is likely to happen again unless much more stringent institutional safeguards are put into place.

During the last four decades governments in wealthy countries have built up large liabilities because they have provided implicit guarantees to their banks and financial institutions. This contributes to the development of moral hazard in lending around the world. Current regulatory reforms will not stop this trend. The real structural challenge is to design an effective mechanism to address the moral hazard of banks and financial institutions. Such a mechanism must, almost certainly, include a provision to ensure that bondholders can be held responsible for losses when their gambling fails. Unless this challenge is addressed effectively we can be assured that banks and financial institutions will behave exactly as they did before and with the same or similar consequences.

Raise Ireland's total tax-take in a fair, equitable and sustainable manner

Social Justice Ireland believes that Ireland should increase its total tax-take to 34.9% of GDP (which would still keep Ireland as a low-tax economy as defined by Eurostat). We also believe that it will be necessary to provide additional tax revenue to cover the annual cost of servicing the banking element of Ireland's debt. A rough estimate of what the latter might require would be €2.5b extra per annum. (In making this calculation we are assuming an Anglo promissory note restructuring and we calculate the cost of servicing €70b of bank debt at an average of 3.5 per cent per annum).

The average tax-take among EU-27 countries is 35.8 per cent of GDP. Ireland's total for 2010 was 28.2 per cent of GDP so there is plenty of scope for movement. Only Romania and Latvia take a lower proportion of GDP in tax.

Increasing Ireland's tax-take is particularly relevant given the recent collapse of taxation revenues (detailed earlier in this chapter) and the obvious and immediate need for Government to rebuild the Irish taxation base. According to the Department of Finance (2011), the total tax-take was slightly higher at 29.9 per cent in 2010, rose to 30.8 per cent in 2011 and is forecast to stay at that exact same level in 2012. The Department's forecast for Ireland's total tax-take in 2015 is 31.9 per cent of GDP. It is this low level of taxation that has placed the exchequer in such a precarious position and put so much unnecessary pressure on public services.

Table 2.8 estimates the scale of tax revenues that could be collected using a benchmark of 34.9 per cent of GDP. The table compares this with the Department of Finance's projected tax take for the years 2012-2015. The total taxation figure represents not just those taxes collected centrally by the exchequer but also contributions to the social insurance fund and revenues collected by local authorities.[14] As we show, if the tax take is increased to the level proposed by *Social Justice Ireland,* significant additional revenue would be raised. We believe Government should move in this direction.

Table 2.8: Potential Irish Total Tax Revenues, 2012-2015 (€m)				
Year	GDP	Tax @ 34.9%	Tax @ DOF %	Difference
2012	159,125	55,535	49,010	6,525
2013	164,550	57,428	51,669	5,759
2014	171,625	59,897	54,748	5,149
2015	179,425	62,619	57,237	5,382

Source: Calculated from Department of Finance Budget 2012: D9 and D19.
Note: See also Table 4.4.

It is obvious that Ireland can never hope to address its longer-term deficits in infrastructure and social provision if we continue to collect substantially less tax income than that required by other European countries. As we outline in some detail in chapter 4 of this review, *Social Justice Ireland* believes that these tax reforms should not be attained through increasing income tax rates, but rather via reforming and broadening the tax base so that Ireland's taxation system becomes fairer.

---

[14] There are also some EU related taxes but these are small in the overall context.

Reverse the ratio of tax increases to expenditure cuts and raise Ireland's infrastructure and social services at least to the EU-average level.
Social Justice Ireland believes that it is important that Ireland should, focus on developing its infrastructure and social services in the years to come to bring them up to EU-average levels. Some progress was made on achieving this target during the period prior to 2008. Now, however, huge reductions in the capital budget mean that infrastructure development is almost at a standstill. Social services are also being seriously reduced as part of the re-balancing of Ireland's budget. It is of serious concern that many of those dependent on services and supports in areas ranging from education to healthcare, from social housing to community development, have experienced severe cutbacks as a result of recent Budgets.

As Ireland recovers from the current crises, it is important that society continues to protect and assist its most vulnerable. It is also important that it continues to improve its infrastructure. To do this however, is very difficult, when Government policy continues to run down the economy. Government has been increasing the total tax-take by €1 for every €2 cut in public expenditure and proposes to continue this up to Budget 2015. By that time expenditure will have been cut by €22,169m while tax will have increased by €10,918 in the period since July 2008. Social Justice Ireland believes this ratio should be reversed. Government needs to adopt policies to stimulate the economy rather than continually run it down. Domestic demand should be given a change to recover through policies which promote Government or European Investment Bank-led investment. Accepting that further adjustments have to be made, there is a clear need to alter the balance of adjustments towards additional taxation measures and away from reduction in public expenditure which is now having a severe impact on basic service provision.

Focus policy to target growth of per-capita national income
Social Justice Ireland believes that a series of new indicators is needed to measure the development of societies. The inadequacy of current metrics was the theme of our 2009 Social Policy conference and the subsequent publication entitled *Beyond GDP: What is progress and how should it be measured?* (Reynolds and Healy, 2009). Later in this review we discuss the need to develop such alternative scorecards and in particular address the commitment to investigate the possibility of developing a set of shadow national accounts (see chapter 12).

In the years to come, as Ireland recovers, we believe that it would be worthwhile for economic policy to focus on growing per capita national incomes rather than just their nominal levels. Per capita national income is calculated by dividing GNP (or GDP) by the population – establishing GNP per person. Reporting and monitoring increases in these indicators would enhance policy making and provide a more realistic yardstick to assess economic developments.

Ensure Ireland's economy is internationally competitive

Ireland lost competitiveness throughout almost all of the last decade. While national income climbed, so too did wages. Simultaneously, our infrastructure, both physical and technological, failed to keep pace with the rest of Europe while many of our public institutions performed badly.[15] Overall, we slipped backwards relative to our international competitors – a dangerous phenomenon for an export-orientated economy.

Without doubt, rebuilding this competitiveness will be a key feature of Ireland's recovery. Already unit labour costs have fallen relative to our EU counterparts and this trend looks set to continue in 2012. Irish wages are likely to be static at best while other EU countries will record small increases. However, as the World Economic Forum's *Global Competitiveness Reports* have pointed out, competitiveness is about more than just labour costs. Therefore, as Ireland recovers attention needs to be paid to the other key areas of competitiveness, including infrastructure, technological connectivity, public sector efficiency, innovation, education/skills and the cost of doing business and living in Ireland.

Address unemployment and target long-term unemployment

The past four years have brought a return to the phenomenon of widespread unemployment. The transition from near full employment to high-unemployment has been a critically important characteristic of this recession. The implications for people, families, social cohesion and the exchequer's finances have been serious. Economic forecasts for the remainder of 2012 indicate that unemployment will persist at a high level. There can be little doubt that Ireland is in a very challenging period, with high levels of long-term unemployment once again a characteristic of Irish society. While Government has unveiled plans aimed at increasing jobs and preparing those who are unemployed to take up employment, it is clear that unemployment is set to persist and that long-term unemployment is likely to continue at a record level for some considerable time unless there is large-scale investment aimed at generating jobs. This almost certainly requires a reduction of the debt burden, as discussed above.

---

[15] See chapter 4 where we examine competitiveness in greater detail.

In chapter 5 of this review we present a detailed outline of the approaches *Social Justice Ireland* believes the new Government should take to comprehensively address this crisis. The scale of these challenges is enormous. The scale of the response is simply not adequate. It is particularly inadequate in respect of long-term unemployment. We outline our own substantial proposal for this in chapter 5. However, it is crucial that Government, commentators and society in general remember that each of the policy priorities identified in this chapter affect people who are experiencing dramatic and, in many cases, unexpected turmoil in their and their families' lives. As Irish society comes to terms with the enormity of this issue, this perspective should remain central.

Reduce poverty

The European wide social survey SILC (*Survey on Income and Living Conditions*) allows accurate comparisons to be made between the levels and rates of various socio-economic phenomena across the member states. The most recent poverty data indicate that throughout the EU-25 the average risk of poverty in 2009 (the latest year for which comparable statistics are available) was 16 per cent. In recent years Ireland's poverty levels had been falling, driven by the increases in social welfare payments delivered in the Budgets of 2005-2007. These increases compensated only partly for the extent to which social welfare rates had fallen behind other incomes in society over the preceding two decades. However, the recent cuts to these payments, combined with reductions in wages and employment numbers, has resulted in Ireland's poverty rising from 14.1 per cent in 2009 to 15.8 per cent in 2010 . This was despite a drop in the poverty line of more than 10 per cent. Inequality grew dramatically in the same period. There is a real danger that Irish society will permit those on the lowest incomes, and in particular those dependent on social welfare, to fall behind once again, as it did in the late 1990s (see chapter 3).

One of the most shocking current social statistics relates to child poverty. Of all the children (under 18 years of age) in Ireland, 19.5 per cent live in poverty – more than 200,000 children. The scale of this statistic, which has increased in recent years, is alarming. Given that our children are our future, this situation is not acceptable. Furthermore, the fact that such a large proportion of our children is living below the poverty line has obvious implications for the education system, for the success of these children within it, for their job prospects in the future and for Ireland's economic potential in the long-run. Addressing child poverty must be a priority.

Despite recent policies, over the next few years *Social Justice Ireland* believes that it is possible to reduce Ireland's poverty rate as most Irish people desire. This can be achieved through policies which continue to benchmark social welfare payments, provide equity of social welfare rates across genders, provide adequate payments for children and deliver higher and universal state pensions and cost of disability payments. We outline our proposals on this in chapter 3 of this review.

As the economy recovers, development of a policy agenda focused on maintaining this position would be equally important. This would demonstrate a clear willingness to include all of society in the fruits of the recovery. It would be a great mistake for Ireland, and Irish policy makers, to repeat the experience of the late 1990s. At that time, economic growth benefited only those who were employed while others, such as those dependent on pensions and other social welfare payments slipped further and further behind.[16]

Develop long-term planning and ensure all actions taken are sustainable economically, environmentally and socially.
Earlier in this review we addressed the issue of a guiding vision for Ireland. In chapter 11 we will argue that Ireland needs an on-going national dialogue on this issue. A vision is required to provide inspiration and energy. A vision is also required to ensure all policy developments move the country in the same direction. Without such a long-term guiding vision it will be very difficult to develop long-term planning. But such an approach to planning is essential if Ireland is to develop coherent and integrated initiatives across the policy spectrum.

We have also argued that economic development, social development and environmental protection are different but interdependent sides of the same coin. This should be recognised and at the core of long-term planning. Ireland has not been well served in some of its long-term planning in the past decade. We still believe that Ireland must take specific steps to ensure that long-term planning becomes a built-in part of its policy development and implementation processes.

Address inequality and develop a rights-based approach
Inequality is a key problem in Irish society. It produces a range of negative outcomes for those who are poor and/or excluded. Growing inequality, which has been the

---

[16] See chapter 3 and the paragraphs on 'Poverty and social welfare recipients' which provide details of the late 1990s experience.

norm for some time, exacerbates the negative effects on people who are poor and/or excluded. Reducing inequality must be a core objective of Government policy. *Social Justice Ireland* also believes strongly in the importance of developing a rights-based approach to social, economic and cultural issues. The need to develop these rights is becoming ever more urgent for Ireland in the context of achieving recovery. Such an approach would go a long way towards addressing the growing inequality Ireland has been experiencing.

Social, economic and cultural rights should be acknowledged and recognised, just as civil and political rights have been. We believe seven basic rights that are of fundamental concern to people who are socially excluded and/or living in poverty should be acknowledged and recognised. These are the rights to:

- sufficient income to live life with dignity;
- meaningful work;
- appropriate accommodation;
- relevant education;
- essential healthcare;
- cultural respect; and
- real participation.

Until these rights are recognised Ireland and the EU will continue to have a major credibility problem, as they will be failing to match their commitment to civil and political rights with an equal commitment to social, economic and cultural rights.

To ensure that the recognition of social, economic and cultural rights goes beyond words, however, it is essential to address the question of how can such rights be made capable of being vindicated in law. In particular, how this can be done in a way that respects the political process and does not destroy the balance of power between the judicial and the governmental dimensions of society while also respecting the social, economic and cultural rights of people.

In previous publications we have developed a detailed proposal showing how this could be done[17]. We believe that movement in this direction would be a very progressive development and would make a major contribution to the emergence of an Ireland which would facilitate and support the well-being of all people equally.

---

[17] For a further discussion of this issue see Healy and Reynolds (2003).

Develop a 'Shared Social Responsibility' approach

The current series of crises risks a regression in rights, social protection and democracy. On the one hand there is a danger that people put all their trust in the market as the only real source of solutions to the challenges being faced. On the other hand, there is a risk that people expect Government to resolve all the challenges effectively and fairly. Both of these extremes must be resisted. Because resources are scarce it is important that all stakeholders recognise the importance of securing the wellbeing of all. There must also be recognition of the need for social, environmental and intergenerational justice. To be effective, an approach is required that is characterised by a spirit of reciprocity, mutual accountability and a shared commitment to reducing social inequalities and inequalities of influence.

We live in a world in which no-one is totally independent or immune from the damaging consequences of other people's actions or failure to act. The most advantaged population groups must not ignore their interdependencies and responsibilities vis-à-vis the rest of society. This is especially important when the least advantaged see their achievements in terms of access to rights, public services and common goods threatened. It is very important that all sectors of society work together and share responsibility for combating the causes of inequalities, poverty, insecurity and discrimination.

Taking a 'shared social responsibility' approach would require individuals and institutions, both public and private, to be accountable for the consequences of their actions or omissions. This would apply to such areas as the protection of human dignity, the environment and common good, poverty and discrimination and the pursuit of justice, development and social cohesion. It is clear that all individuals and institutions do not have equal responsibility in each of these areas. Some have much greater resources, power or capacity and, consequently, have greater responsibility. But all have some capacity and, consequently, some responsibility.

For such an approach to work effectively would require much greater transparency and accountability, much greater access to knowledge and a deliberative approach to decision-making. It would require a new approach to responsibility in a context of interdependence. The Council of Europe agreed a new Charter on Shared Social Responsibilities in 2011. (Council of Europe 2011) It could provide a very good basis for proceeding on this issue.

Avoid upwards redistribution

The need to address the crisis created by the incompetent management and regulation of our banking institutions is an unavoidable element of Ireland's recovery. A similar, and related, crisis needs to be addressed following the illogical behaviour of numerous property developers, large and small, ranging from those who built unwanted housing to those who dramatically over-paid, and over-borrowed to buy development land. In addressing both these related problems Government must avoid adopting policies whereby the exchequer, representing society as a whole, provides huge resources to bail out a few companies, individuals and bondholders while inequality is allowed to continue growing and the most vulnerable are left further behind. Overpaying for bank assets as they transfer to state control or allowing insolvent developers keep 'performing assets' while the state carries the burden for their un-performing ones is simply unacceptable. Similarly, burdening society with the debts of reckless banks while not sharing some of that burden with all bondholders who financed it is unfair and irresponsible. As we rebuild the financial system of this country we must avoid upwards redistribution in supporting banks, bondholders and developers.

What are the implications for policy in Ireland flowing from this analysis? What are the specific issues to be addressed in areas such as taxation or education or rural development? What specific policy initiatives should Government take in areas such as income distribution or healthcare or unemployment? The following 12 chapters address these and similar questions. Each chapter addresses one specific area:

- Income Distribution
- Taxation
- Work, Unemployment and Job creation
- Public Services
- Housing and Accommodation
- Healthcare

- Education and Educational Disadvantage
- Intercultural & Migration issues
- Participation
- Sustainability and the Environment
- Rural Development
- The Developing World

On each of these issues, we propose a core policy objective. We also provide an analysis of the present situation, review relevant initiatives and outline key policy priorities aimed at securing a fair and just Ireland. In doing this, we clearly indicate the choices *Social Justice Ireland* believes should be made in the years immediately ahead. In chapter 15 we set out the values-base from which we provide this analysis and critique.

3. INCOME DISTRIBUTION

> ## CORE POLICY OBJECTIVE:
> ## INCOME DISTRIBUTION
> To provide all with sufficient income to live life with dignity. This would require enough income to provide a minimum floor of social and economic resources in such a way as to ensure that no person in Ireland falls below the threshold of social provision necessary to enable him or her to participate in activities that are considered the norm for society generally.

High rates of poverty and income inequality in Ireland require greater attention than they currently receive. Tackling these problems effectively is a multifaceted task. It requires action on many fronts ranging from healthcare and education, to accommodation and employment. However, the most important requirement in tackling poverty is the provision of sufficient income to enable people to live life with dignity. No anti-poverty strategy can possibly be successful without an effective approach to addressing low incomes.

This chapter addresses the issue of income in four parts. The first examines the extent and nature of poverty in Ireland today while the second profiles our income distribution. The final two sections address potential remedies to these problems by outlining the issues and arguments surrounding achieving and maintaining an adequate social welfare income and the introduction of a basic income.

(a) Poverty
While there is still considerable poverty in Ireland, there has been much progress on this issue over recent years. Driven by increases in social welfare payments, in particularly payments to the unemployed, the elderly and people with disabilities, the rate of poverty significantly declined between 2001 and 2009. However, the most recent data, analysed in this section, indicates that poverty has once again begun to increase. It climbed from a record low level in 2009 to a higher level in 2010, driven by recent budgetary policy which has reversed earlier social welfare increases.[18]

---

[18] Irish household Income data has been collected since 1973 and all surveys up to 2009 and 2010 have recorded poverty levels above 15 per cent.

Data on Ireland's income and poverty levels are now provided by the annual *SILC* survey *(Survey on Income and Living Conditions)*. This survey replaced the *European Household Panel Survey* and the *Living in Ireland Survey* which had run throughout the 1990s. Since 2003 the *SILC / EU-SILC* survey has collected detailed information on income and living conditions from up to 130 households in Ireland each week; giving a total sample of between 5,000 and 6,000 households each year.

Social Justice Ireland welcomes this survey and in particular the speed and accessibility of the data produced. Because this survey is conducted simultaneously across all of the EU states, the results are an important contribution to the on-going discussion on relative income and poverty levels across the EU member states. It also provides the basis for informed analysis of the relative position of the citizens of member states. In particular, this analysis is informed by a set of agreed indicators of social exclusion which the EU Heads of Government adopted at Laeken in 2001. These indicators (known as the updated-Laeken indicators) are calculated from the survey results and cover four dimensions of social exclusion: financial poverty, employment, health and education.[19]

What is poverty?

The National Anti-Poverty Strategy (NAPS) published by government in 1997 adopted the following definition of poverty:

> *People are living in poverty if their income and resources (material, cultural and social) are so inadequate as to preclude them from having a standard of living that is regarded as acceptable by Irish society generally. As a result of inadequate income and resources people may be excluded and marginalised from participating in activities that are considered the norm for other people in society.*

This definition was reiterated in the 2007 *National Action Plan for Social Inclusion 2007-2016 (NAPinclusion)*.

Where is the poverty line?

How many people are poor? On what basis are they classified as poor? These and related questions are constantly asked when poverty is discussed or analysed.

In trying to measure the extent of poverty, the most common approach has been to identify a poverty line (or lines) based on people's disposable income (earned

---

[19] For more information on these indicators see Nolan (2006:171-190).

income after taxes and including all benefits). In recent years the European Commission and the UN among others have begun to use a poverty line located at 60 per cent of median income. The median income is the income of the middle person in society's income distribution. This poverty line is the one adopted in the *SILC* survey and differs from the Irish poverty line up to 2003 which was set at 50 per cent of mean, or average, income. This switch to median income removes many of the technical criticisms that had been levelled against the use of relative income measures to assess poverty.[20] In cash terms, however, there is very little difference between the poverty line drawn at either 60 per cent of median income or 50 per cent of mean income.[21] While the 60 per cent median income line has been adopted as the primary poverty line, alternatives set at 50 per cent and 70 per cent of median income are also used to clarify and lend robustness to assessments of poverty.

The most up-to-date data available on poverty in Ireland comes from the 2010 *SILC* survey, conducted by the CSO. In that year the CSO gathered data from a statistically representative sample of more than 5,000 households containing 11,587 individuals. The data gathered by the CSO is very detailed. It incorporates income from work, welfare, pensions, rental income, dividends, capital gains and other regular transfers. This data was subsequently verified anonymously using PPS numbers.

According to the CSO the median disposable income per adult in Ireland during 2010 was €18,502 per annum or €346.22 per week. Consequently, the income poverty lines for a single adult derived from this are:

50 per cent line	€173.11 a week
60 per cent line	€207.73 a week
70 per cent line	€242.35 a week

Updating the 60 per cent median income poverty line to 2012 levels, using the ESRI's (2012:iv) predicted changes in wage levels for 2011 (+0.1 per cent) and 2012 (0 per cent), produces a relative income poverty line of €207.94 for a single person. In 2012, any adult below this weekly income level will be counted as being

---

[20] In particular the use of median income ensures that it is possible to eliminate poverty (a rate of 0 per cent), a feature that was theoretically impossible when poverty lines were calculated using mean income.
[21] For example in 2003 the CSO reported that the 60 per cent median income line was €14 higher than the 50 per cent mean income line. In some other European countries the opposite situation was found.

at risk of poverty. It is noteworthy that the value of the 2012 poverty line is not much different to the 2010 figure shown above and is in fact lower than the poverty line value for 2009 (€231.37). This is because wages have fallen since 2009 and are projected to remain almost static for 2012 while throughout that period taxes have increased and most social welfare rates of payment have decreased. Taken together, these factors have had a negative impact on disposable income and, because the poverty line is a relative measure, it adjusts accordingly.

Table 3.1 applies the poverty line to a number of household types to show what income corresponds to each household's poverty line. The figure of €207.94 is an income per adult equivalent figure. It is the minimum weekly disposable income (after taxes and including all benefits) that one adult needs to be above the poverty line. For each additional adult in the household this minimum income figure is increased by €137.24 (66 per cent of the poverty line figure) and for each child in the household the minimum income figure is increased by €68.62 (33 per cent of the poverty line).[22] These adjustments reflect the fact that as households increase in size they require more income to stay above the poverty line. In all cases a household below the corresponding weekly disposable income figure is classified as living at risk of poverty. For clarity, corresponding annual figures are also included.

Table 3.1: The Minimum Weekly Disposable Income Required to Avoid Poverty in 2012, by Household Types		
Household containing:	Weekly poverty line	Annual poverty line
1 adult	€207.94	€10,842
1 adult + 1 child	€276.56	€14,420
1 adult + 2 children	€345.18	€17,998
1 adult + 3 children	€413.79	€21,576
2 adults	€345.18	€17,998
2 adults + 1 child	€413.79	€21,576
2 adults + 2 children	€482.41	€25,154
2 adults + 3 children	€551.03	€28,732
3 adults	€482.41	€25,154

One immediate implication of this analysis is that most weekly social assistance rates paid to single people are €19.94 below the poverty line.

---

[22] For example the poverty line for a household with 2 adults and 1 child would be calculated as €207.94 + €137.24 + €68.62 = €413.79.

How many have incomes below the poverty line?

Table 3.2 outlines the findings of various poverty studies since 1994, when detailed poverty studies commenced. Using the EU poverty line set at 60 per cent of median income, the findings reveal that in 2010 approximately 16 out of every 100 people in Ireland were living in poverty. The table shows that the rates of poverty decreased significantly after 2001, reaching a record low in 2009. These recent decreases in poverty levels are welcome. They are directly related to the increases in social welfare payments delivered over the Budget's spanning these years.[23] However poverty increased once again in 2010 as the effect of budgetary changes to welfare and taxes, as well as the effects of wage reductions and unemployment, drove more low income households into poverty.

Table 3.2: Percentage of population below various relative income poverty lines, 1994-2010

	1994	1998	2001	2005	2006	2007	2009	2010
50% line	6.0	9.9	12.9	10.8	8.9	★	6.9	8.5
60% line	**15.6**	**19.8**	**21.9**	**18.5**	**17.0**	**15.8**	**14.1**	**15.8**
70% line	26.7	26.9	29.3	28.2	26.7	★	24.5	25.1

Source: CSO (2011:10) and Whelan et al (2003:12), using national equivalence scale.
Notes: All poverty lines calculated as a percentage of median income.
★ Data not published for 2007.

Because it is sometimes easy to overlook the scale of Ireland's poverty problem, it is useful to translate the poverty percentages into numbers of people. Using the percentages for the 60 per cent median income poverty line and population statistics from CSO population projections and Census results, we can calculate the numbers of people in Ireland who have been in poverty for the years 1994, 1998, 2001, 2003-2010 (CSO 2010:45, 2011:7). These calculations are presented in table 3.3. The results give a better picture of just how significant this problem really is in Ireland today.

---

[23] See table 3.14 below for further analysis of this point.

Table 3.3: The numbers of people below relative income poverty lines in Ireland, 1994-2010			
	% of persons in poverty	Population of Ireland	Numbers in poverty
1994	15.6	3,585,900	559,400
1998	19.8	3,703,000	733,194
2001	21.9	3,847,200	842,537
2003	19.7	3,978,900	783,843
2004	19.4	4,045,200	784,769
2005	18.5	4,133,800	764,753
2006	17.0	4,239,800	720,766
2007	15.8	4,339,000	685,562
2008	13.9	4,422,100	614,672
2009	14.1	4,459,300	628,761
2010	15.8	4,470,700	706,371

Source: Calculated using CSO (2011:11), Whelan et al (2003:12), using national equivalence scale and CSO SILC results for various years.

The table's figures are telling. Over the past decade more than 135,000 people have been lifted out of poverty. Furthermore, over the period from 2004-2008, the period corresponding with consistent Budget increases in social welfare payments, over 170,000 people left poverty. Despite this, it is of concern that between 2009 and 2010 the numbers in poverty increased once again, by 77,000 in that year.

However, the fact that there are now just over 700,000 people in Ireland living life on a level of income that is this low must be a major concern. As we have shown earlier (see table 3.1) these levels of income are low and those below them clearly face difficulty in achieving what the NAPS described as "*a standard of living that is regarded as acceptable by Irish society generally*".

Who are the poor?

In recent years two interchangeable phrases have been used to describe those living on incomes below the poverty line: '*living in poverty*' and '*at risk of poverty*'. The latter term is the most recent, introduced following a European Council meeting in Laeken in 2001 where it was agreed that those with incomes below the poverty line should be termed as being 'at risk of poverty'.

The results of the *SILC* survey provided a breakdown of those below the poverty line. This section reviews those findings and provides a detailed assessment of the different groups in poverty.

Table 3.4 presents figures for the risk of poverty facing people when they are classified by their principal economic status (the main thing that they do). These risk figures represent the proportion of each group that are found to be in receipt of a disposable income below the 60 per cent median income poverty line. In 2010 the groups within the Irish population that were at highest risk of poverty included the unemployed and those not at work due to illness or a disability. Almost one in five classified as being "on home duties", mainly women, have an income below the poverty line. The "student and school attendees" category represents a combination of individuals living in poor families while completing their secondary education and those attending post-secondary education but with low incomes. The latter element of this group are not a major policy concern, given that they are likely to only experience poverty while they gain education and skills which should ensure they live with sufficient income subsequently. Those still in school and experiencing poverty are more aligned to the issue of child poverty, which is examined later in this chapter.

Despite the increase in poverty between 2009 and 2010, the table also reveals the groups which have driven the overall reduction in poverty over the period (falling from 19.7 per cent to 15.8 per cent). Comparing 2003 and 2009, the poverty rate has fallen for all groups other than students and those in jobs while there have been pronounced falls among the welfare-dependent groups, i.e. the unemployed, retired and those not at work due to illness or a disability.

Table 3.4: Risk of poverty among all persons aged 16yrs + by principal economic status, 2003-2010			
	2003	**2006**	**2010**
At work	7.6	6.5	7.8
Unemployed	41.5	44.0	26.1
Students and school attendees	23.1	29.5	24.0
On home duties	31.8	23.8	20.3
Retired	27.7	14.8	9.0
Unable to work as ill/disabled	51.7	40.8	20.9
Total	**19.7**	**17.0**	**15.8**

Source: CSO SILC reports (2005:11, 2007:15, 2011:7), using national equivalence scale

One obvious conclusion from table 3.4 is that any further progress in reducing poverty should be driven by continuing to enhance the adequacy of welfare payments. However, recent budgetary decisions seem likely to undermine progress in this area and have begun to drive poverty up once again (see analysis later in this chapter).

The working poor

Having a job is not, of itself, a guarantee that one lives in a poverty-free household. As table 3.4 indicates 7.8 per cent of those who are employed are living at risk of poverty. Despite decreases in poverty among most other groups, poverty figures for the working poor have remained very high. In 2010, almost 120,000 people in employment were still at risk of poverty.[24]

This is a remarkable statistic and it is important that policy makers begin to recognise and address this problem. Many working families on low earnings struggle to achieve a basic standard of living. Policies which protect the value of the minimum wage and attempt to keep those on that wage out of the tax net are relevant policy initiatives in this area. Similarly, attempts to increase awareness among low income working families of their entitlement to the Family Income Supplement (FIS) are also welcome; although evidence suggests that FIS is experiencing dramatically low take-up and as such has questionable long-term potential. However, one of the most effective mechanisms available within the present system to address the problem of the working poor would be to make tax credits refundable. We will address this proposal later in this review

Child poverty

Children are one of the most vulnerable groups in any society. Consequently the issue of child poverty deserves particular attention. Child poverty is measured as the proportion of all children aged 17 years or younger that live in households with an income below the 60 per cent of median income poverty line. The 2010 *SILC* survey indicates that 19.5 per cent were at risk of poverty and, as table 3.5 shows, in recent years the rate of child poverty has begun to increase (2011:7).

---

[24] See table 3.14.

Table 3.5: Child Poverty – % Risk of Poverty Among
Children in Ireland.

	2006*	2007*	2008	2010
Children, 0-17 yrs	19.0	17.4	18.0	19.5

Source: CSO (various editions of SILC)
Note: * 2006 and 2007 data exclude SSIA effect.

Translating the data in table 3.5 into numbers of children implies that in 2010 just over 200,000 children lived in households that were experiencing poverty.[25] The scale of this statistic is alarming. Furthermore, it is of note that between 2008 and 2010, the 1.5 per cent increase in the child poverty rate suggests a further 30,000 children have slipped below the poverty line. Given that our children are our future, this situation is not acceptable. Furthermore, the fact that such a large proportion of our children are living below the poverty line has obvious implications for the education system, for the success of these children within it, for their job prospects in the future and for Ireland's economic potential in the long-term.

Child benefit remains a key route to tackling child poverty and is of particular value to those families on the lowest incomes. Similarly, it is a very effective component in any strategy to improve equality and childcare. It is of concern, therefore, that child payments were cut in recent Budgets. On foot of these policies, it is likely that child poverty will increase further over the next few years. This will represent a major setback in an area in which the state already has a dismal record.

Older people
According to the CSO's *Population and Migration Estimates 2011* 11.7 per cent of the Irish population are aged over 65 years – some 524,100 people (CSO, 2011:7). Earlier data from the 2006 Census also indicated that just over a quarter of this group live alone (CSO, 2007: 36). When poverty is analysed by age group the 2010 figures show that 9.6 per cent of those aged above 65 years live in relative income poverty (CSO, 2011:7).

Among all those in poverty, the retired have experienced the greatest volatility in their poverty risk rates. As table 3.6 shows, in 1994 some 5.9 per cent of this group

---

[25] See table 3.14.

ere classified as poor; by 1998 the figure had risen to 32.9 per cent and in 2001 it peaked at 44.1 per cent. The most recent data record a decrease in poverty rates. While recent decreases are welcome, it remains a concern that so many of this county's senior citizens are living on so little.

Table 3.6: Percentage of older people (65yrs+) below the 60 per cent median income poverty line.								
	1994	1998	2001	2003	2004	2005	2006	2010
Aged 65 +	5.9	32.9	44.1	29.8	27.1	20.1	13.6	9.6

Source: Whelan et al (2003: 28) and CSO (various editions of SILC)

The Ill /Disabled

As table 3.4 showed, those not employed due to illness or a disability are one of the groups at highest risk of poverty with 20.9 per cent of this group classified in this category. Much like the experience of Ireland's older people, the situation of this group has varied significantly over the last decade and a half. The group's risk of poverty climbed from approximately three out of every ten persons in 1994 (29.5 per cent) to over six out of every ten in 2001 (66.5 per cent) before decreasing to approximately two out of every ten in the period 2008-2010. As with other welfare dependent groups, these fluctuations parallel a period where policy first let the value of payments fall behind wage growth before ultimately increasing them to catch-up.

Overall, although those not at work due to illness or a disability only account for a small proportion of those in poverty, their experience of poverty is high. Furthermore, given the nature of this group *Social Justice Ireland* believes there is an on-going need for targeted policies to assist them. These include job creation, retraining (see chapter 5 on work) and further increases in social welfare supports. There is also a very strong case to be made for introducing a non-means tested cost of disability allowance. This proposal, which has been researched and costed in detail by the National Disability Authority (NDA, 2006) and advocated by Disability Federation of Ireland (DFI), would provide an extra weekly payment of between €10 and €40 to somebody living with a disability (calculated on the basis of the severity of their disability). It seems only logical that if people with a disability are to be equal participants in society, the extra costs generated by their disability should not be borne by them alone. Society at large should act to level the playing field by covering those extra but ordinary costs. The *NESC Strategy 2006* also supported this policy development, urging that "the Government strongly consider the case for a separate 'cost of disability payment' that, in line with its analysis in the Developmental Welfare State, would be personally tailored and portable across the employment/non-employment divide" (NESC, 2005:168). In their *2008 Pre-Budget Submission* (for Budget 2008) DFI anticipate such a scheme would cost €183m per annum (DFI, 2007).

Poverty and education

The 2010 *SILC* results provide an interesting insight into the relationship between poverty and completed education levels. Table 3.7 reports the risk of poverty by completed education level and shows, as might be expected, that the risk of living on a low income is strongly related to low education levels. These figures underscore the relevance of continuing to address the issues of education disadvantage and early-school leaving (see chapter 9). Government education policy should ensure that these high risk groups are reduced. The table also suggests that when targeting anti-poverty initiatives, a large proportion should be aimed at those with low education levels, including those with low levels of literacy.[26]

Table 3.7: Risk of poverty among all persons aged 16yrs + by completed education level, 2007–2010			
	2007	**2008**	**2010**
Primary or below	24.0	20.4	17.8
Lower secondary	20.7	16.4	19.8
Higher secondary	13.8	12.4	15.7
Post leaving certificate	10.9	10.9	13.2
Third level non–degree	8.4	5.4	8.6
Third level degree or above	4.2	5.5	7.8
Total	**15.8**	**13.9**	**15.8**

Source: CSO (2008:15; 2009:45, 2011:7), using national equivalence scale and excluding SSIA effect for 2007 and 2008.

Poverty and Nationality

A feature of the last decade has been the growth in the number of people living in Ireland but born outside the state. The CSO refers to this group as "non-Irish nationals" and the 2006 *SILC* report presented data on poverty levels among this group vis-à-vis "Irish Nationals". For sampling reasons subsequent surveys did not

---

[26] We address the issues of unemployment and completed education levels in chapter 5 and adult literacy in chapter 9.

publish an update of this figure. The definitions used by the CSO in examining this issue are necessarily broad given the difficulty of collecting accurate statistical samples among nationals of individual countries.

Table 3.8: Risk of poverty by nationality, 2005-2006			
	2005	**2006**	**Change**
Irish Nationals	18.0	16.6	-1.4
Non-Irish Nationals	26.9	23.5	-3.4
Overall Population	**18.5**	**17.0**	**-1.5**

Source: CSO (2007:15), using national equivalence scale.

The findings, reported in table 3.8, reveal a stark contrast between the poverty risk levels of the two groups. Non-Irish nationals face a much higher risk of poverty, overall and by gender. As the data does not allow for a more detailed breakdown of these figures by nationality, we cannot say with certainty who these non-Irish nationals in poverty are or where they came from originally. However, it is likely that many of those experiencing poverty are recent migrants, many from the new member states of the EU.

Social Justice Ireland welcomed the provision of this data, although it is of some concern that the data was excluded from the most recent reports. The poverty data suggests that migration issues, including issues with regard to the participation of migrants in Irish society, deserve greater attention. We consider many of these issues in chapter 10.

Poverty by region and area

Recent SILC reports have provided a regional breakdown of poverty levels. The data, presented in table 3.9 suggests a very uneven national distribution of poverty. Using 2009 data, in Dublin less than one in ten people lived in poverty while the figures are twice this in the Mid-West, South-East and the Midlands. The table also reports that poverty is more likely to occur in rural areas than urban areas. In 2010 the risk of poverty in rural Ireland was 7 per cent higher than in urban Ireland with at risk rates of 20.0 per cent and 13.1 per cent respectively.

Table 3.9: Risk of poverty by region and area, 2005-2010				
	2005	**2007**	**2009**	**2010**
Border	–	17.8	14.1	n/a
Midlands	–	29.7	23.5	n/a
West	–	19.4	14.1	n/a
Dublin	–	11.5	8.3	n/a
Mid-East	–	8.1	14.6	n/a
Mid-West	–	19.0	18.9	n/a
South-East	–	18.0	18.3	n/a
South-West	–	17.1	14.7	n/a
Border, Midland and West			16.2	14.9
South and East			13.3	16.2
Urban Areas	16.0	14.3	11.8	13.1
Rural Areas	22.5	18.4	17.8	20.0
Overall Population	**18.5**	**15.8**	**14.1**	**15.8**

Source: CSO (2008:15; 2009:45, 2011:7), using national equivalence scale and excluding SSIA effect for 2007.

Note: Regional NUTS 3 data only available for 2007-2009 and NUTS 2 for 2009-2010.

The poverty gap

As part of the 2001 Laeken indicators, the European Union requested that all member countries begin to measure the relative "at risk of poverty gap". This indicator assesses how far below the poverty line the income of the median (middle) person in poverty is. The size of that difference is calculated as a percentage of the poverty line and therefore represents the gap between the income of the middle person in poverty and the poverty line. The higher the percentage figure, the greater the poverty gap and the further people are falling beneath the poverty line. As there is a considerable difference between being 2 per cent and 20 per cent below the poverty line this approach is significant.

Table 3.10: The Poverty Gap, 2003–2010							
	2003	**2004**	**2005**	**2006**	**2007★**	**2009**	**2010**
Poverty gap size	21.5	19.8	20.6	17.5	17.4	16.2	18.9

Source: CSO SILC reports (2008:16; 2011:10)
Note: ★ Data for 2007 not excluding SSIA effect as not published by CSO.

The *SILC* results for 2010 showed that the poverty gap was 18.9 per cent, compared to 16.2 per cent in 2009. Over time the gap had decreased from a figure of 21.5 per cent in 2003. The 2010 poverty gap figure implies that 50 per cent of those in poverty had an equivalised income below 81.1 per cent of the poverty line. As the depth of poverty is an important issue, we will monitor closely the movement of this indicator in future editions of the *SILC*. It is crucial that as part of Ireland's approach to addressing poverty that this figure decline and it is of concern that the 2010 figures once again records an increase.

The incidence of poverty

Figures detailing the incidence of poverty reveal the proportion of all those in poverty that belong to particular groups in Irish society. Tables 3.11 and 3.12 report all those below the 60 per cent of median income poverty line, classifying them by their principal economic status. The first table examines the population as a whole, including children, while the second table focuses exclusively on adults (using the ILO definition where adults are considered all those aged 16 years and above).

Table 3.11 shows that in 2010, the largest group of the population who are poor, accounting for 28.4 per cent of the total, were children. The second largest group were those working in the home (16.7 per cent). Of all those who are poor, 30.7 per cent were in the labour force and the remainder (69.3 per cent) were outside the labour market[27]

---

[27] This does not include the ill and disabled, some of whom will be active in the labour force. The SILC data does not distinguish between those are temporally unable to work due to illness and those permanently outside the labour market due to their illness or disability.

Table 3.11: Incidence of persons below 60% of median income by principal economic status, 2003-2010

	2003	2005	2006	2007*	2009	2010
At work	16.0	15.7	16.1	16.8	14.3	17.3
Unemployed	7.6	7.5	8.3	9.2	12.9	13.4
Students/school	8.6	13.4	15.0	14.1	14.6	12.1
On home duties	22.5	19.7	18.4	18.7	18.0	16.7
Retired	9.0	7.5	5.8	7.1	4.7	4.2
Ill/disabled	9.1	7.9	8.0	7.4	6.4	5.3
Children (under 16 years)	25.4	26.8	26.6	25.9	27.6	28.4
Other	1.9	1.6	1.8	0.8	1.5	2.6
Total	**100.0**	**100.0**	**100.0**	**100.0**	**100.0**	**100.0**

Source: Collins (2006:141), CSO SILC Reports (2007:19; 2008:25; 2009:48; 2011:13).
Note: * Data for 2007 not excluding SSIA effect as not published by CSO.

Table 3.12 looks at adults only and provides a more informed assessment of the nature of poverty. This is an important perspective as children depend on adults for their upbringing and support. Irrespective of how policy interventions are structured, it is through adults that any attempts to reduce the number of children in poverty must be directed. The table shows that in 2010 almost one-quarter of Ireland's adults with an income below the poverty line were employed. Overall, 43 per cent of adults at risk of poverty in Ireland were associated with the labour market.

The incidence of being at risk of poverty amongst those in employment is particularly alarming. Many people in this group do not benefit from Budget changes in welfare or tax. They would be the main beneficiaries of any move to make tax credits refundable, a topic we will address in chapter 4.

Table 3.12: Incidence of adults (16yrs+) below 60% of median income by principal economic status, 2003–2010						
	2003	2005	2006	2007★	2009	2010
At work	21.4	21.4	21.9	22.7	19.8	24.2
Unemployed	10.2	10.2	11.3	12.4	17.8	18.7
Students/school	11.5	18.3	20.4	19.0	20.2	16.9
On home duties	30.1	26.9	25.1	25.2	24.9	23.3
Retired	12.0	10.2	7.9	9.6	6.5	5.9
Ill/disabled	12.2	10.8	10.9	10.0	8.8	7.4
Other	2.5	2.2	2.5	1.1	2.1	3.6
Total	**100.0**	**100.0**	**100.0**	**100.0**	**100.0**	**100.0**

Source: Calculated from Collins (2006:141), CSO SILC Reports (2007:19; 2008:25; 2009:48; 2011:13).

Note: ★ Data for 2007 not excluding SSIA effect as not published by CSO.

Finally, table 3.13 examines the composition of poverty by household type. Given that households are taken to be the 'income receiving units' (income flows into households who then collectively live off that income) there is a value in assessing poverty by household type. *Social Justice Ireland* welcomes the fact that the CSO has, at our suggestion, begun to publish the *SILC* poverty data broken down by household category, even though this data has yet to be released for the 2010 SILC. From a policy making perspective this information is crucial as anti-poverty policy is generally focused on households (households with children, pensioner households, single person households etc.). The 2009 data shows that 22.8 per cent of households who were at risk of poverty were headed by somebody who was employed. Almost 44 per cent of households at risk of poverty were found to be headed by a person outside the labour force.[28]

---

[28] Those on home duties, students and school attendees, retired plus a proportion of the ill and disabled.

Table 3.13: Households below 60% of median income classified by principal economic status of head of household, 2004-2009					
	2004	2006	2007*	2008*	2009
At work	29.8	29.5	31.3	39.6	22.8
Unemployed	12.0	14.7	12.3	11.5	26.0
Students/school	2.8	4.6	5.1	4.1	5.4
On home duties	28.0	30.7	28.7	25.7	26.7
Retired	13.5	8.5	10.9	7.9	6.6
Ill/disabled	12.0	11.5	11.2	10.1	10.9
Other	1.9	0.7	0.4	1.1	1.6
Total	**100.0**	**100.0**	**100.0**	**100.0**	**100.0**

Source: CSO SILC Reports (2007:39; 2008:36; 2009:49; 2010:49)
Note: * Data for 2007 and 2008 not excluding SSIA effect as not published by CSO.

The Scale of Poverty - Numbers of People

As the three tables in the last section deal only in percentages it is useful to transform these proportions into numbers of people. Table 3.3 revealed that in 2010 706,371 people were living below the 60 per cent of median income poverty line. Using this figure, table 3.14 presents the number of people in poverty in that year within various categories. Comparable figures are also presented for 2005 2007 and 2009.

The data in table 3.14 is particularly useful in the context of framing anti-poverty policy. Groups such as the retired and the ill/disabled, although carrying a high risk of poverty, involve much smaller numbers of people than groups such as adults who are employed (the working poor), people on home duties and children/students. The primary drivers of the 2005-09 poverty reductions were increasing incomes among those who are on home duties, those who are classified as ill/disabled, the retired and children. Between 2007 and 2009 the numbers of workers in poverty declined while the numbers of unemployed people in poverty notably increased. This reflected the rise in unemployment in the labour market as a whole during those years. As the table shows, the increase in poverty between 2009 and 2010 can be principally explained by the increase in poverty among people with jobs, people who are unemployed and children.

Table 3.14: Poverty Levels Expressed in Numbers of People, 2005-2010				
	2005	**2007**	**2009**	**2010**
Overall	764,753	685,562	628,761	706,371
Adults				
On home duties	150,656	128,200	113,177	117,964
At work	120,066	115,174	89,913	122,202
Students/school	102,477	96,664	91,799	85,471
Unemployed	57,356	63,072	81,110	94,654
Ill/disabled	60,415	50,732	40,241	37,438
Retired	57,356	48,675	29,552	29,668
Other	12,236	5,484	9,431	18,366
Children				
Children (under 16 yrs)	204,954	177,561	173,538	200,609
Children (under 18 yrs)	n/a	224,179	219,438	235,928

Source: Calculated using CSO SILC Reports (2011:13; 2009:48, 2008:25, 2006:13) and data from table 3.3.

Moving to Persistent Poverty

Social Justice Ireland is committed to using the best and most up-to-date data in its ongoing socio-economic analysis of Ireland. We believe that to do so is crucial to the emergence of accurate evidence-based policy formation. It also assists in establishing appropriate and justifiable targeting of state resources.

At the intergovernmental conference in Laeken during 2001, the EU adopted a set of commonly measured indicators to monitor socio-economic progress across all of the member states. Data for these measures is to be collected annually in the *SILC* survey. The availability of annual data on poverty, incomes and living conditions is an important move. It facilitates a more informed and timely assessment of these issues than was achievable in the past. It will also allow us to track changes more closely over time and to make accurate comparisons across all 27 EU member states.

Among the Laeken indicators is an indicator of persistent poverty. This indicator measures the proportion of those living below the 60 per cent of median income poverty line in the current year and for two of the three preceding years. Persistent poverty therefore identifies those who have experienced sustained exposure to poverty which is seen to harm their quality of life seriously and to increase their levels of deprivation. To date the *SILC* survey has not produced any detailed results and breakdowns for this measure (although the survey has run for more than four full years and it is therefore possible to provide this insight). The CSO had indicated that it would publish such a breakdown during 2009; however this did not occur due to sampling reasons. We regret this delay and hope that the technical impediments to the publication of this data are overcome. *Social Justice Ireland* believes that this data should be used as the primary basis for setting poverty targets and monitoring changes in poverty status. Existing measures of relative and consistent poverty should be maintained as secondary indicators. As the persistent poverty indicator will identify the long-term poor, we believe that the CSO should produce comprehensive breakdowns of those in persistent poverty, similar to the approach it currently takes with relative income poverty.

However, the available *SILC* data has provided some insight into the likely persistent poverty numbers. In the 2009 SILC report the CSO presented '*tentative estimates for persistent poverty*' which indicated that in 2009 the persistent poverty rate was 7.7 per cent and that this figure had decreased from 9.5 per cent in 2008 and 15.5 per cent in 2007 (2010:123-124). These figures, while preliminary, are worryingly high. The 2009 figure implies that more than half of all those in poverty (the overall population figure was 14.1 per cent) have been in poverty for a number of years. They also imply that most of Ireland's poor are long-term poor and that poverty in Ireland is a structural problem which requires focused policies to address and reduce it.

Poverty and social welfare recipients

Social Justice Ireland believes in the very important role that social welfare plays in addressing poverty. As part of the *SILC* results the CSO has provided an interesting insight into the role that social welfare payments play in tackling Ireland's poverty levels. It has calculated the levels of poverty before and after the payment of social welfare benefits.

Table 3.15 shows that without the social welfare system 51 per cent of the Irish population would have been living in poverty in 2010. Such an underlying poverty rate suggests a deeply unequal distribution of direct income – an issue we address further in the income distribution section of this chapter. In 2010, the actual poverty figure of 15.8 per cent reflects the fact that social welfare payments reduced poverty by 35.2 percentage points.

Looking at the impact of these payments on poverty over time, it is clear that the increases in social welfare over the period 2005-2007 yielded noticeable reductions in poverty levels. The small increases in social welfare payments in 2001 are reflected in the smaller effects achieved in that year. Conversely, the larger increases, and therefore higher levels of social welfare payments, in subsequent years delivered greater reductions. This has occurred even as poverty levels before social welfare increased. *Social Justice Ireland* warmly welcomed these social welfare increases and the CSO's data proves the effectiveness of this policy approach.

Table 3.15: The role of social welfare (SW) payments in addressing poverty						
	2001	**2005**	**2006**	**2007★**	**2009**	**2010**
Poverty pre SW	35.6	40.1	40.3	41.0	46.2	51.0
Poverty post SW	21.9	18.5	17.0	16.5	14.1	15.8
The role of SW	**-13.7**	**-21.6**	**-23.3**	**-24.5**	**-32.1**	**-35.2**

Source: CSO SILC Reports (2006:7; 2007:13; 2011:10, using national equivalence scale.
Note: ★ Data for 2007 not excluding SSIA effect as not published by CSO.

As social welfare payments do not flow to everybody in the population, it is interesting to examine the impact they have on alleviating poverty among certain groups, such as older people, for example. Using data from SILC 2009, the CSO found that without any social welfare payments 88 per cent of all those aged over 65 years would have been living in poverty. Benefit entitlements reduce the poverty level among this group to 9.6 per cent in 2009. Similarly, social welfare payments (including child benefit) reduce poverty among those under 18 years from 47.3 per cent to 18.6 per cent – a 60 per cent reduction in poverty risk (CSO, 2009:47). These findings, combined with the social welfare impact data in table 3.15, underscore the importance of social transfer payments in addressing poverty; a point that needs to be borne in mind as Government continues to address Ireland's ongoing crisis.

Table 3.4 and the subsequent analysis has shown that many of the groups in Irish society which experienced increases in their poverty levels over the last decade have been dependent on social welfare payments. These include pensioners, the unemployed, lone parents and those who are ill or disabled. Table 3.16 presents the results of an analysis of five key welfare recipient groups performed by the ESRI using poverty data for five of the years between 1994 and 2001. These are the years that the Irish economy grew fastest and the core years of the famed 'Celtic Tiger' boom. Between 1994 and 2001 all categories experienced large growth in their poverty risk. For example, in 1994 only 5 out of every 100 old age pension recipients were in poverty; in 2001 this had increased ten-fold to almost 50 out of every 100. The experience of widow's pension recipients is similar.

Table 3.16: Percentage of persons in receipt of welfare benefits/assistance who were below the 60 per cent median income poverty line, 1994/1997/1998/2000/2001

	1994	1997	1998	2000	2001
Old age pension	5.3	19.2	30.7	42.9	49.0
Unemployment benefit/assistance	23.9	30.6	44.8	40.5	43.1
Illness/disability	10.4	25.4	38.5	48.4	49.4
Lone Parents allowance	25.8	38.4	36.9	42.7	39.7
Widow's pension	5.5	38.0	49.4	42.4	42.1

Source: Whelan et al (2003: 31)

Table 3.16 highlights the importance of adequate social welfare payments to prevent people becoming at risk of poverty. Over the period covered by these studies groups similar to *Social Justice Ireland* repeatedly pointed out that these payments had failed to rise in proportion to earnings elsewhere in society. The primary consequence of this was that recipients slipped further and further back and as a consequence more and more fell into poverty. It is clear that adequate levels of social welfare need to be maintained and we outline our proposals for this later in this chapter.

Poverty and deprivation

Income alone does not tell the whole story concerning living standards and command over resources. As we have seen in the NAPS definition of poverty, it is necessary to look more broadly at exclusion from society because of a lack of resources. This requires looking at other areas where "as a result of inadequate income and resources people may be excluded and marginalised from participating in activities that are considered the norm for other people in society" (NAPS, 1997). Although income is the principal indicator used to assess well-being and ability to participate in society, there are other measures. In particular these measures assess the standards of living people achieve by assessing deprivation through use of different indicators. To date assessments of deprivation in Ireland have been limited and confined to a small number of items. While this is regrettable, the information gathered is worth considering.

Deprivation in the SILC survey

Since 2007 the CSO has presented 11 measures of deprivation in the *SILC* survey, compared to just eight before that. While this increase is welcome, *Social Justice Ireland and* others have expressed serious reservations about the overall range of measures employed. We believe that a whole new approach to measuring deprivation should be developed. Continuing to collect information on a limited number of static indicators is problematic in itself and does not present a true picture of the dynamic nature of Irish society.

Table 3.17: Levels of deprivation for eleven items among the population in 2009 and 2010 (%)		
	2009	**2010**
Without heating at some stage in the past year	7.3	10.6
Unable to afford a morning, afternoon or evening out in the last fortnight★	14.9	19.3
Unable to afford two pairs of strong shoes	2.1	2.9
Unable to afford a roast once a week	3.4	5.5
Unable to afford a meal with meat, chicken or fish every second day	2.1	3.0
Unable to afford new (not second-hand) clothes	4.5	7.6
Unable to afford a warm waterproof coat	1.1	2.0
Unable to afford to keep the home adequately warm★	4.1	6.8
Unable to replace any worn out furniture★	16.3	20.3
Unable to afford to have family or friends for a drink or meal once a month★	9.4	14.4
Unable to afford to buy presents for family or friends at least once a year★	3.4	5.1

Source: CSO (2011:12)

Note: ★ New deprivation indicator, used from 2007 onwards.

The details presented in table 3.17, therefore, should be seen in the context of the above reservation. The table shows that the rates of deprivation recorded across the set of eleven items varied between 2 and 20 per cent of the Irish population. Overall 63.8 per cent of the population were not deprived of any item, while 13.7 per cent were deprived of one item, 8.3 per cent were without two items and 14.2 per cent were without three or more items. It is of interest that from 2007 onwards, as the economic crisis unfolded, the proportion of the population who experienced no deprivation fell steadily from 75.6 per cent in 2007 to 63.8 per cent in 2010.

Simultaneously, the proportion of the population experiencing deprivation on two and three items almost doubled, reaching 8.3 per cent and 14.2 per cent respectively (CSO, 2011:11).

Deprivation and poverty combined: consistent poverty

'Consistent poverty' combines deprivation and poverty into a single indicator. It does this by calculating the proportion of the population simultaneously experiencing poverty and registering as deprived of two or more of the items in table 3.17. As such, it captures a sub-group of the poor.

The 2007 *SILC* data marked an important change for this indicator. Coupled with the expanded list of deprivation items, the definition of consistent poverty was changed. From 2007 onwards, to be counted as experiencing consistent poverty individuals must be both below the poverty line and experiencing deprivation of at least two items. Up to2007 the criteria was below the poverty line and deprivation of at least one item. The *National Action Plan for Social Inclusion 2007-2016 (NAPinclusion)* published in early 2007 set its overall poverty goal using this earlier consistent poverty measure. One of its aims was to reduce the number of people experiencing consistent poverty to between 2 per cent and 4 per cent of the total population by 2012, with a further aim of totally eliminating consistent poverty by 2016. A revision to these targets is currently being considered and *Social Justice Ireland* is participating in this process as part of the Governments Technical Advisory Group on Poverty and in the context of the Europe 2020 process (see Mallon and Healy, 2012: 45).

Using these new indicators and definition, the 2010 *SILC* data indicates that 6.2 per cent of the population experience consistent poverty, an increase from 4.2 per cent in 2008 and 5.5 per cent in 2009 (CSO, 2011:10). In terms of the population, the 2010 figures indicate that 277,183 people live in consistent poverty.

Deprivation of food: food poverty

A report on the nature and extent of income-related constraints on food consumption in Ireland entitled *Food Poverty and Policy* defined food poverty as "the inability to access a nutritionally adequate diet and the related impacts on health, culture and social participation" (Society of St.Vincent de Paul et al, 2004). It found that poverty imposed three main constraints on their food consumption. It:

- affected food affordability, both in terms of the choice and quantity of food that can be bought and the share of the household budget that could be allocated to food;

- constraints in terms of transport and physical ability restricted access to food retail options; and
- interacted with issues such as personal skills and knowledge, social pressure and cultural norms as well as with structural and economic constraints to produce a complex set of factors contributing to food poverty.

Consequently, the experience of food poverty among poor people was that they: eat less well compared to better off groups; have difficulties accessing a variety of nutritionally balanced good quality and affordable foodstuffs; spend a greater proportion of their weekly income on food; and may know what is healthy but are restricted by a lack of financial resources to purchase and consume it.

A recent study entitled *Food on a Low Income* (Safefood 2011) confirms these findings and notes that the priority of most poor people was to put food on the table rather than ensuring nutritional value.

Deprivation of heat in the home: fuel poverty

Deprivation of heat in the home, often also referred to as fuel poverty, is another area of deprivation that has received attention in recent times. A 2007 policy paper from the Institute for Public Health (IPH) entitled "*Fuel Poverty and Health*" highlighted the sizeable direct and indirect effects on health of fuel poverty. Overall the IPH found that the levels of fuel poverty in Ireland remain "unacceptably high" and that they are responsible for "among the highest levels of excess winter mortality in Europe, with an estimated 2,800 excess deaths on the island over the winter months" (2007:7). They also highlighted the strong links between low income, unemployment and fuel poverty with single person households and households headed by lone parents and pensioners found to be at highest risk. Similarly, the policy paper shows that older people are more likely to experience fuel poverty due to lower standards of housing coupled with lower incomes.

More recently, The Society of St Vincent de Paul's (SVP) has defined energy poverty as the inability to attain an acceptable level of heating and other energy services in the home due to a combination of three factors: income; energy price and energy efficiency of the dwelling. The SILC study 2009 found that 7.3 per cent of households in the country were without heating at some stage in that year. The SVP points out that households in receipt of energy-related welfare supports account for less than half of the estimated energy poor households. Clearly, welfare payments need to address energy poverty. Other proposals made by the SVP include detailed initiatives on issues such as: the prevention of disconnections; investing in efficiency measures in housing; education and public awareness to promote energy saving; and the compensation of Ireland's poorest households for the existing carbon tax.

Social Justice Ireland supports the IPH's call for the creation of a national fuel poverty strategy similar to the model currently in place in Northern Ireland. Addressing this issue, like all issues associated with poverty and deprivation, requires a multi-faceted approach. The proposals presented by the SVP should form the core of such a fuel poverty strategy.[29]

The experience of poverty

A recently published research report from the Vincentian Partnership for Social Justice (VPSJ) and Trinity College Dublin casts new light on the challenges faced by people living on low incomes in Ireland (Collins et al, 2012). Entitled '*A Minimum Income Standard for Ireland*', the research establishes the cost of a minimum essential standard of living for individuals and households across the entire lifecycle; from children to pensioners. Subsequently the study calculates the minimum income households require to be able to afford this standard of living.

A minimum essential standard of living is defined by the United Nations as one which meets a person's physical, psychological, spiritual and social needs. To establish this figure, the research adopted a consensual budgets standards approach whereby representative focus groups established budgets on the basis of a households minimum needs, rather than wants. These budgets, spanning over 2,000 goods, were developed for sixteen areas of expenditure including: food, clothing, personal care, health related costs, household goods, household services, communication, social inclusion and participation, education, transport, household fuel, personal costs, childcare, insurance, housing, savings and contingencies. These budgets were then benchmarked, for their nutritional and energy content, to ensure they were sufficient to provide appropriate nutrition and heat for families, and priced. The study establishes the weekly cost of a minimum essential standard of living for five household types., These included: a single person of working age living alone; a two parent household with two children; a single parent household with two children; a pensioner couple; and a female pensioner living alone. Within these household categories, the analysis distinguishes between the expenditure for urban and rural households and between those whose members are unemployed or working, either part-time or full-time. The study also established the expenditure needs of a child and how these change across childhood.

---

[29] We address these issues further in the context of a carbon tax in chapter 4.

Table 3.18 summarises the findings of this research for two adult plus two children urban households dependent on unemployment benefit. When the weekly income of these households is compared to the weekly expenditure they require to experience a basic standard of living, the report found that almost all these households received an inadequate income. These households have to cut back on the basics to make ends meet (Collins et al, 2012:105-107). The report found similar results for rural welfare dependent households. It also found that many low income working households, in particular those working at the minimum wage, were unable to earn sufficient income to afford a basic standard of living – a phenomenon which underscores the focus on the scale of the working poor problem earlier in this review.

Table 3.18: Comparisons of minimum expenditure levels with certain income levels for a 2 adult 2 child urban household (€ per week)

Ages of Children	9 Months & Pre-School	Both Pre-School	Pre & Primary School	Both Primary School	Primary & Second Level	Both Second Level
Household Expenditure	464.03	421.14	451.5	481.87	547.77	613.67
Household Income	437.02	437.02	440.87	444.71	446.73	448.75
Income – Expenditure	–27.02	+15.88	–10.64	–37.17	–101.04	–164.92
Income Adequacy	Inadequate	Adequate	Inadequate	Inadequate	Inadequate	Inadequate

Source: Collins et al, 2012: 105-107.

Overall this study, which complements earlier research by the VPSJ (2006, 2010), contains major implications for government policy if poverty is to be eliminated. These include the need to address child poverty, the income levels of adults on social welfare, the 'working poor' issue and access to services ranging from social housing to fuel for older people and the distribution of resources between urban and rural Ireland.[30]

Poverty: a European perspective
It is helpful to compare Irish measures of poverty with those elsewhere in Europe. Eurostat, the European Statistics Agency, produces comparable 'at risk of poverty'

[30] Data from these studies are available at www.budgeting.ie

figures (proportions of the population living below the poverty line) for each EU member state. The data is calculated using the 60 per cent of median income poverty line in each country. Comparable EU wide definitions of income and equivalence scale are used.[31] The latest data available is for the year 2010.

As table 3.19 shows, in 2010 Irish people experienced a below average risk of poverty when compared to all other EU member states. Eurostat's 2008 figures marked the first time Ireland's poverty levels fell below average EU levels. This phenomenon was driven, as outlined earlier in this review, by sustained increases in welfare payments in the years prior to 2008. Ireland's poverty levels remained below average EU levels in 2009 and 2010, although over that time poverty rates increased. In 2010, across the EU the highest poverty levels were found in the recent accession countries of Latvia, Romania and Bulgaria while the lowest levels were in countries such as Austria, Slovakia and the Netherlands.

Table 3.19: The risk of poverty in the European Union in 2010

Country	Poverty Risk	Country	Poverty Risk
Latvia	21.3	Malta	15.5
Romania	21.1	Belgium	14.6
Bulgaria	20.7	Luxembourg	14.5
Spain	20.7	France	13.5
Lithuania	20.2	Denmark	13.3
Greece	20.1	Finland	13.1
Italy	18.2	Sweden	12.9
Portugal	17.9	Slovenia	12.7
Poland	17.6	Hungary	12.3
United Kingdom	17.1	Austria	12.1
Cyprus	17.0	Slovakia	12.0
IRELAND	16.1	Netherlands	10.3
Estonia	15.8	Czech Republic	9.0
Germany	15.6	**EU-27 average**	**16.4**

Source: Eurostat online database

Note: Table uses the most up-to-date comparable data available for countries and corresponds to the year 2010.

[31] Differences in definitions of income and equivalence scales result in slight differences in the poverty rates reported for Ireland when compared to those reported earlier which have been calculated by the CSO using national definitions of income and the Irish equivalence scale.

The average risk of poverty in the EU-27 for 2010 was 16.4 per cent. Chart 3.1 further develops the findings of table 3.19 and shows the difference between national poverty risk levels and the EU-27 average.

Chart 3.1: Percentage difference in National Poverty risk from EU-27 average

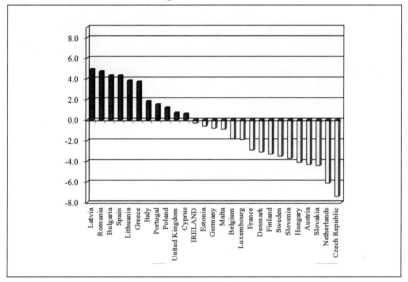

Source: Eurostat online database
Note: Chart uses the most up-to-date comparable data available for countries and corresponds to the year 2010.

While there have been some reductions in poverty in recent years across the EU, the data does suggest that poverty remains a large and on-going EU wide problem. In 2010, the average EU-27 level implies that more than 80 million people are in poverty across the EU. As part of the Europe 2020 Strategy, European Governments have begun to adopt policies to target these poverty levels and are using as their main benchmark the proportion of the population at risk of poverty or social exclusion. This indicator has been defined by the European Council on the basis of three indicators: the aforementioned 'at risk of poverty' rate after social transfers, the index of material deprivation and the percentage of people living in households with very low work intensity. It is calculated as the sum of persons relative to the national population who are at risk of poverty or severely materially deprived or living in households with very low work intensity, where a person is only counted once even if recorded in more than one indicator.[32]

Table 3.20 summarises the latest data on this indicator for Europe and chart 3.2 summarises the latest Irish data for 2010. While *Social Justice Ireland* regrets that the Europe 2020 process shifted its indicator focus away from an exclusive concentration on the at risk of poverty rate, we welcome the added attention at a European level to issues regarding poverty, deprivation and joblessness. Together with Caritas Europa, we intend to monitor progress on this strategy over the years to come. However, it is clear already that the austerity measures which are being pursued in many EU countries will result in the erosion of social services and lead to the further exclusion of people who already find themselves on the margins of society. This is in direct contradiction to the inclusive growth focus of the Europe 2020 Strategy. It is reflected in the figures in table 3.20 which show an increase in risk levels in 2010.

Table 3.20: People at risk of poverty or social exclusion, Ireland and the EU 2007–2010				
	2007	**2008**	**2009**	**2010**
Ireland % Population	23.1	23.7	25.7	29.9
Ireland 000s people	1,005	1,050	1,150	1,335
EU % Population	24.4	23.6	23.1	23.5
EU 000s people	119,316	115,730	113,716	115,790

Source: Eurostat online database

Income Distribution

As previously outlined, despite some improvements poverty remains a significant problem. The purpose of economic development should be to improve the living standards of all of the population. A further loss of social cohesion will mean that large numbers of people continue to experience deprivation and the gap between them and the better off will widen. This has implications for all of society, not just those who are poor.

---

[32] See European Commission (2011) for a more detailed explanation of this indicator.

Chart 3.2: Population at risk of poverty or social exclusion, Ireland 2010

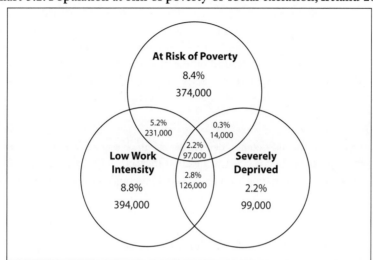

Source: Compiled from Eurostat online database

Analysing the annual income and expenditure accounts provides us with information on trends in the distribution of national income. However, the limitations of this accounting system need to be acknowledged. Measures of income are far from perfect gauges of a society. They ignore many relevant non-market features, such as volunteerism, caring and environmental protection. Many environmental factors, such as the depletion of natural resources, are registered as income but not seen as a cost. Pollution is not registered as a cost but cleaning up after pollution is seen as income. Increased spending on prisons and security, which are a response to crime, are seen as increasing national income but not registered as reducing human well-being.

The point is, of course, that national accounts do not include items that cannot easily be assigned a monetary value. Progress cannot be measured by economic growth alone. Many other factors are required, as we highlight elsewhere in this review.[33] However, when judging economic performance and making judgements about how well Ireland is really doing, it is important to look at the distribution of national income as well as its absolute amount.[34]

---

[33] We return to critique National Income statistics in chapter 12. There, we also propose some alternatives.
[34] We examine the issue of the world's income and wealth distribution in chapter 14.

Ireland's income distribution: current situation

The most recent data on Ireland's income distribution, from the 2010 SILC survey, was published in preliminary form by the CSO in November 2011. While the publication provided considerable detail on poverty figures (see earlier in this chapter) it provided limited detailed on the structure of the income distribution. A further report is to be published later in 2012. However, it did show that over recent years Ireland's income distribution has widened further – a point we return to later.

Chart 3.3 shows the most comprehensive data on the income distribution available, which was published by the CSO in late 2010. It examines the income distribution by household deciles, starting with the 10% of households with the lowest income (the bottom decile) up to the 10% of households with the highest income (the top decile). The data presented is for disposable income. This is the amount of money households have in their pocket to spend after they have received any employment/pension income, paid all their income taxes and received any welfare entitlements.

Chart 3.3: Ireland's Income Distribution by 10% (decile) group, 2009

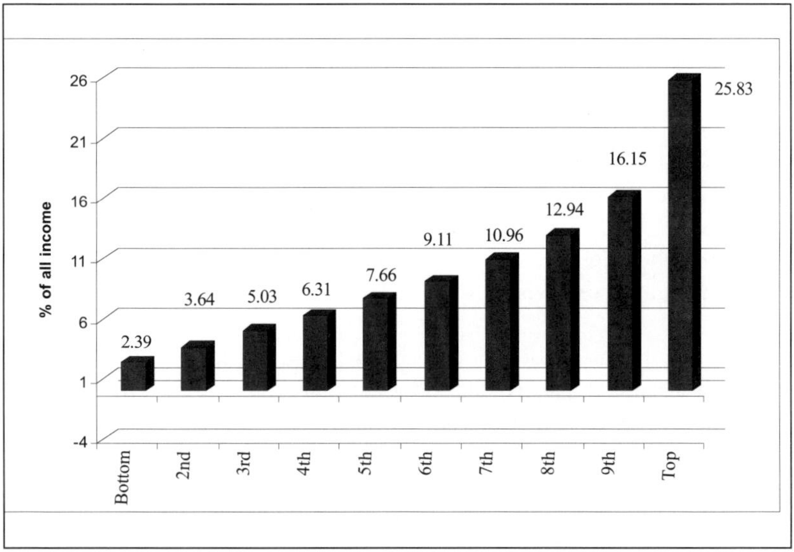

Source: Calculated from CSO, 2010:24-25

In 2009, the top 10 per cent of Irish households received 25.83 per cent of the total disposable income while the bottom decile received 2.39 per cent. Collectively, the poorest 50 per cent of households received a very similar share (25.02 per cent) to the top 10 per cent. Overall the share of the top 10 per cent is nearly 11 times the share of the bottom 10 per cent. Table 3.21 outlines the cash values of these income shares in 2009. It shows that the top 10 per cent of households receive an average weekly disposable income (after all taxes and having received all benefits) of €2,276 while the bottom decile receives €210 per week. In 2009 the average household disposable income was €880 a week / €45,926 per annum (CSO, 2010: 24-25). While the nominal value of these shares is likely to have declined since 2009, the spread of income reflected in the table has become more unequal according to the CSOs preliminary SILC report for 2010.

Table 3.21: Amounts of disposable income, by decile in 2009.

Decile	Weekly disposable income	Annual disposable income
Bottom	€210.45	€10,973
2nd	€320.37	€16,705
3rd	€443.07	€23,103
4th	€555.88	€28,985
5th	€675.19	€35,206
6th	€802.53	€41,846
7th	€965.83	€50,361
8th	€1,140.49	€59,468
9th	€1,422.84	€74,191
Top	€2,276.00	€118,677

Source: Calculated from CSO (2010:24-25)
Note: Annual figures are rounded to the nearest Euro to ease interpretation.

Ireland's income distribution: trends from 1987-2010

The results of studies by Collins and Kavanagh (1998, 2006) combined with the recent CSO income figures provide a useful insight into the pattern of Ireland's income distribution over 23 years. Table 3.22 combines the results from these studies and reflects the distribution of income in Ireland as tracked by five surveys. Overall, across the period 1987-2009 income distribution is very static. However, within the period there were some notable changes, with shifts in distribution towards higher deciles in the period 1994/95 to 2004.

Table 3.22: The distribution of household disposable income, 1987–2009 (%)					
Decile	**1987**	**1994/95**	**1999/00**	**2004**	**2009**
Bottom	2.28	2.23	1.93	2.10	2.39
2nd	3.74	3.49	3.16	3.04	3.64
3rd	5.11	4.75	4.52	4.27	5.03
4th	6.41	6.16	6.02	5.69	6.31
5th	7.71	7.63	7.67	7.43	7.66
6th	9.24	9.37	9.35	9.18	9.11
7th	11.16	11.41	11.20	11.11	10.96
8th	13.39	13.64	13.48	13.56	12.94
9th	16.48	16.67	16.78	16.47	16.15
Top	24.48	24.67	25.90	27.15	25.83
Total	**100.00**	**100.00**	**100.00**	**100.00**	**100.00**

Source: Collins and Kavanagh (2006:156) and CSO (2006:18-19, 2010: 24-58).

Note: Data for 1987, 1994/95 and 1999/00 are from various Household Budget Surveys. 2004 and 2009 data from SILC.

Using data from the two ends of this period, 1987 and 2009, chart 3.4 examines the change in the income distribution over the intervening 22 years. While a lot changed in Ireland over that period, income distribution did not change significantly. Compared with 1987, only two deciles saw their share of the total income distribution increase – the bottom decile and the top decile. However, the change for the former is small (+0.11 per cent) while the change for the latter is more notable (+1.34 per cent). All other deciles witnessed a decrease in their share of the national income distribution.

Looking at only the last six available SILC surveys (2004-2009), the CSO found that the bottom two deciles saw their share of income increase. Similar to the earlier changes in the poverty figures, it is likely that these improvements were related to budgetary policy over that period which increased social welfare payments. The CSO data show that households in these deciles receive a large proportion of their income from social welfare payments (CSO, 2010: 24-25). As shown earlier, during this period they experienced increases in welfare payments representing a partial catch-up in their relative income position given the declines experienced in the late 1990s.

Chart 3.4: Change in Ireland's Income Distribution, 1987-2009

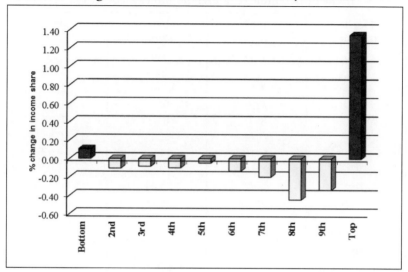

Source: Calculated from CSO, 2010:24-25

Preliminary data for 2010 suggests that changes in this reasonably static income distribution picture may have occurred. Although precise information on each decile share is not available yet, the CSO has reported that the overall level of income inequality has grown to its highest level since the SILC survey began in 2003. Using the Gini coefficient measure of inequality, which ranges from 0-100 with higher scores indicating greater inequality, Ireland's inequality levels grew from 29.3 in 2009 to 33.9 in 2010. Furthermore, the initial 2010 data indicates that the share of the top 20 per cent of households has climbed further to reach 5.5 times the share of the bottom 20 per cent. The comparable ratio in 2009 was 4.3 times.

It is noteworthy that Ireland's disposable income distribution (after redistribution through taxes and transfers) has been largely static while there have been improvements in welfare payments which reduced poverty, as highlighted in table 3.15. The implication of this is that simultaneous with improvements in welfare payments and redistributive taxes, the underlying distribution of direct or market income has become more unequal. Collins and Kavanagh (2006: 155, 162) highlighted the "marked increase in the level of direct income inequality" over the period from 1973 to 2004.

Table 3.23: The distribution of household direct income, 1987-2009 (%)			
Decile	**1987**	**2004**	**2009**
Bottom	0.38	0.19	0.23
2nd	1.00	0.48	0.71
3rd	1.40	1.05	1.35
4th	3.30	2.64	2.57
5th	6.10	5.70	4.69
6th	8.70	8.65	7.69
7th	11.60	11.49	10.68
8th	15.09	14.96	14.47
9th	20.08	19.54	21.02
Top	32.46	35.31	36.59
Total	**100.00**	**100.00**	**100.00**
Bottom 20%	1.38	0.67	0.94
Bottom 50%	12.08	10.06	9.55
Top 10:Bot 10	85 times	185 times	160 times

Source: Collins and Kavanagh (2006:155) and CSO (2010: 24-25).
Note: Data for 1987 is from the Household Budget Survey, 2004 and 2009 data from SILC.

Table 3.23 suggests that the level of direct income inequality has continued to widen. Over the period from 1987 to 2009 the direct income shares of all deciles except the top two have declined. Compared to the situation in 1987 the gap between the bottom and top deciles has dramatically widened. By 2009 the share of the top 10 per cent was almost four times that of the bottom 50 per cent. While the role of the redistribution system is to intervene and address this inequality via taxation and welfare payments, the fact that the underlying nature of income inequality continues to worsen suggests that the challenges faced by the redistribution system have become much greater over time.

Income changes – a 25 year assessment

It has been suggested in recent times that there should be a reduction in the basic social welfare payment, the jobseekers allowance. It has been asserted by some that this rate increased too fast and reached too high a level during the last decade. The earlier analysis (see tables 3.15 and 3.16) highlighted that over the period since 2000 welfare increases were essentially attempting to catch-up given the dramatic worsening of the position of those dependent on social welfare relative to the rest of society. This was most significantly demonstrated by the large increases in the poverty levels of welfare recipients between 1994 and 2001. However, it is worth broadening this perspective to compare the income gains of those on welfare compared to a range of others in Irish society over the past quarter of a century. Chart 3.5 presents the results of such an analysis undertaken by *Social Justice Ireland* for the years between 1986 and 2012 (incorporating all changes to earnings and take home pay in Budget 2011).

The following should be noted about the calculations:

* Taxation is calculated on a single person basis under normal rules as this yields the lowest net pay. It could be calculated differently which would result in the net weekly pay increase being higher for those in paid employment included in the table.
* Irish punt values have been converted from pounds to euros.
* The pay for a TD is calculated on the 2011 rate for a TD with 10 years service or more. When the next Dáil is elected there will be no increments available to TDs and all will earn the same basic pay of €92,672 a year.
* To allow like for like comparison, the figures do not take account of pension contributions or deductions as these are neither available nor comparable across sectors. In this context it should be noted that those at the higher income range have a much greater gain for their pension contributions compared to the others listed in the table.

Chart 3.5: Increases in weekly pay, 1986-2011

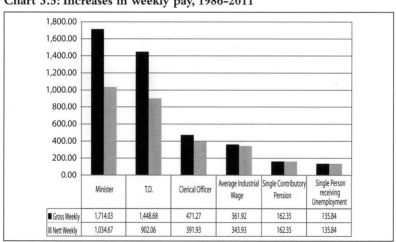

	Minister	T.D.	Clerical Officer	Average Industrial Wage	Single Contributory Pension	Single Person receiving Unemployment
■ Gross Weekly	1,714.03	1,448.68	471.27	361.92	162.35	135.84
▦ Nett Weekly	1,034.67	902.06	391.93	343.93	162.35	135.84

The analysis shows that over the quarter century 1986-2011 the take-home pay of TDs rose by €902 a week while jobseekers benefit rates for a single person only increased by €136 a week in the same period. Government ministers' take-home pay rose by more than €1,035 a week in the same period. Similarly, the take-home pay of clerical officers in the public sector rose by €392 a week; the take-home pay of a person on the average industrial wage rose by €344 a week; and the contributory old age pension for a single person rose by €162.35 a week.

These are dramatic numbers in the context of the on-going calls for welfare and pension cuts. As we have pointed out in our various pre-Budget submission over recent years, other choices exist that would have enabled Government not to cut social welfare rates. These choices should have been taken in the past and should be taken in the period ahead. The figures also underscore the massive increases in direct income inequality over recent decades demonstrated earlier in this review.

Income distribution: a European perspective

Another of the 18 indicators adopted by the EU at Laeken assesses the income distribution of member states by comparing the ratio of equivalised disposable income received by the bottom quintile (20 per cent) to that of the top quintile. This indicator reveals how far away from each other the shares of these two groups are – the higher the ratio the greater the income difference. Table 3.24 presents the most up-to-date results of this indicator for the 27 states that were members of the EU in 2010. The 2010 data indicate that the Irish figure increased to 5.3 from a ratio of 4.2 in 2009, reflecting the already noted increase in income inequality in 2010. Ireland now has a ratio above the EU average and, given recent economic and budgetary policy, this looks likely to persist and may even worsen. Overall, the greatest differences in the shares of those at the top and bottom of income distribution are found in many of the newer and poorer member states. However, some EU-15 members, including the UK, Italy, Spain, Greece and Portugal, also record large differences.

Table 3.24: Ratio of Disposable Income received by bottom quintile to that of the top quintile in the EU-27.

Country	Ratio	Country	Ratio
Lithuania	7.3	Denmark	4.4
Spain	6.9	Cyprus	4.4
Latvia	6.9	Malta	4.3
Romania	6.0	Luxembourg	4.1
Bulgaria	5.9	Belgium	3.9
Portugal	5.6	Slovakia	3.8
Greece	5.6	Netherlands	3.7
United Kingdom	5.4	Austria	3.7
IRELAND	**5.3**	Finland	3.6
Italy	5.2	Sweden	3.5
Poland	5.0	Czech Republic	3.5
Estonia	5.0	Slovenia	3.4
Germany	4.5	Hungary	3.4
France	4.5	**EU-27 average**	**5.0**

Source: Eurostat online database

Note: Table uses the most up-to-date comparable data available for countries and corresponds to the year 2010.

Maintaining an Adequate Level of Social Welfare

From 2005 onwards there was major progress on benchmarking social welfare payments. Budget 2007 benchmarked the minimum social welfare rate at 30 per cent of Gross Average Industrial Earnings (GAIE). This was a key achievement and one that we correctly predicted would lead to reductions in poverty rates, complementing those already achieved and detailed earlier.

The process of benchmarking social welfare payments centred on three elements: the 2001 *Social Welfare Benchmarking and Indexation Working Group* (SWBIG), the 2002 *National Anti-Poverty Strategy (NAPS) Review* and the *Budgets 2005-2007*.

Social welfare benchmarking and indexation working group

In its final report the SWBIG agreed that the lowest social welfare rates should be benchmarked. A majority of the working group, which included a director of *Social Justice Ireland*, also agreed that this benchmark should be index-linked to society's standard of living as it grows and that the benchmark should be reached by a definite date. The working group chose Gross Average Industrial Earnings (GAIE) to be the index to which payments should be linked.[35] The group further urged that regular and formal review and monitoring of the range of issues covered in its report should be provided for. The group expressed the opinion that this could best be accommodated within the structures in place under the NAPS and the *National Action Plan for Social Inclusion* (now combined as *NAPinclusion*). The SWBIG report envisaged that such a mechanism could involve:

- the review of any benchmarks/targets and indexation methodologies adopted by government to ensure that the underlying objectives remain valid and were being met
- the assessment of such benchmarks/targets and indexation methodologies against the various criteria set out in the group's terms of reference to ensure their continued relevance
- the assessment of emerging trends in the key areas of concern – e.g. poverty levels, labour market performance, demographic changes, economic performance, competitiveness, etc.
- identification of gaps in the area of research and assessment of any additional research undertaken in the interim.

National Anti-Poverty Strategy (NAPS) review 2002

In 2002, the NAPS review set the following as key targets:

To achieve a rate of €150 per week in 2002 terms for the lowest rates of social welfare to be met by 2007 and the appropriate equivalence level of basic child income support (i.e. Child Benefit and Child Dependent Allowances combined) to be set at 33 per cent - 35 per cent of the minimum adult social welfare payment rate.

We, among others, welcomed this target. It was a major breakthrough in social, economic and philosophical terms. We also welcomed the reaffirmation of this target in *Towards 2016*. That agreement contained a commitment to "achieving the NAPS target of €150 per week in 2002 terms for lowest social welfare rates by 2007" (2006:52). The target of €150 a week was equivalent to 30 per cent of Gross Average Industrial Earnings (GAIE) in 2002.[36]

---

[35] The group recommended a benchmark of 27 per cent although we argued for 30 per cent.

[36] GAIE is calculated by the CSO on the earnings of all individuals (male and female) working in all industries. The GAIE figure in 2002 was €501.51 and 30 per cent of this figure equals €150.45 (CSO, 2006: 2).

In response to this commitment we calculated the projected growth in €150 between 2002 and 2007 when it is indexed to the estimated growth in GAIE. Table 3.25 outlines these expected growth rates and calculates that the lowest social welfare rates for single people should have reached €185.80 by 2007.

Table 3.25: Estimating growth in €150 a week (30% GAIE) for 2002-2007						
	2002	2003	2004	2005	2006	2007
% Growth of GAIE	–	+6.00	+3.00	+4.50	+3.60	+4.80
30% GAIE	150	159.00	163.77	171.14	177.30	185.80

Source: GAIE growth rates from CSO Industrial Earnings and Hours Worked (September 2004:2) and ESRI Medium Term Review (Bergin et al, 2003:49).

Budgets 2005-2007

The NAPS commitment was very welcome and was one of the few areas of the anti-poverty strategy that was adequate to tackle the scale of the poverty, inequality and social exclusion being experienced by so many people in Ireland today.

In 2002, we set out a pathway to reaching this target by calculating the projected growth of €150 between 2002 and 2007 when it is indexed to the estimated growth in GAIE. Progress towards achieving this target had been slow until Budget 2005. At its first opportunity to live up to the NAPS commitment the government granted a mere €6 a week increase in social welfare rates in Budget 2003. This increase was below that which we proposed and also below that recommended by the government's own tax strategy group. In Budget 2004 the increase in the minimum social welfare payment was €10. This increase was again below the €12 a week we sought and at this point we set out a three-year pathway (see table 3.26).

Table 3.26: Proposed approach to addressing the gap, 2005-2007			
	2005	2006	2007
Min. SW. payment in €'s	148.80	165.80	185.80
€ amount increase each year	14.00	17.00	20.00
Delivered	✓	✓	✓

Following Budget 2004 we argued for an increase of €14 in Budget 2005. The Government's decision to deliver an increase equal to that amount in that Budget marked a significant step towards honouring this commitment which we warmly welcomed. Budget 2006 followed suit, delivering an increase of €17 per week to those in receipt of the minimum social welfare rate. Finally, Budget 2007's decision to deliver an increase of €20 per week to the minimum social welfare rates brought the minimum social welfare payment up to the 30 per cent of the GAIE benchmark.

Social Justice Ireland believes that these increases, and the achievement of the benchmark in Budget 2007, marked a fundamental turning point in Irish public policy. Budget 2007 was the third budget in a row where the government delivered on its NAPS commitment. In doing so the government moved to meet the target so that in 2007 the minimum social welfare rate increased to €185.80 per week; a figure equivalent to the 30 per cent of GAIE.

We warmly welcomed this achievement. It marked major progress and underscored the delivery of a long overdue commitment to sharing the fruits of this country's economic growth since the mid-1990s. An important element of the NAPS commitment to increasing social welfare rates was the acknowledgement that the years from 2002-2007 marked a period of 'catch-up' for those in receipt of welfare payments. Once this income gap had been bridged, the increases necessary to keep social welfare payments at a level equivalent to 30 per cent of GAIE became much smaller. In that context we welcomed the commitment by Government in *NAPinclusion* to "maintain the relative value of the lowest social welfare rate at least at €185.80, in 2007 terms, over the course of this Plan (2007-2016), subject to available resources" (2007:42). Whether or not 30 per cent of GAIE is adequate to eliminate the risk of poverty is an issue to be monitored through the SILC studies and in particular to be addressed when fresh data on persistent poverty emerges.

Setting a Benchmark: 2011 onwards

In late 2007 the CSO discontinued their *Industrial Earnings and Hours Worked* dataset and replaced it with a more comprehensive set of income statistics for a broader set of Irish employment sectors. The end of that dataset also saw the demise of the GAIE figure from Irish official statistics. It has been replaced with a series of measures, including a new indicator measuring average earnings across all the employment sectors now covered. While the improvement to data sources is welcome, the end of the GAIE figure poses problems for continuing to calculate the social welfare benchmark. To this end, *Social Justice Ireland* commissioned a report in late 2010 to establish an appropriate way of continuing to calculate this benchmark.

A report entitled *'Establishing a Benchmark for Ireland's Social Welfare Payments'* (Collins, 2011) is available on our website. It established that 30 per cent of GAIE is equivalent to 27.5 per cent of the new average earnings data being collected by the CSO. A figure of 27.5 per cent of average earnings is therefore the appropriate benchmark for minimum social welfare payments and reflects a continuation of the previous benchmark using the new CSO earnings dataset.

Table 3.27 applies this benchmark using CSO data for second quarter 2011 (published November 23rd 2011). The data is updated using ESRI projections for wage growth in 2012 (0 per cent) and 2013 (0 per cent). In 2011 and 2012, 27.5 per cent of average weekly earnings equal €189.24; marginally more than the current minimum social welfare rate (€188). As a consequence of this benchmark, *Social Justice Ireland* believes that the appropriate budgetary policy in 2013 would be to leave minimum social welfare rates static at €188 per week. While such a figure is challenging for individuals to survive on, it would be completely unacceptable to reduce this payment below its current level. In that regard we welcome the commitment from the Government not to reduce these rates further.

Table 3.27: Benchmarking Social Welfare Payments for 2012 and 2013 (€)

Year	Average Weekly Earnings	27.5% of Average Weekly Earnings
2011	688.14	189.24
2012	688.14	189.24
2013	688.14	189.24

Notes: 2011 data from Quarter 2 2011 (CSO, November 2011).
Earnings Growth rates for 2012 and 2013 from ESRI QEC Winter 2011/Spring 2012.

Individualising social welfare payments

The issue of individualising payments so that all recipients receive their own social welfare payments has been on the policy agenda in Ireland and across the EU for several years. We welcomed the report of the Working Group, *Examining the Treatment of Married, Cohabiting and One-Parent Families under the Tax and Social Welfare Codes*, which addressed some of the individualisation issues.

At present the welfare system provides a basic payment for a claimant, whether that be, for example, for a pension, a disability payment or a job-seeker's payment. It then adds an additional payment of about two-thirds of the basic payment for the second person. For example, following Budget 2012 a couple on the lowest social welfare rate receive a payment of €312.80 per week. This amount is approximately 1.66 times the payment for a single person (€188). Were these two people living separately they would receive €188 each; giving a total of €376. Thus by living as a household unit such a couple receive a lower income than they would were they to live apart.

Social Justice Ireland believes that this system is unfair and inequitable. We also believe that the system as currently structured is not compatible with the Equal Status Acts (2000-2004), a point we strongly made in a submission to the *Department of Social and Family Affairs Review of the Social Welfare Code* with regard to its compatibility with the Equal Status Acts. People, often women, are disadvantaged by living as part of a household unit because they receive a lower income. We believe that where a couple are in receipt of welfare payments, the payment to the second person should be increased to equal that of the first. Such a change would remove the current inequity and bring the current social welfare system in line with the terms of the Equal Status Acts (2000-2004). An effective way of doing this would be to introduce a basic income system which is far more appropriate for the world of the 21st century.

Basic Income

Over the past decade major progress has been achieved in building the case for the introduction of a basic income in Ireland. This includes the publication of a *Green Paper on Basic Income* by the government in September 2002 and the publication of a book by Clark entitled *The Basic Income Guarantee* (2002). A major international conference on basic income was also held in Dublin during Summer 2008 at which more than 70 papers from 30 countries were presented. These are available on *Social Justice Ireland*'s website.

The case for a Basic Income

Social Justice Ireland has argued for a long time that the present tax and social welfare systems should be integrated and reformed to make them more appropriate to the changing world of the 21st century. To this end we have argued for the introduction of a basic income system. This proposal is especially relevant at the present moment of economic upheaval.

A basic income is an income that is unconditionally granted to every person on an individual basis, without any means test or work requirement. In a basic-income system every person receives a weekly tax-free payment from the Exchequer while all other personal income is taxed, usually at a single rate. For a person who is unemployed, the basic-income payment would replace income from social welfare. For a person who is employed, the basic-income payment would replace tax credits in the income-tax system.

Basic income is a form of minimum income guarantee that avoids many of the negative side effects inherent in social welfare payments. A basic income differs from other forms of income support in that:

- it is paid to individuals rather than households;
- it is paid irrespective of any income from other sources;
- it is paid without conditions; it does not require the performance of any work or the willingness to accept a job if offered one; and
- it is always tax free.

There is real danger that the plight of large numbers of people excluded from the benefits of the modern economy will be ignored. Images of rising tides lifting all boats are often offered as government's policy makers and commentators assure society that prosperity for all is just around the corner. Likewise, the claim is often made that a job is the best poverty fighter and consequently priority must be given to securing a paid job for everyone. These images and claims are no substitute for concrete policies to ensure that all are included. Twenty-first-century society needs a radical approach to ensure the inclusion of all people in the benefits of present economic growth and development. Basic Income is such an approach.

As we are proposing it, a basic income system would replace social welfare and income tax credits. It would guarantee an income above the poverty line for everyone. It would not be means tested. There would be no "signing on" and no restrictions or conditions. In practice a basic income recognises the right of every person to a share of the resources of society.

The Basic Income system ensures that looking for a paid job and earning an income, or increasing one's income while in employment, is always worth pursuing, because for every euro earned the person will retain a large part. It thus removes the poverty traps and unemployment traps in the present system. Furthermore, women and men would receive equal payments in a basic income system. Consequently the basic income system promotes gender equality because it treats every person equally.

It is a system that is altogether more guaranteed, rewarding, simple and transparent than the present tax and welfare systems. It is far more employment friendly than the present system. It also respects other forms of work besides paid employment. This is crucial in a world where these need to be recognised and respected. It is also very important in a world where paid employment cannot be permanently guaranteed for everyone seeking it. There is growing pressure and need in Irish society to ensure recognition and monetary reward for such work. Basic income is a transparent, efficient and affordable mechanism for ensuring such recognition and reward.

Basic income also lifts people out of poverty and the dreadful dependency mode of survival. In doing this, it also restores self-esteem and broadens horizons. Poor people, however, are not the only ones who should welcome a basic income system. Employers, for example, should welcome it because its introduction would mean they would not be in competition with the social welfare system. Since employees would not lose their basic income when taking a job, there would always be an incentive to take up employment.

Ten reasons to introduce basic income
- It is work and employment friendly.
- It eliminates poverty traps and unemployment traps.
- It promotes equity and ensures that everyone receives at least the poverty level of income.
- It spreads the burden of taxation more equitably.
- It treats men and women equally.
- It is simple and transparent.
- It is efficient in labour-market terms.
- It rewards types of work in the social economy that the market economy often ignores, e.g. home duties, caring, etc.
- It facilitates further education and training in the labour force.
- It faces up to the changes in the global economy.

Key policy priorities on income distribution
- If poverty rates are to fall in the years ahead, *Social Justice Ireland* believes that the following are required:
  - benchmarking of social welfare payments,
  - equity of social welfare rates,
  - adequate payments for children,
  - refundable tax credits,

- a universal state pension, and
- a cost of disability payment.

Social Justice Ireland believes that in the period ahead Government and policy-makers generally should:

- Acknowledge that Ireland has an on-going poverty problem.

- Assess the impact on society's most vulnerable people of any proposed policy initiatives aimed at achieving the fiscal adjustments required by the EU/IMF bailout and the Government's multi-year budgetary plan.

- Change the ratio of expenditure cuts to tax increases in forthcoming budgets. Tax increases should account for two thirds of the required fiscal adjustment.

- Examine and support viable, alternative policy options aimed at giving priority to protecting vulnerable sectors of society.

- Provide substantial new measures to address long-term unemployment. This should include programmes aimed at re-training and re-skilling those at highest risk.

- Recognise the problem of the 'working poor'. Make tax credits refundable to address the situation of households in poverty which are headed by a person with a job.

- Introduce a cost of disability allowance to address poverty and social exclusion of people with a disability.

- Poverty-proof all public policy initiatives and provision.

- Recognise the reality of poverty among migrants and adopt policies to assist this group. In addressing this issue also reform and increase the 'direct provision' allowances paid to asylum seekers.

- Accept that persistent poverty should be used as the primary indicator of poverty measurement once this data becomes available.

- Move towards introducing a basic income system. No other approach has the capacity to ensure all members of society have sufficient income to live life with dignity.

4. TAXATION

CORE POLICY OBJECTIVE: TAXATION

To collect sufficient taxes to ensure full participation in society for all, through a fair tax system in which those who have more, pay more, while those who have less, pay less.

The fiscal adjustments as a consequence of the economic crisis have underscored the centrality of taxation in budget deliberations and to policy development at both macro and micro level. Taxation plays a key role in shaping Irish society through funding public services, supporting economic activity and redistributing resources to enhance the fairness of society. Consequently, it is crucial that clarity exist with regard to both the objectives and instruments aimed at achieving these goals. To ensure the creation of a fairer and more equitable tax system, policy development in this area should adhere to our core policy objective outlined above. In that regard, *Social Justice Ireland* is committed to increasing the level of detailed analysis and debate addressing this area.

The need for a wider tax base is a lesson painfully learnt by Ireland during the past four years. A disastrous combination of a naïve housing policy, a failed regulatory system and foolish fiscal policy and economic planning combined to cause a collapse in exchequer revenues. The narrowness of the Irish tax base resulted in almost 25 per cent of expected tax revenues disappearing, plunging the exchequer and the country into a series of fiscal policy crises. As shown in chapter 2, tax revenues collapsed from over €59 billion in 2007 to €47.8 billion in 2010[3]. It is only through a determined effort to reform Ireland's taxation system that these mistakes can be addressed and avoided in the future.

This chapter outlines Ireland's relative taxation position, the anticipated future taxation needs, further approaches to reforming and broadening the tax base and proposals for building a fairer tax system.

---

[37] Cf. Table 2.2 in chapter 2.

Ireland's total tax take up to 2009

The most recent comparative data on the size of Ireland's total tax-take has been produced by Eurostat (2011) and is detailed alongside that of 26 other EU states in table 4.1. The definition of taxation employed by Eurostat comprises all compulsory payments to central government (direct and indirect) alongside social security contributions (employee and employer) and the tax receipts of local authorities.[38] The tax-take of each country is established by calculating the ratio of total taxation revenue to national income as measured by gross domestic product (GDP). Table 4.1 also compares the tax-take of all EU member states against the average tax-take of 35.8 per cent.

Table 4.1: Total tax revenue as a % of GDP, for EU-27 Countries in 2009

Country	% of GDP	+/- from average	Country	% of GDP	+/- from average
Denmark	48.1	+12.3	United Kingdom	34.9	-0.9
Sweden	46.9	+11.1	Czech Rep	34.5	-1.3
Belgium	43.5	+7.7	**Ireland GNP**	**34.3**	**-1.5**
Italy	43.1	+7.3	Malta	34.2	-1.6
Finland	43.1	+7.3	Poland	31.8	-4.0
Austria	42.7	+6.9	Portugal	31.0	-4.8
France	41.6	+5.8	Spain	30.4	-5.4
Germany	39.7	+3.9	Greece	30.3	-5.5
Hungary	39.5	+3.7	Lithuania	29.3	-6.5
Netherlands	38.2	+2.4	Bulgaria	28.9	-6.9
Slovenia	37.6	+1.8	Slovakia	28.8	-7.0
Luxembourg	37.1	+1.3	**Ireland GDP**	**28.2**	**-7.6**
Estonia	35.9	+0.1	Romania	27.0	-8.8
Cyprus	35.1	-0.7	Latvia	26.6	-9.2

Source: Eurostat (2011:50) and CSO National Income and Expenditure Accounts (2011:3)

Notes: All data is for 2009. EU-27 average is 35.8 per cent.

---

[38] See Eurostat (2011:373-378) for a more comprehensive explanation of this classification.

Of the EU-27 states, the highest tax ratios can be found in Denmark, Sweden, Belgium, Italy, Finland and Austria while the lowest appear in Latvia, Romania, Slovakia, Bulgaria, Lithuania and Ireland. Overall, Ireland possesses the third lowest tax-take at 28.2 per cent, some 7.6 per cent below the EU average. Furthermore, Ireland's overall tax take has continued to fall over the past few years with the 2009 figure representing the lowest tax-take since Eurostat began compiling records in. 1995 (see chart 4.1). The increase in the overall level of taxation between 2002 and 2006 can be explained by short-term increases in construction related taxation sources (in particular stamp duty and construction related VAT) rather than any underlying structural increase in taxation levels.

Chart 4.1: Trends in Ireland and EU-27 overall taxation levels, 2000-2009

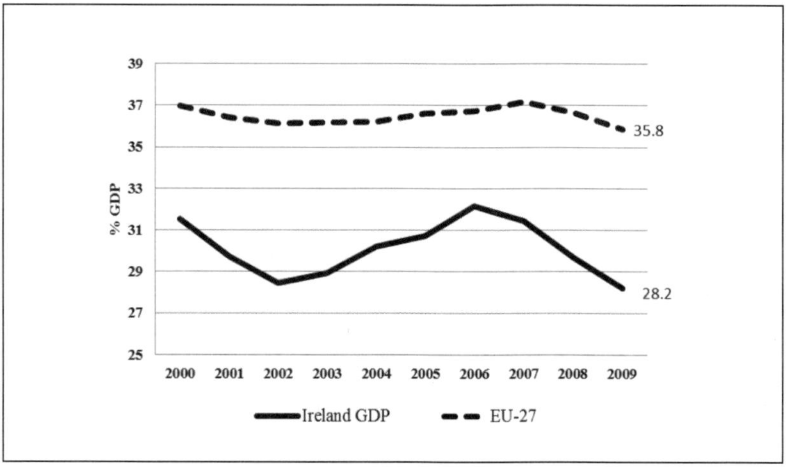

Source: Eurostat (2011:50) and CSO National Income and Expenditure Accounts (2011:3)

GDP is accepted as the benchmark against which tax levels are measured in international publications. However, it has been suggested that for Ireland gross national product (GNP) is a better measure. This is because Ireland's large multinational sector is responsible for significant profit outflows which, if included (as they are in GDP but not in GNP), exaggerate the scale of Irish economic activity.[39] Commenting on this, Collins stated that "while it is clear that

---

[39] Collins (2004:6) notes that this is a uniquely Irish debate and not one that features in other OECD states such as New Zealand where noticeable differences between GDP and GNP also occur.

multinational profit flows create a considerable gap between GNP and GDP, it remains questionable as to why a large chunk of economic activity occurring within the state should be overlooked when assessing its tax burden" and that "as GDP captures all of the economic activity happening domestically, it only seems logical, if not obvious, that a nations' taxation should be based on that activity" (2004:6).[40] He also noted that using GNP will understate the scale of the tax base and overstate the tax rate in Ireland because it excludes the value of multinational activities in the economy but does include the tax contribution of these companies. In this way, the size of the tax-take from Irish people and firms is exaggerated.

Social Justice Ireland believes that it would be more appropriate to calculate the tax-take by comparing GNP and using an adjusted tax-take figure which excludes the tax paid by multi-national companies. As figures for their tax contribution are currently unavailable, we have simply used the unadjusted GNP figures and presented the results in table 4.1. In 2009 this stood at 34.3 per cent. This also suggests to international observers and internal policy makers that the Irish economy is not as tax-competitive as it truly is. This issue should be addressed by Government and appropriate adjustments made when calculating Ireland's tax-take as a percentage of GNP.

In the context of the figures in table 4.1 and the trends in chart 4.1, the question needs to be asked: if we expect our economic and social infrastructure to catch up to that in the rest of Europe, how can we do this while simultaneously gathering less taxation income than it takes to run the infrastructure already in place in most of those other European countries? In reality, we will never bridge the social and economic infrastructure gaps unless we gather a larger share of our national income and invest it in building a fairer and more successful Ireland.

Social Justice Ireland believes that Ireland should increase its total tax-take to 34.9% (which would still keep Ireland as a low-tax economy as defined by Eurostat).
Prior to the recent recession (see below) the Irish tax take had begun to increase. Using the GDP benchmark, it climbed from 28.4 per cent in 2002 to 30.2 per cent in 2004 and to 30.7 per cent in 2005 (Eurostat, 2011: 282). The 2006 figure climbed further to 32.2 per cent of GDP but, as mentioned earlier, this increase principally reflected large inflows of transaction taxes from stamp duty, VRT and construction/housing related VAT – the taxes that have since collapsed. However,

---

[40] See also Collins (2011:90) and Bristow (2004:2) who make a similar argument.

the fact remains that increases towards the European average are certainly feasible and are unlikely to have any significant negative impact on the economy in the long term. *Social Justice Ireland* continues to propose that over the next few years Ireland increase its total tax-take to 34.9 per cent of GDP, We also believe that it will be necessary to provide additional tax revenue to cover the annual cost of servicing the banking element of Ireland's debt. A rough estimate of what the latter might require would be €2.5b extra per annum. (In making this calculation we are assuming an Anglo promissory note restructuring and we calculate the cost of servicing €70b of bank debt at an average of 3.5 per cent per annum). This proposal is explored further in the next section of this chapter.

Ireland's total tax take to 2015

Despite significant increases in the tax-take from the PAYE sector in the last four Budgets, the scale of collapse in Ireland's tax revenues has been dramatic. National taxes announced in the Budget and collected centrally (as detailed in table 4.2) have fallen by €14b since 2007 with the largest fall in areas such as capital gains taxes, stamp duties, corporation taxes and VAT. Decreases in income taxes have been somewhat offset by increased revenues from the income levy (2009-2010), the introduction of the Universal Social Charge (USC) and the merging of the health levy into the USC structure. Overall, total tax receipts have fallen from over €59 billion in 2007 to €43 billion in 2011.

As we have shown earlier, the impact of these declines in taxation income, reflecting the scale of the national and international recession and the instability and narrowness of the national tax base, have had dramatic effects on the overall tax-take. Looking to the years immediately ahead, Budget 2012 provided some insight into the expected future shape of Ireland's current taxation revenues and this is shown in table 4.3. The Budget provided a detailed breakdown of current taxes for 2011 and 2012 and overall projections for 2013-2015. Over the next four years, assuming these policies are followed, overall current revenue will climb to €43.2 billion. A property tax, intended to replace the 2012 €100 household levy, will also yield revenues from 2014 onwards but this is classified as local government income rather than exchequer taxation income (i.e. it does not feature in the totals in table 4.3).

Table 4.2: The changing nature of Ireland's tax revenue (€m)				
	2007	2008	2009	2010
Taxes on income and wealth				
Income tax (including sur tax)	13563	13148	11684	11237
Corporation tax	6393	5071	3889	3944
Motor tax - Estimated portion paid by households etc.	526	583	582	563
Other taxes	5	6	5	8
Fees under the Petroleum and Minerals Development Acts	5	10	2	3
Training and Employment Levy	411	414	373	309
Social Insurance contribution	9053	9259	8924	8709
Total taxes on income and wealth	**29957**	**28491**	**25458**	**24773**
Taxes on capital				
Capital gains tax	3097	1424	545	345
Capital acquisitions tax	391	343	256	237
Total taxes on capital	**3488**	**1767**	**801**	**582**
Taxes on expenditure				
Custom duties (€ml)	30	21	11	23
Excise duties including VRT	5993	5547	4909	4820
Value added tax	14057	12842	10175	9609
Rates	1267	1353	1467	1413
Motor tax - Estimated portion paid by businesses	431	477	476	461
Stamps (excluding fee stamps)	3244	1763	1003	962
Other fees	171	219	201	259
Total taxes on expenditure	**25193**	**22223**	**18243**	**17547**
EU Taxes	**519**	**484**	**359**	**400**
Total Taxation (i.e. sum of the rows in bold above)	**59157**	**52964**	**44861**	**43301**

Source: CSO Statistical Data Bank, National Income and Expenditure annual results, various years, selected from table N1022:T22. Details on Taxation by Statistical Indicator and Year

Table 4.3: Projected current tax revenues, 2011–2015					
	2011 €m	2012 €m	2013 €m	2014 €m	2015 €m
Customs	240	245			
Excise Duties	4,690	4,815			
Capital Gains Tax	310	355			
Capital Acquis. Tax	240	295			
Stamp Duties	1,400	1,350			
Income Tax ★	13,835	15,000			
Corporation Tax	3,730	3,770			
Value Added Tax	9,730	9,995			
Total Tax Receipts★★	**34,175**	**35,825**	**38,350**	**41,020**	**43,175**

Source: Department of Finance, Budget 2012: D11 and D18.
Notes: ★Including USC and health levy income from 2011 onwards
★★These figures do not incorporate other tax sources including revenues to the social insurance fund and local government charges. These are incorporated into the totals reported in table 4.4 below.

Budget 2012 also set out projections for the overall scale of the national tax-take (as a proportion of GDP) up to 2015. These figures are reproduced in table 4.4 and have been used to calculate the cash value of the overall levels of tax revenue expected to be collected. While the estimates in this table are based on the tax-take figures published by the Department of Finance in Budget 2012 – that document provided only limited details on the nature and composition of these figures. It should be borne in mind that over recent years the Department's projections for the overall taxation burden have continually undershot the end-of-year outcomes. However, even taking the Department's projections as the likely outcome, Chart 4.2 extends the assessment of Chart 4.1 and highlights just how far below average EU levels (assuming these remain at a record low of 35.8 per cent of GDP) and the *Social Justice Ireland* target (34.9 per cent of GDP) these taxation revenue figures are.

Table 4.4: Ireland's projected total tax take, 2010-2015 (% GDP)★

Year	GDP (nominal)	Tax as % GDP	Total Tax Receipts
2010	€156,000m	29.9	€46,614m
2011	€155,250m	30.8	€47,817m
2012	€159,125m	30.8	€49,011m
2013	€164,550m	31.4	€51,669m
2014	€171,625m	31.9	€54,748m
2015	€179,425m	31.9	€57,237m

Source: Department of Finance, Budget 2012: D9, D19 and D20.
Notes: ★ Total tax take = current taxes (see table 4.2 and 4.3) + Social Insurance Fund income + health levy (2010 only) + charges by local government.

Chart 4.2: Ireland's Projected Taxation Levels to 2015 and comparisons with EU-27 averages and Social Justice Ireland target

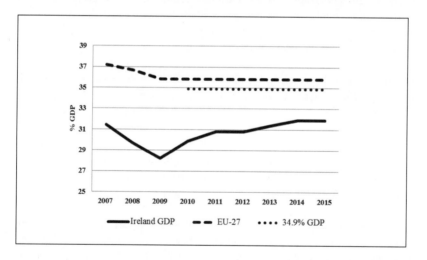

While a proportion of the recent tax decline is related to the recession, a large part is structural and requires attention. As detailed in chapter 2, *Social Justice Ireland* believes that over the next few years policy should focus on increasing Ireland's tax-take to 34.9 per cent of GDP, a figure defined by Eurostat as 'low-tax' (Eurostat, 2008:5). As a policy objective, Ireland should remain a low-tax economy, but not one incapable of adequately supporting the economic, social and infrastructural requirements necessary to support our society and complete our convergence with the rest of Europe. We also believe that it will be necessary to provide additional tax revenue to cover the annual cost of servicing the banking element of Ireland's debt. A rough estimate of what the latter might require would be €2.5b extra per annum. (In making this calculation we are assuming an Anglo promissory note restructuring and we calculate the cost of servicing €70b of bank debt at an average of 3.5 per cent per annum).

Effective tax rates

Effective tax rates are central to the on-going debate on personal/income taxation in Ireland. These rates are calculated by comparing the total amount of income tax a person pays with their pre-tax income. For example, a person earning €50,000 who pays a total of €10,000 in tax, PRSI and USC will have an effective tax rate of 20 per cent. Calculating the scale of income taxation in this way provides a more accurate reflection of the burden of income taxation faced by earners.

Following Budget 2012 we have calculated effective tax rates for a single person, a single income couple and a couple where both are earners. Table 4.5 presents the results of this analysis. For comparative purposes, it also presents the effective tax rates which existed for people with the same income levels in 2000 and 2008.

In 2012, for a single person with an income of €15,000 the effective tax rate will be 2.7 per cent, rising to 14.0 per cent on an income of €25,000 and 42.7 per cent on an income of €120,000. A single income couple will have an effective tax rate of 2.7 per cent at an income of €15,000, rising to 7.2 per cent at an income of €25,000, 26.2 per cent at an income of €60,000 and 39.1 per cent at an income of €120,000. In the case of a couple, both earning and a combined income of €40,000, their effective tax rate is 9.2 per cent, rising to 33.4 per cent for combined earnings of €120,000.

While these rates have increased since 2008 for almost all earners they are still low compared to those which prevailed in 2000. Few people complained at that time about tax levels being excessive and the recent increases should be seen in this context. Taking a longer view, chart 4.3 illustrates the downward trend in effective tax rates for three selected household types since 1997. These are a single earner on €25,000; a couple with one earner on €40,000; and a couple with two earners on €60,000. Their experiences are similar to those on other income levels and are similar to the effective tax rates of the self-employed over that period (see Department of Finance, Budget 2012, taxation annex).

Table 4.5: Effective Tax Rates following Budgets 2000 / 2008 / 2012			
Income Levels	Single Person	Couple 1 earner	Couple 2 Earners
€15,000	13.9% / 0.0% / 2.7%	2.5% / 0.0% / 2.7%	0.8% / 0.0% / 2.0%
€20,000	13.9% / 0.0% / 9.8%	8.3% / 2.7% / 6.3%	6.1% / 0.0% / 2.3%
€25,000	24.0% / 8.3% / 14.0%	12.3% / 2.9% / 7.2%	11.0% / 0.0% / 2.5%
€30,000	28.4% / 12.9% / 16.8%	15.0% / 5.1% / 8.6%	14.6% / 1.7% / 4.7%
€40,000	33.3% / 18.6% / 24.2%	20.2% / 9.4% / 14.2%	17.5% / 3.6% / 9.2%
€60,000	37.7% / 27.5% / 33.4%	29.0% /19.8% / 26.2%	28.0% /12.2% / 16.8 %
€100,000	41.1% / 33.8% / 40.9%	35.9% /29.2% / 36.5%	35.9% /23.8% / 29.7 %
€120,000	41.9% / 35.4% / 42.7%	7.6% /31.6% / 39.1%	37.7% /27.2% / 33.4 %

Source: Social Justice Ireland (2011:8).

Notes: Tax = income tax + PRSI + levies/USC

Couples assume 2 children and 65%/35% income division

Chart 4.3: Effective tax rates in Ireland, 1997-2012

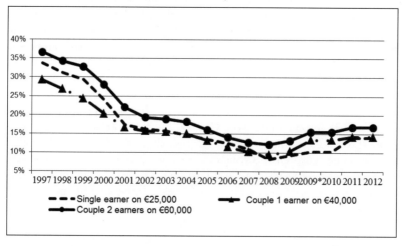

Source: Department of Finance, Budget 2012.

Notes: Tax = income tax + PRSI + levies/USC

Couples assume 2 children and 65%/35% income division

2009★= Supplementary Budget 2009 (April 2009)

The two 2009 Budgets produced notable increases in these effective taxation rates. Both Budgets required government to raise additional revenue and with some urgency - increases in income taxes providing the easiest option. Similarly, the introduction of the USC in Budget 2011 increased these rates, most notably for lower income earners, The subsequent Budget 2012 provided a welcome reduction for the lowest earners through raising the income level at which the USC applies. However, income taxation is not the only form of taxation and, as the rest of this chapter will show, there are many in Ireland not paying their fair share.

Income taxation and the income distribution

An insight into the distribution of income taxpayers across the income distribution is provided each year by the Revenue Commissioners in its Statistical Report. The Revenue's ability to profile taxpayers is limited by the fact that it only examines 'tax cases' which may represent either individual taxpayers or couples who are jointly assessed for tax. A further disadvantage of these figures is that there is a considerable delay between the tax year being reported on and the publication of the data for that year. The latest data, published in 2011, is for 2009.

The progressivity of the Irish income taxation system is well demonstrated in table 4.6 – as incomes increase the average income tax paid also increases. The table also underscores the issues highlighted in chapter 3; that a large proportion of the Irish population survive on low incomes. Summarising the data in the table, almost 20 per cent of cases have an income below €10,000; 54 per cent have an income below €30,000 and 90 per cent of cases are below €75,000. At the top of the income distribution, 5 per cent of households (almost 110,000) receive an income in excess of €100,000. The table also highlights the dependence of the income taxation system on higher income earners, with 27 per cent of income tax coming from cases with incomes of between €60,000 and €100,000 and 46 per cent of income tax coming from cases with incomes above €100,000. While such a structure is not unexpected, a symptom of progressivity rather than a structural problem, it does underscore the need to broaden the tax base beyond income taxes – a point we have made for some time and develop further later in this chapter.

Indirect taxation and the income distribution

As table 4.3 detailed, the second largest source of taxation revenue is VAT and the third largest is excise duties. These indirect taxes tend to be regressive – meaning they fall harder on lower income individuals and households (Barrett and Wall, 2006:17-23; Collins, 2011: 102-103).

Table 4.6: Income taxation and Ireland's income distribution, 2009					
From €	To €	No. of cases	Av. income	Av. Tax	% Total Tax
–	10,000	394,539	€4,397	€9	0.03
10,000	12,000	71,794	€11,033	€31	0.02
12,000	15,000	112,979	€13,503	€51	0.05
15,000	17,000	74,477	€16,009	€64	0.05
17,000	20,000	124,386	€18,515	€113	0.13
20,000	25,000	204,127	€22,498	€486	0.94
25,000	27,000	76,215	€25,993	€905	0.65
27,000	30,000	106,521	€28,498	€1,226	1.23
30,000	35,000	155,769	€32,430	€1,770	2.60
35,000	40,000	137,980	€37,456	€2,596	3.37
40,000	50,000	204,688	€44,647	€4,330	8.35
50,000	60,000	136,972	€54,684	€6,827	8.81
60,000	75,000	131,135	€66,894	€9,713	12.00
75,000	100,000	110,765	€85,608	€14,824	15.47
100,000	150,000	70,116	€119,004	€25,562	16.88
150,000	200,000	18,383	€170,611	€42,307	7.33
200,000	275,000	9,933	€231,519	€61,196	5.73
Over 275,000		10,677	€562,993	€162,784	16.37
Totals		**2,151,456**	**€38,138**	**€4,934**	**100.00**

Source: Calculated from Revenue Commissioners (2011).

An assessment of how these indirect taxes impact on households across the income distribution is possible using data from the CSO's Household Budget Survey (HBS), which collects details on household expenditure and income every five years. Chart 4.4 and table 4.7 presents the results of Barrett and Wall's examination of the 2004/05 HBS data.[41] They show that indirect taxation consumes more than 20 per cent of the lowest decile's income and more than 18 per cent of the income of the bottom five deciles. These findings reflect the fact that lower income households tend to spend almost all of their income while higher income households both spend and save.

---

[41] A subsequent study by Leahy et al (2010) found similar results but provides less data on the income distribution impacts of indirect taxes.

Dealing specifically with VAT, the study also found that lower income households paid more at the 21 per cent (now 23 per cent) rate than did higher income households. Consequently in its *Analysis and Critique of Budget 2012*, *Social Justice Ireland* highlighted the way that the Budget increase in VAT was regressive and unnecessarily undermined the living standards of low income households. Other, fairer approaches to increasing taxation were available and we regret that the Government did not take them.

Chart 4.4: VAT and excise duties as a % of household income, by decile

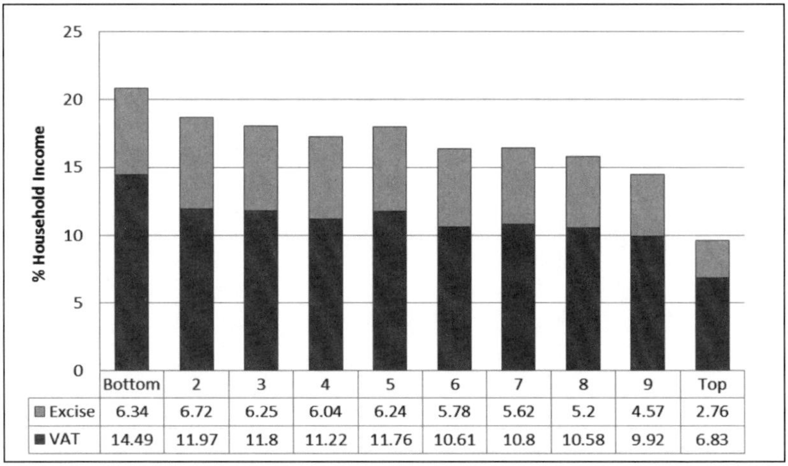
% Household Income
25
20
15
10
5
0
Bottom 2 3 4 5 6 7 8 9 Top
Excise 6.34 6.72 6.25 6.04 6.24 5.78 5.62 5.2 4.57 2.76
VAT 14.49 11.97 11.8 11.22 11.76 10.61 10.8 10.58 9.92 6.83

Source: Barrett and Wall (2006:19-20).

Table 4.7: VAT Payments at reduced and standard rates as a % of income, by selected deciles						
% income paid in VAT	**Bottom**	**2nd**	**3rd**	**8th**	**9th**	**Top**
@ 13.5% rate (reduced)	3.6	3.0	2.7	2.0	1.8	1.3
@ 21% rate (standard)*	11.5	9.1	9.4	8.9	8.4	5.8

Source: Barrett and Wall (2006:19-20).

Note: * Rate subsequently decreased and increased – latest increase to 23% in Budget 2012.

Future taxation needs

Government decisions to raise or reduce overall taxation revenue needs to be linked to the demands on its resources. These demands depend on what Government is required to address or decides to pursue. The effects of the current economic crisis, and the way it has been handled, carry significant implications for our future taxation needs. The rapid increase in our national debt, driven by the need to borrow both to replace disappearing taxation revenues and to fund emergency 'investments' in the failing commercial banks, has increased the on-going annual costs associated with servicing the national debt.

National debt has increased from a level of 25 per cent of GDP in 2007, low by international standards, to 107 per cent of GDP in 2011. It is projected to peak at 119 per cent in 2013. Data in Budget 2012 projected the cost relative to GDP of servicing the national debt over the next four years and these figures have been used to calculate the figures in table 4.8. Over recent years the costs of interest payments on the national debt has climbed from 5 per cent of current taxation revenues to over 17.5 per cent in 2012 and is projected to increase further to 23 per cent by 2014 – reaching a cost of almost €10 billion that year. The size of these payments underscores the need for government to restructure the cost and scale of Ireland's debt, in particular that associated with the bailing out of the banking system – see chapter 2. Furthermore, the erosion of the National Pension Reserve Fund (NPRF) through its use for funding various bank rescues has transferred the liability for future public sector pensions onto future exchequer expenditure. Again, this will require additional taxation resources.

Table 4.8:Cost of interest payments on the national debt, 2011-2015				
	Debt service % GDP	Debt service costs €	Debt service % total taxes	Debt service % current taxes
2011	3.3%	€5,123m	10.7%	13.9%
2012	4.2%	€6,683m	13.6%	17.5%
2013	5.6%	€9,215m	17.8%	22.7%
2014	5.8%	€9,954m	18.2%	23.0%
2015	5.7%	€10,227m	17.9%	22.4%

Source: Calculated from Department of Finance (2011: D19-23).
Note: Definitions for current and total taxation are provided earlier in this chapter.

These new future taxation needs add to those which already exist for funding local government, repairing our water infrastructure, paying for the health and pension needs of an ageing population, paying EU contributions, paying Kyoto protocol fines and purchasing any carbon credits that are required. Collectively, they mean that Ireland's overall level of taxation has to rise significantly in the years to come – a reality Irish society and the political system need to begin to seriously address.

Research by Bennett et al (2003) has provided some insight into future exchequer demands associated with healthcare and pensions in Ireland in the years 2025 and 2050. As the population ages these figures will increase substantially, almost doubling between 2002 and 2050 from 8.9 to 16.7 per cent of GDP. Dealing purely with the pension issue, an ESRI study reached similar conclusions and projected that social welfare spending that is focused on older people will rise from 3.1 per cent in 2004 to 5.5 per cent in 2030 and to 9.3 per cent in 2050. The 2008 OECD Economic Survey of Ireland reached similar conclusions, suggesting a 2050 peak of 11.1 per cent of GDP (2008:80-84).[42]

Table 4.9: Projected Costs of Healthcare and Pensions in Ireland, as % GDP			
	2002	2025	2050
Healthcare	6.0	6.3	8.8
Pensions	2.9	4.5	7.9
Healthcare + Pensions	**8.9**	**10.9**	**16.7**

Source: Bennett et al (2003)

Is a higher tax-take problematic?

Suggesting that any country's tax take should increase normally produces negative responses. People think first of their incomes and increases in income tax, rather than more broadly of reforms to the tax base. Furthermore, proposals that taxation should increase are often rejected with suggestions that they would undermine economic growth. However, a review of the performance of the British and US economies over recent years sheds a different light on this issue.

In the years prior to the current international economic crisis, Britain achieved low unemployment and higher levels of growth compared to other EU countries

---

[42] The 2010 National Pensions Strategy suggested a higher overall cost of pensions in 2050 as equivalent to 15.5% of GDP but provided no verifiable explanation for his forecast and why it differs so much from other research on the topic.

(OECD, 2004). These were achieved simultaneously with increases in its tax/GDP ratio. In 1994 this stood at 33.7 per cent and by 2004 it had increased 2.3 percentage points to 36.0 per cent of GDP. Furthermore, in his March 2004 Budget the then British Chancellor Gordon Brown indicated that this ratio would reach 38.3 per cent of GDP in 2008-09 (2004:262). His announcement of these increases was not met with predictions of economic ruin or doom for Britain and its economic growth remained high compared to other EU countries (IMF, 2004 & 2008).

Taxation and competitiveness

Another argument made against increases in Ireland's overall taxation levels is that it will undermine competitiveness. However, the suggestion that higher levels of taxation would damage our position relative to other countries is not supported by international studies of competitiveness. Annually the World Economic Forum publishes a *Global Competitiveness Report* ranking the most competitive economies across the world.

Table 4.10 outlines the top fifteen economies in this index for 2011-12 as well as the ranking for Ireland (which comes 29th). It also presents the difference between the size of the tax-take in these, the most competitive, economies in the world, and Ireland for 2009.[43]

Only the US and Japan reports a lower taxation level than Ireland. All the other leading competitive economies collect a greater proportion of national income in taxation. Over time Ireland's position on this index has varied, most recently falling from 22nd to 29th. When Ireland has slipped back the reasons stated for Ireland's loss of competitiveness included decreases in economic growth and fiscal stability, poor performances by public institutions and a decline in the technological competitiveness of the economy (WEF, 2003: xv; 2008:193; 2011: 25-26; 210-211). Interestingly, a major factor in that decline is related to underinvestment in state funded areas: education; research; infrastructure; and broadband connectivity. Each of these areas is dependent on taxation revenue and they have been highlighted by the report as necessary areas of investment to achieve enhanced competitiveness.[44] As such, lower taxes do not feature as a significant priority; rather it is increased and targeted efficient government spending.

---

[43] This analysis updates that first produced by Collins (2004:15-18).

[44] A similar conclusion was reached in another international competitiveness study by the International Institute for Management Development (2007).

Table 4.10: Differences in taxation levels between the world's 15 most competitive economies and Ireland.

Competitiveness Rank	Country	Taxation level versus Ireland
1	Switzerland	+1.9%
2	Singapore	*not available*
3	Sweden	+18.9%
4	Finland	+14.8%
5	United States	-3.7%
6	Germany	+9.5%
7	Netherlands	+10.4%
8	Denmark	+20.3%
9	Japan	-0.9%
10	United Kingdom	+6.5%
11	Hong Kong SAR	*not available*
12	Canada	+4.2%
13	Taiwan,	*not available*
14	Qatar	*not available*
15	Belgium	+15.4%
29	**IRELAND**	-

Source: World Economic Forum (2011:15)
Notes: a) Taxation data from OECD for the year 2009 (2011)
b) For some countries comparable data is *not available*.
c) The OECD's estimate for Ireland in 2009 = 27.8 per cent of GDP

A similar point was expressed by the Nobel Prize winning economist Professor Joseph Stiglitz while visiting Ireland in June 2004. Commenting on Ireland's long-term development prospects he stated that "all the evidence is that the low tax, low service strategy for attracting investment is short-sighted" and that "far more important in terms of attracting good businesses is the quality of education, infrastructure and services." Professor Stiglitz, who chaired President Clinton's Council of Economic Advisors, added that "low tax was not the critical factor in the Republic's economic development and it is now becoming an impediment".[45]

---

[45] In an interview with John McManus, Irish Times, June 2nd 2004.

Reforming and broadening the tax base

Social Justice Ireland believes that there is merit in developing a tax package which places less emphasis on taxing people and organisations on what they earn by their own useful work and enterprise, or on the value they add or on what they contribute to the common good. Rather, the tax that people and organisations should be required to pay should be based more on the value they subtract by their use of common resources. Whatever changes are made should also be guided by the need to build a fairer taxation system, one which adheres to our already stated core policy objective.

There are a number of approaches available to Government in reforming the tax base. Recent Budgets have made some progress in addressing some of these issues while the 2009 Commission on Taxation Report highlighted many areas that require further reform. A short review of the areas we consider a priority are presented below across the following subsections:

> *Tax Expenditures / Tax Reliefs*
> *Minimum Effective Tax Rates of Higher Earners*
> *Corporation Taxes*
> *Site Value Tax*
> *Second Homes*
> *Taxing Windfall Gains*
> *Financial Speculation Taxes*

A separate and related section on environment taxes follows.

Tax Expenditures / Tax Reliefs

A significant outcome from the Commission on Taxation is contained in part eight of its Report which details all the tax breaks (or "tax expenditures" as they are referred to officially). For years we have sought to have a full list of these tax breaks and their actual cost published. However, despite our best endeavours, neither the Department of Finance nor the Revenue Commissioners have been either able or willing to produce such a list. Subsequently, two members of the Commission have produced a detailed report for the Trinity College Policy Institute which offered further insight into this issue (Collins and Walsh, 2010). Table 4.11 reproduces their findings which highlight that the annual cost of tax expenditures in 2006 (the year where most data was available) totalled in excess of €11.5b per annum and that of the 131 tax expenditures in the Irish system, cost estimates are only available for 89 of them (68 per cent). Given the scale of public expenditure involved, this is a bizarre and totally unacceptable situation.

Table 4.11:Estimate of the Annual Cost of Ireland's Tax Expenditures			
Tax Expenditures relating to:	No. of tax expenditures	No. with available costs	Estimated Cost €m
Children	8	8	723
Housing	6	6	3,256
Health	10	7	579
Philanthropy	16	7	89
Enterprise	28	12	457
Employment	28	18	2,816
Savings and investment	8	6	2,995
Age-related and other	7	5	144
Property investment	20	20	435
Total	**131**	**89**	**11,494++**

Source: Collins and Walsh (2010:4).

Some progress has been made in addressing and reforming these tax breaks in recent Budgets, and we welcome this progress. However, despite this the 2012 Finance Bill (Department of Finance, 2012) introduced new tax breaks targeted at high earning multinational executives – with no accompanying documentation evaluating the cost, distributive impacts or appropriateness of these proposals.

There is further potential to reduce the cost of this area. Recipients of these tax expenditures use them to reduce their tax bills, so it needs to be clearly understood that this is tax which is being forgone. *Social Justice Ireland* has highlighted a number of these reforms in its pre-Budget Policy Briefings, *Budget Choices*, and will further address this issue in advance of Budget 2013. We will have particular regard to the need to reform the most expensive tax break, which is associated with pensions.[46] *Social Justice Ireland* believes that reforming the tax break system would make the tax system fairer. It would also provide substantial additional resources which would contribute to achieving the adjustment Government has proposed for the years to come.

---

[46] See Budget 2012 *Policy Briefing* on 'Budget Choices' pages 8, 9, 10, 15, 18-19 - available on social Justice Ireland's website.

Both the Commission on Taxation (2009:230) and Collins and Walsh (2010:20-21) have also highlighted and detailed the need for new methods for evaluation/introducing tax reliefs. We strongly welcome these proposals, which are similar to the proposals the directors of *Social Justice Ireland* made to the Commission in written and oral submissions. The proposals focus on prior evaluation of the costs and benefits of any proposed expenditure, the need to collect detailed information on each expenditure, the introduction of time limits for expenditures, the creation of an annual tax expenditures report as part of the Budget process and the regular scrutiny of this area by an Oireachtas committee. *Social Justice Ireland* believes that these proposals should be adopted as part of the necessary reform of this area.

Minimum Effective Tax Rates for Higher Earners

Evidence from both Department of Finance studies and Revenue Commissioner reports has shown that the major beneficiaries of the aforementioned tax breaks are those on the highest incomes.

In 2005 the Department of Finance commissioned a number of reports on the scale, extent, merit and distribution of the existing tax break schemes. The findings of these reports run to some 1,000 pages (see Department of Finance 2006 Vols I, II, III). While it is impossible to summarise these findings in a few paragraphs, three examples provide a good indication of what the reports found.

In 2000 the government introduced a tax relief scheme for capital investments in Hotels and Holiday Camps. An assessment by Indecon Consultants for the Department of Finance found that up to 2006 these schemes resulted in a net loss in tax revenue (revenue forgone) of €120.5m (Department of Finance, 2006 Vol. I: 73).[47] The report recommended that the scheme be abolished, which it was in Budget 2006. As part of this review, Indecon also considered the distribution of these tax reliefs. Table 4.12 presents the results of a confidential survey of Ireland's accountancy and tax professionals carried out by the consultants. In the survey these professionals were asked to indicate where the beneficiaries of these schemes came in terms of income levels.[48] They indicated that all these benefits flowed to investors with gross incomes of over €100,000 per annum and two thirds had gross

---

[47] These estimates pre-date the economic crash which, via the banking system and NAMA will have further increased these costs to the exchequer.

[48] Accurate income distribution figures are unavailable as the Revenue Commissioners did not collect detailed information on these schemes.

incomes in excess of €200,000. Table 4.12 shows a similar distribution analysis of those investors who availed of tax reliefs for multi-storey car parks. It presents an even more skewed allocation to those with incomes in excess of €200,000. In terms of tax revenue forgone, this scheme cost the exchequer €15.9m.

Table 4.12: The % distribution of investors utilising two tax relief schemes according to the views of accountancy and tax professionals – by likely annual gross income

Gross Annual Income of Investors	Hotels and Holiday Camps	Multi-storey Car Parks
€200,000 +	66.7%	83.3%
€100,000 to €200,000	33.3%	16.7%
€50,000 to €100,000	0.0%	0.0%
Less than €50,000	0.0%	0.0%
Total	**100.0%**	**100.0%**
Net tax forgone up to 2006	**€120.5m**	**€15.9m**

Source: Department of Finance (2006, Vol I: 73-76, 297-298)

The suggestion that it is the better-off who principally gain from the provision of tax exemption schemes is underscored by a series of reports published by the Revenue Commissioners entitled *Effective Tax Rates for High Earning Individuals* (2002, 2005, 2006 and 2007). These reports provided details of the Revenue's assessment of the top 400 earners in Ireland and the rates of effective taxation they faced.[49] The reports led to the introduction of a minimum 20 per cent effective tax rate as part of the 2006 and 2007 Finance Acts for all those with incomes in excess of €500,000.

During 2011 the Revenue Commissioners published an analysis of the operation of this new minimum rate using data for 2009 (Revenue Commissioners, 2011). Table 4.13 gives the findings of that analysis for 183 individuals with income in excess of €500,000. The report also includes information on the distribution of effective tax rates among the 269 earners with incomes between €250,000 and €500,000.

---

[49] The effective taxation rate is calculated as the percentage of the individual's total pre-tax income paid in taxation.

Table 4.13: The Distribution of Effective Tax Rates among those earning in excess of €250,000 in 2009 (% of total)		
Effective Tax Rate	**Individuals with incomes of €500,000+**	**Individuals with incomes of €250,000 – €500,000**
0%–5%	0%	27.5%
5% < 10%	0%	21.9%
10% < 15%	0%	20.1%
15% < 20%	78.7%	23.4%
20% < 25%	21.3%	7.1%
25% < 30%	0%	0%
30% +	0%	0%
Average effective rate	**20.05%**	**12.32%**
Total Cases	**183**	**269**

Source: Revenue Commissioners (2011)

Social Justice Ireland welcomed the introduction of this scheme which marked a major improvement in the fairness of the tax system. However, it should be noted that the average effective tax rate faced by earners above €500,000 in 2009 (20.05 per cent) was equivalent to the amount of income tax paid by a single PAYE worker with a gross income of €40,000 in that year. Similarly, the average effective tax rate faced by people earning between €250,000 – €500,000 in 2009 (12.32 per cent) was equivalent to the amount of income tax paid by a single PAYE worker with a gross income of between €25,000 – €30,000 in that year. The contrast in these income levels for the same overall rate of income taxation brings into question the fairness of the taxation system as a whole.

Social Justice Ireland also welcomed the Budget 2010 and Budget 2012 decisions to increase the minimum effective rate of income tax to 30 per cent (equivalent to the rate faced by a single PAYE worker on approximately €55,000 gross) and to apply this to high earners, with a tapering effect for those above €150,000 but below €500,000. It is important that Government to continue to raise this minimum effective rate so that it is in-line with that faced by PAYE earners on equivalent high-income levels. Following Budget 2012 a single individual on an income of €120,000 gross will pay an effective tax rate of 42.7 per cent; a figure which suggests that the minimum threshold for high earners has potential to adjust upwards over the next few years.

Corporation Taxes

In Budget 2003 the standard rate of corporation tax was reduced from 16 per cent to 12.5 per cent, at a full year cost of €305m. This followed another reduction in 2002, which had brought the rate down from 20 per cent to 16 per cent. At the time the total cost in lost revenue to the exchequer of these two reductions was estimated at over €650m per annum. Serious questions remain concerning the advisability of pursuing this policy approach. Ireland's corporation tax rate is now considerably below the corresponding rates in most of Europe. Windfall profits are flowing to a sector that is already extremely profitable. Furthermore, Ireland's low rate of corporation tax is being abused by multi-national companies which channel profits through units, often very small units, in Ireland to avail of the lower Irish rate of tax. In many cases this is happening at a cost to fellow EU member's exchequers and with little benefit in terms of jobs and additional real economic activity in Ireland. Understandably, Ireland is coming under increasing pressure to reform this system.

There is no substantive evidence in any of the relevant literature to support the contention that corporations would leave if the corporate tax rate were higher – at 17.5 per cent for example. Furthermore, the logic of having a uniform rate of corporation tax for all sectors is questionable. David Begg of ICTU has stated, "there is no advantage in having a uniform rate of 12.5 per cent corporation tax applicable to hotels and banks as well as to manufacturing industry" (2003:12). In the last few years there has been some improvement in this situation with special, and higher, tax rates being charged on natural resource industries. *Social Justice Ireland* welcomes this as an overdue step in the right direction.

As the European Union expands corporation tax competition is likely to intensify. Already Estonia and the Isle of Man have put in place a zero per cent corporation tax rate, Cyprus and Bulgaria have set their rate at 10 per cent and others continue to reduce their headline rates and provide incentives targeted at reducing the effective corporate tax rate. Over the next decade Ireland will be forced to either ignore tax rates as a significant attraction/retention policy for foreign investors, which would be a major change in industrial policy, or to follow suit, despite the exchequer costs, and compete by further cutting corporation tax. Sweeney has warned of a dangerous situation in which Ireland could end up "leading the race to the bottom" (2004:59). The costs of such a move, in lost exchequer income, would be enormous.

An alternative direction could be to agree a minimum effective rate for all EU countries. Given the international nature of company investment, these taxes are fundamentally different from internal taxes and the benefits of a European agreement which would set a minimum effective rate are obvious. They include protecting Ireland's already low rate from being driven down even lower, protecting the jobs in industries which might move to lower taxing countries and protecting the revenue generated for the exchequer by corporate taxes. *Social Justice Ireland* believes that an EU wide agreement on a minimum effective rate of corporation tax should be negotiated and this could evolve from the current discussions around a Common Consolidated Corporate Tax Base (CCCTB). *Social Justice Ireland* believes that the minimum rate should be set well below the 2011 EU-27 average rate of 23.1 per cent but above the existing low Irish level.[50] A rate of 17.5 per cent seems appropriate. Were such a rate in place in Ireland in 2011, corporate tax income would have been between €1 billion and €1.5 billion higher – a significant sum given the current economic challenges.

Site Value Tax

Taxes on wealth are minimal in Ireland, which is unique amongst developed countries in having no tax on immovable property. Revenue is negligible from capital acquisitions tax (CAT) because it has a very high threshold in respect of bequests and gifts within families are the rates of tax on transfers of family farms and firms are very generous (see tax revenue tables at the start of this chapter). While the Budget 2012 increase in the rate of CAT is welcome, the likely future revenue from this area remains limited given the tax's current structure.

The requirement, as part of the EU/IMF/ECB bailout agreement, to introduce a recurring property tax led Government in Budget 2012 to introduce a flat €100 per annum household charge. The Government has indicated that this charge is an interim measure – a point we welcome as its current structure is unfair because it fails to discriminate between those with large well located dwellings with many public services and those living in areas with limited public services or in more modest accommodation. While consideration is being given to introducing a value-based property tax, *Social Justice Ireland* believes that a Site Value Tax, also known as a Land Rent Tax, is a more appropriate and fairer approach.

The issue of site value taxation is one that has received on-going attention over the past few years. Two papers at a 2004 Social Policy Conference directly addressed this issue (see O'Siochru, 2004:23-57; and Dunne, 2004:93-122) and the Chambers of Commerce of Ireland has published a report entitled *Local Authority Funding –*

---

[50] Data from Eurostat (2011:130).

Government in Denial (2004) which called for an annual site tax. More recently, Collins and Larragy (2011) have outlined how such a charge would work and operate using the Property Registration Authority of Ireland's (PRAI) database as the basis for operation of the tax.

A 'land value', 'land rent' or 'site-value' tax (all three names are used to describe the same concept) is based on the annual rental value of land. The annual rental site value is the rental value that a particular piece of land would have if there were no buildings or improvements on it. It is the value of a site, as provided by nature and as affected for better or worse by the activities of the community at large. The tax falls on the annual value of land at the point where it enters into economic activity, before the application of capital and labour to it.

The arguments for a land-rent tax are to do with fairness and economic efficiency. Most of the reward of rising land values goes to those who own land, while most of the cost of the activities that create rising land values does not. This is because rising land values - for example, in prosperous city centres or prime agricultural areas - are largely created by the activities of the community as a whole and by government regulations and subsidies, while the higher value of each particular site is enjoyed by its owner. This often results in land owners retaining unused sites in the hope of selling them later when land values will have risen. Speculation on rising land values distorts land prices, generally making them significantly higher than they would be otherwise. NESC (2003:96) points out that given the immobility of land the introduction of a tax on development land would have minimal economic effects.

A land value tax is positive on both efficiency and equity grounds. From an efficiency perspective, a site value tax would be a major step toward securing the tax base as it could not move to any location providing greater tax reductions. In doing this it would move the tax away from a transaction, such as stamp duty, which can make the tax base vulnerable because it is dependent on maintaining and increasing the scale of the transactions, and switch it instead to an immovable physical asset which is a much securer base. It would have other efficiency impacts, such as ensuring that derelict sites are developed and that land would not be held over, as appears to be the situation at present, in an attempt to increase its value by creating artificial scarcity of land for development.

A land value tax is also positive on equity grounds. High land values in urban areas of Ireland are mainly a product of the economic and social activity in those areas.

Consequently, it can be argued that a substantial portion of the benefits of these land values should be enjoyed by all the members of the community and not just the site owners. In addition, the increasing site values are closely linked to the level of investment in infrastructure those areas have received. Much of that investment has been paid for by taxpayers. It can be argued, therefore, that a substantial portion of the benefits of the increasing site value should go to the whole community through the taxation system. After all, the site owner may well have made little or no contribution to the investment that produced the increased value in the first place.

Social Justice Ireland believes that the introduction of a site value tax would lead to more efficient land use within the structure of social, environmental and economic goals embodied in planning and other legislation. We believe that Government should move as fast as possible to phase out the current €100 flat-rate household charge and replace it with a clearly structured site value tax whose revenue would flow to local authorities.

Second Homes

A feature of the housing boom of the last decade was the rapid increase in ownership of holiday homes and second homes. For the most part these homes remained empty for at least nine months of the year. It is a paradox that many and they were built at the same time as he rapid increases in housing waiting lists (see chapter 7).

Preliminary results from Census 2011 indicated that since 2006 there had been an increase in the number of vacant dwellings on census night – rising from 266,332 units in 2006 to 294,202 units in April 2011 (+27,880 units). The precise breakdown of these units, into holiday homes, temporarily vacant principal residences, properties in the course of being sold etc, will be revealed in further census reports due in mid-2012. However, the CSO has noted that these vacant properties were more heavily distributed along western coastal areas from Donegal to Cork (CSO, 2011: 18-19). Results from the 2006 Census showed that on census night (April 23rd) there were 49,789 unoccupied holiday homes in Ireland, representing approximately 3 per cent of the national housing stock. Table 4.14 outlines the county-by-county distribution of these holiday homes as found in 2006.

Table 4.14 The Number and Distribution of Holiday homes in Ireland, from Census 2006.

County	No. Holiday Homes	County	No. Holiday Homes
Donegal	8,275	Louth	575
Wexford	6,601	Dublin City and County	418
Cork City and County	6,561	Kilkenny	406
Kerry	5,990	Meath	346
Mayo	4,216	Limerick City and County	346
Clare	3,624	Carlow	308
Galway City and County	3,172	Westmeath	271
Sligo	1,540	Longford	261
Waterford City and County	1,326	Offaly	220
Leitrim	1,192	Monaghan	171
Wicklow	1,156	Kildare	116
Roscommon	942	Laois	103
Tipperary	874		
Cavan	779	**State**	**49,789**

Source: CSO (2007:92)

What is often overlooked when this issue is being discussed is that the infrastructure to support these houses is substantially subsidised by the taxpayer. Roads, water, sewage and electricity infrastructure are just part of this subsidy which goes, by definition, to those who are already better off as they can afford these second homes in the first place. *Social Justice Ireland* supports the views of the ESRI (2003) and the Indecon report (2005:183-186; 189-190) on this issue. We believe that people purchasing second houses should have to pay these full infrastructural costs, much of which is currently borne by society through the Exchequer and local authorities. There is something perverse in the fact that the taxpayer should be providing substantial subsidies to the owners of these unoccupied houses at a time when so many people do not have basic adequate accommodation.

The second house issue should be addressed so that priority can be given to supplying needed accommodation which will be lived in all year round. The introduction of the Non Principal Private Residence (NPPR) charge in 2009 was a welcome step forwards. However, despite increases, the charge is still very low relative to the previous and on-going benefits that are derived from these properties. The charge should therefore be increased and the NPPR retained as a separate substantial second homes payment once a system of recurring annual property charges is introduced.

Taxing Windfall Gains

The vast profit made by property speculators on the rezoning of land by local authorities was a particularly undesirable feature of the recent economic boom. For some time *Social Justice Ireland* has called for a substantial tax to be imposed on the profits earned from such decisions. While this may not be an issue in Ireland at this time of austerity, it is best to make the system fairer before any further unearned gains are reaped by speculators. Re-zonings are made by elected representatives supposedly in the interest of society generally. It therefore seems appropriate that a sizeable proportion of the windfall gains they generate should be made available to local authorities and used to address the ongoing housing problems they face (see chapter 7). In this regard, *Social Justice Ireland* welcomes the decision to put such a tax in place. The windfall tax level of 80 per cent is appropriate and. as table 4.15 illustrates. This still leaves speculators and land owners with substantial profits from these rezoning decisions. The profit from this process should be used to fund local authorities. We fear that when the property market recovers in years to come there will be lobbying for this tax to be reduced or removed. Government should anticipate and resist this.

Table 4.15: Illustrative examples of the Operation of an 80% Windfall Gain Tax on Rezoned Land					
Agricultural Land	Rezoned Value	Profit	Tax @ 80%	Post-Tax Profit	Profit as % Original Value
€50,000	€400,000	€350,000	€280,000	€70,000	140%
€100,000	€800,000	€700,000	€560,000	€140,000	140%
€200,000	€1,600,000	€1,400,000	€1,120,000	€280,000	140%
€500,000	€4,000,000	€3,500,000	€2,800,000	€700,000	140%
€1,000,000	€8,000,000	€7,000,000	€5,600,000	€1,400,000	140%

Note: Calculations assume an eight-fold increase on the agricultural land value upon rezoning.

Financial Speculation taxes

As the international economic chaos of the past few years has shown, the world is now increasingly linked via millions of legitimate, speculative and opportunistic financial transactions. Similarly, global currency trading increased sharply throughout recent decades. It is estimated that a very high proportion of all financial transactions traded are speculative currency transactions which are completely free of taxation.

There is growing support worldwide for the introduction of a tax on such speculative transactions. The Tobin tax, proposed by the Nobel Prize winner James Tobin, proposes such a solution. It is a progressive tax, designed to target only those profiting from currency speculation. Therefore, it is neither a tax on citizens nor on business. Given the recent world economic experience, such a tax would also have value in assisting Governments and regulators to continually monitor the risk that financial institutions, and implicitly Governments and Central Banks, are taking. As the recent crisis has demonstrated, for the most part Central Banks and Governments are unable to adequately track and monitor these transactions.

An insight into the scale of these transactions is provided by the the latest edition of the Bank for International Settlements (BIS) Triennial Central Bank Survey of Foreign Exchange and Derivatives Market Activity, published in December 2010. The key findings from that report were:

- In April 2010 the average daily turnover in global foreign exchange markets was US$3.98 trillion; an increase of almost 20 per cent since 2007 and 160 per cent since 2001.
- The major components of these activities were: $1.490 trillion in spot transactions, $475 billion in outright forwards, $1.765 trillion in foreign exchange swaps, $43 billion currency swaps, and $207 billion in options and other products.
- 65 per cent of trades were cross-border and 35 per cent local.
- The vast majority of trades involved four currencies: US Dollar, Euro, Japanese Yen and Pound Sterling.
- Most of this activity (55 per cent) occurred in the US and UK, as did most activity involving interest rate derivatives (71 per cent).

The scope of the proposed Tobin tax varies. Initially, James Tobin suggested a tax on all purchases of financial instruments denominated in another currency. Since then, Canadian economist Rodney Schmidt broadened the proposal to include all foreign exchange transactions. These would include simple exchanges of one currency for another (spot transactions) as well as complex derivative financial instruments such as forwards, swaps, futures and options involving two currencies. The proposals in the UK for a 'Robin-Hood Tax' and from the European

Commission for an EU Financial Transactions Tax (FTT) represent a further development of these proposals.

The rate would be determined by each country enacting the tax, but the tax range recommended to produce moderate market calming and revenue-raising outcomes is between 0.1 and 0.25 per cent. For example, the October 2011 EU Commission proposal for a FTT, proposes that it would be levied on transactions between financial institutions when at least one party to the transaction is located in the EU. The exchange of shares and bonds would be taxed at a rate of 0.1 per cent and derivative contracts, at an even lower rate of 0.01 per cent. Overall, the Commission projects that the FTT would raise €57 billion per annum and proposes that it should come into effect from 1st January 2014. While the proposed rates may seem to consumers very small relative to VAT rates and income taxes, the impact on the margins of currency speculators would be sufficient to generate significant funds and in some cases curb excessive speculative activities. The FTT is aimed at taxing the 85 per cent of financial transactions that take place between financial institutions. Loans, mortgages, insurance contracts and other normal financial activities carried out by individuals or small businesses would fall outside the scope of the FTT proposal.

It is proposed that the revenue generated by this tax be used for national economic and social development and international development co-operation purposes. According to the United Nations, the amount of annual income raised from a Tobin tax would be enough to guarantee to every citizen of the world basic access to water, food, shelter, health and education. Therefore, this tax has the potential to wipe out the worst forms of material poverty throughout the world.

When James Tobin first put forward his idea he envisaged the tax being adopted by every country in the world simultaneously. Otherwise, he argued, speculators would "flock" to those countries without Tobin tax laws. Since such international agreement seemed improbable, the tax was seen by many as a worthy but impracticable proposal. However, over recent years the work of economists and financial experts has demonstrated that universal simultaneous adoption would not be vital for a successful implementation. Foreign currency markets may be global but the vast majority of transactions take place in a small number of key markets. If the principal countries implement the tax, this would suffice to cover the planet as a whole. Eight major countries account for more than 80 per cent of world exchange transactions, the top four for 65 per cent. In the City of London, the largest financial centre with 33 per cent of the world total, the 10 biggest banks account for 50 per cent of transactions.

What is needed is for one major region of the world to implement the tax. Consequently, *Social Justice Ireland* welcomed the EU Commission proposals in late 2011. While debate and consideration continues at Commission and Heads of Government level on this issue, the interest of many EU Governments and the European Parliament in this issue is welcome. We also encourage the Irish Government to be more open to this proposal and to support it at EU level. To date the Government has been hesitant to heed the lessons it should be learning from our recent economic and banking history.

Social Justice Ireland believes that the time has come for such a tax. Potentially, it could simultaneously facilitate and fund the required regulation of financial speculation while providing substantial funds to adequately address the world development issues highlighted in the Millennium Development Goals (chapter 14). *Social Justice Ireland* urges the European Commission and the Irish Government to act swiftly on this issue which offers significant practical benefits.

Introducing Environmental Taxes

Environmental taxes also have a role to play in broadening Ireland's tax base. We address this issue over the following two subsections on carbon taxes and "Cap and Share".

Carbon Taxes

Budget 2010 announced the long-overdue introduction of a carbon tax. This had been promised in Budget 2003 and committed to in the *National Climate Change Strategy* (2007). The tax has been structured along the line of the proposal from the Commission on Taxation (2009: 325-372) and is linked to the price of carbon credits which was set at an initial rate of €15 per tonne of CO_2 and subsequently increased in Budget 2012 to €20 per tonne. Products are taxed based on the level of the emissions they create.

While *Social Justice Ireland* welcomed the introduction of this tax, it regrets the lack of accompanying measures to protect those most affected by it, in particular low income households and rural dwellers. *Social Justice Ireland* believes that as the tax increases the Government should be more specific in defining how it will assist these households. Furthermore, there is a danger that given the difficult fiscal circumstances Ireland now finds itself in, any increases in the carbon tax over the next few years may divert from the original intention, to encourage behavioural change, towards a focus on raising revenue.

Cap and Share

'Cap and Share' (C&S) is another approach in the area of environmental taxation. This is a personal carbon trading scheme aimed at supporting the transition to a lower carbon intensity economy. C&S envisages the establishment of an overall cap on greenhouse gas emissions and, the subsequent allocation of 'entitlements' to every resident based on an equal division of the overall cap. Upstream companies, such as fuel importers and refineries, would be required to purchase sufficient entitlements to match the emissions from their operations. C&S is founded on the philosophy of equal rights for all to emit to the atmosphere. At the downstream end, C&S rewards individuals who consume electricity and fuel at below average levels, whilst those with greater than average carbon intensity would be penalised. Design of the scheme needs to ensure that it does not result in disadvantaged sectors of society being made worse off.

At a 2004 Social Policy Conference Richard Douthwaite provided some detail on this approach (2004: 125-137). He suggested the introduction of a tradable quota system. Under his proposal Ireland would divide the total tonnage of carbon dioxide it is allowed to emit under the agreement it reached with its EU partners under the Kyoto arrangements – its 1990 emissions plus 13 per cent - by its current population. It would issue permits for that amount – roughly 15.5 tonnes of CO_2 per head – to the population, perhaps at the rate of 1.3 tonnes each month. Citizens could then trade these permits through the financial institutions, with polluters, such as large firms and oil distribution companies, required to purchase them. The price received for these permits would vary according to the demand for fossil energy and just how well Ireland and the rest of the EU was doing in reducing emission levels. If the EU economy was booming and a lot of energy was being used, the price of the permits would be high but, so would the price of petrol, electricity and home-heating oil. Similarly, if the economy was depressed, these prices and the value of permits would fall. This automatic cushion against higher energy prices would protect, in particular, the least well-off.

Such a cushion would be important because, as energy is used in the production of everything we use and consume all prices would rise as a result of any restrictions on energy use. The proceeds from the permit sales would also provide the average person with enough additional purchasing power to cover the higher costs of the fuels and (because of the higher energy prices) the other goods and services they buy – provided that their purchases are not excessively energy-intensive. However, if some individuals were able to cut their direct and indirect fuel use below their entitlement, they would become better off financially. Those continuing to use energy intensive products, such as large automobiles, for example, would in effect have to pay for that privilege. The fact that fossil fuels themselves and goods made with significant amounts of fossil energy would cost more would encourage people to find lower-fossil-energy alternatives and enable the transition to renewable energy sources to gather pace. In short, a quota system would give people the price signals to move in the right direction.[51] A detailed report from Comhar (2008) advanced a similar proposal.

Building a fairer taxation system

The need for fairness in the tax system was clearly recognised in the first report of the Commission on Taxation more than 25 years ago. It stated:
"…in our recommendations the spirit of equity is the first and most important consideration. Departures from equity must be clearly justified by reference to the needs of economic development or to avoid imposing unreasonable compliance costs on individuals or high administrative costs on the Revenue Commissioners." (1982:29)

The need for fairness is just as obvious today and *Social Justice Ireland* believes that this should be a central objective of the current reform of the taxation system. While we recognise that many of the reforms below can only occur once the current crisis in the exchequer's finances has been resolved, we include them here because they represent necessary reforms that would greatly enhance the fairness of Ireland's taxation system. This section is structured in eight parts:

> *Standard rating discretionary tax expenditures*
> *Keeping the minimum wage Out of the tax net*
> *Favouring changes to tax credits rather than tax rates*
> *Favouring changes to tax credits rather than tax bands*
> *Introducing Refundable Tax Credits*
> *Introducing a Refundable Tax Credit For Children*
> *Reforming individualisation*
> *Standard rating discretionary tax expenditures*

---

[51] A more comprehensive outline of this proposal is presented in Douthwaite (2004) and in Feasta/NEF (2006).

Making all discretionary tax reliefs/expenditures available at the standard 20 per cent rate only would represent a crucial step towards achieving a fairer tax system. If there is a legitimate case for making a tax relief/expenditure available, then it should be made available in the same way to all. It is inequitable that people on higher incomes should be able to claim certain tax reliefs at their top marginal tax rates while people with less income are restricted to claim benefit for the same relief at the lower standard rate of 20 per cent. The standard rating of tax expenditures, otherwise known as reliefs, offers the potential to simultaneously make the tax system fairer and fund the necessary developments they are designed to stimulate without any significant macroeconomic implications.[52] Recent Budgets have made substantial progress towards achieving this objective and we welcome these developments. Furthermore, we encourage the Government to standard rate the tax relief on pension contributions. This is an overdue reform with an ability to generate almost €700m per annum in savings for the exchequer (Collins and Walsh, 2010:22).

Keeping the minimum wage out of the tax net

The decision by the Minister for Finance to remove those on the minimum wage from the tax net was a major achievement of Budget 2005. This had an important impact on the growing numbers of working-poor and addressed an issue with which *Social Justice Ireland* is highly concerned.

The fiscal and economic crisis of 2008-12 lead to Government reversing this policy, first via the income levy in second Budget 2009 and then via the Universal Social Charge (USC) in Budget 2011. Since Budget 2012 the USC is charged on all the income of those who earn more than €10,036 per annum. Using the unadjusted minimum wage of €8.65 per hour, the threshold implies that a low-income worker on the minimum wage and working more than 23 hours per week (earning €199 per week) is subject to the tax. *Social Justice Ireland* believes that this threshold is far too low and unnecessarily depresses the income and living standards of the working poor. Budget 2012 raised the entry point for the USC from €4,004 per annum to €10,036 per annum, a move welcomed by Social *Justice Ireland*. However, the imposition of the USC at such low income levels raises a very small amount of funds for the exchequer. Forthcoming Budgets should continue to raise the point at which the USC commences and in the years to come, as more resources hopeful become available to the Exchequer, *Social Justice Ireland* will urge Government to restore the policy of keeping the minimum wage fully outside the tax net.

---

[52] See O'Toole and Cahill (2006:215) who also reach this conclusion.

Favouring changes to tax credits rather than tax rates

Social Justice Ireland believes that any future income tax changes should be restricted to changes in either tax credits or tax bands rather than tax rates. This is more desirable in the context of achieving fairness in the taxation system.

To emphasise this point, we start by comparing a change in tax credits against a change in tax rates (the next section makes a comparison with tax bands). One of the initiatives announced in Budget 2007 was a cut in the top tax rate of one per cent (from 42 to 41 per cent). In his Budget speech the Minister indicated that the full year cost of this change was €186m. The Budget documentation also indicated that the full-year cost of a €90 increase in the tax credits of every tax payer equalled €185m. Therefore, both policy changes have roughly the same exchequer cost. Chart 4.5 compares these two changes and the increased income they delivered to earners across the income distribution.

An increase in tax credits would provide the same value to all taxpayers across the income distribution provided they are earning sufficient to pay more than €90 in income taxes. Therefore, the increased income received by an earner on €25,000 and on €80,000 is the same – an extra €90. However, a decrease in the top tax rate only benefits those paying tax at that rate. Therefore, the earner on €25,000 gains nothing from this change while those on €50,000 gain €160 per annum and those on €80,000 gain €460 per annum. The higher the income, the greater the gain.

As chart 4.5 shows, in Budget 2007 all single people earning less than €43,000 would have gained more from an increase in tax credits rather than a decrease in the top tax rate. For a couple (not shown in the diagram), all those earning less than €86,000 would have been better off had the government used the same money to deliver an increase in tax credits rather than a decrease in the top tax rate. In terms of fairness, changing tax credits is a fairer option than changing tax rates.

Favouring changes to tax credits rather than tax bands

In reforming income taxation policy over the years and decades to come, Government should always seek to enhance fairness. The following example, based on numbers from Budget 2008, illustrates the choices between changing either tax credits or tax bands.

Chart 4.5: Budget 2007 comparison of a 1% cut in the top tax rate and an increase in tax credits of €90 for each taxpayer.

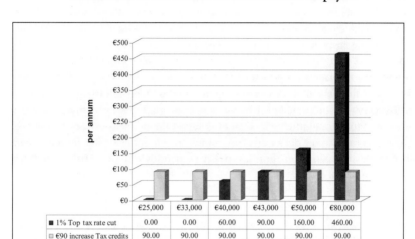

	€25,000	€33,000	€40,000	€43,000	€50,000	€80,000
■ 1% Top tax rate cut	0.00	0.00	60.00	90.00	160.00	460.00
▢ €90 increase Tax credits	90.00	90.00	90.00	90.00	90.00	90.00

If €535 million were available for distribution in a Budget it could be used to either increase the 20 per cent tax band by €5,000 (full year cost €536.1m) or increase personal tax credits by €250 a year (full-year cost €533.75m).[53] While the exchequer cost of these two alternatives is roughly the same, their impact is notably different:

Increasing the 20 per cent tax band by €5,000 would be of no benefit to anyone with incomes at or below the top of that band (i.e. €35,400 for a single person) but would provide a benefit of €1,000 a year to a single person earning more than €40,400. Single people with incomes in the €35,400–€40,400 range would benefit by a proportion of the €1,000. (The thresholds for married people with one or two incomes are different but the impacts are along the same lines as identified for single people here).

Increasing the tax credit by €250 a year would mean that every earner with a tax bill in excess of €250 a year would benefit by that amount.

---

[53] Figures from Department pre-Budget 2008 income tax ready reckoner.

In terms of fairness, increasing tax credits is a better option than widening the standard rate tax band. Government should always take this option when it has money available to reduce income taxes. It has the additional advantage of helping to address the 'working poor' issue which, as we have highlighted earlier, is emerging as a growing problem that requires a policy response.

Introducing refundable tax credits

The move from tax allowances to tax credits was completed in Budget 2001. This was a very welcome change because it put in place a system that had been advocated for a long time by a range of groups. One problem persists however. If a low income worker does not earn enough to use up his or her full tax credit then he or she will not benefit from any tax reductions introduced by government in its annual budget.

Making tax credits refundable would be a simple solution to this problem. It would mean that the part of the tax credit that an employee did not benefit from would be "refunded" to him/her by the state.

Chart 4.6: How much better off would people be if tax credits were made refundable?

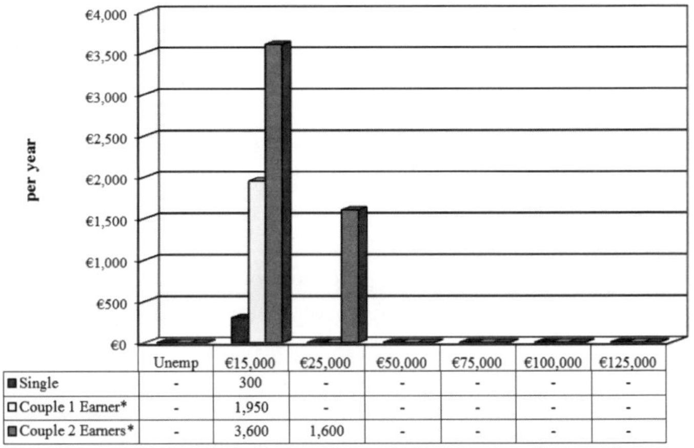

	Unemp	€15,000	€25,000	€50,000	€75,000	€100,000	€125,000
■ Single	-	300	-	-	-	-	-
□ Couple 1 Earner*	-	1,950	-	-	-	-	-
■ Couple 2 Earners*	-	3,600	1,600	-	-	-	-

Note: * Except where unemployed as there is no earner

The major advantage of making tax credits refundable lies in addressing the disincentives currently associated with low-paid employment. The main beneficiaries of refundable tax credits would be low-paid employees (full-time and part-time). Chart 4.6 displays the impacts of the introduction of this policy across various gross income levels. It clearly shows that all of the benefits from introducing this policy would go directly to those on the lowest incomes.

With regard to administering this reform, the central idea recognises that most people with regular incomes and jobs would not receive a cash refund of their tax credit because their incomes are too high. They would simply benefit from the tax credit as a reduction in their tax bill. Therefore, as chart 4.6 shows, no change is proposed for these people and they would continue to pay tax via their employers, based on their net liability after deduction of their tax credits by their employers on behalf of the Revenue Commissioners. For other people on low or irregular incomes, the refundable tax credit could be paid via a refund by the Revenue at the end of the tax year. Following the introduction of refundable tax credits, all subsequent increases in the level of the tax credit would be of equal value to all employees.

To illustrate the benefits of this approach, charts 4.7 and 4.8 compare the effects of a €100 increase in tax credits before and after the introduction of refundable tax credits. Chart 4.7 shows the effect as the system is currently structured – an increase of €100 in credits, but these are not refundable. It shows that the gains are allocated equally to all categories of earners above €50,000. However, there is no benefit for those workers whose earnings are not in the tax net.

Chart 4.8 shows how the benefits of a €100 a year increase in tax credits would be distributed under a system of refundable tax credits. This simulation demonstrates the equity attached to using the tax-credit instrument to distribute budgetary taxation changes. The benefit to all categories of income earners (single/couple, one-earner/couple, two-earners) is the same. Consequently, in relative terms, those earners at the bottom of the distribution do best.

Overall the merits of adopting this approach are: that every beneficiary of tax credits could receive the full value of the tax credit; that the system would improve the net income of the workers whose incomes are lowest, at modest cost; and that there would be no additional administrative burden placed on employers.

Outside Ireland, the refundable tax credits approach has gathered more and more attention outside Ireland, including a detailed Brooking Policy Briefing on the issue published in the United States in late 2006 (see Goldberg et al, 2006). In reviewing this issue in the Irish context Colm Rapple stated that "the change is long overdue" (2004:140).

Chart 4.7: How much better off would people be if tax credits were increased by €100 per person?

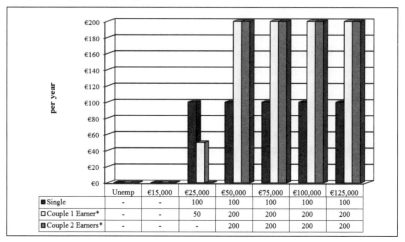

	Unemp	€15,000	€25,000	€50,000	€75,000	€100,000	€125,000
■ Single	-	-	100	100	100	100	100
□ Couple 1 Earner*	-	-	50	200	200	200	200
▨ Couple 2 Earners*	-	-	-	200	200	200	200

Note: * Except where unemployed, as there is no earner

Chart 4.8: How much better off would people be if tax credits were increased by €100 per person and this was refundable?

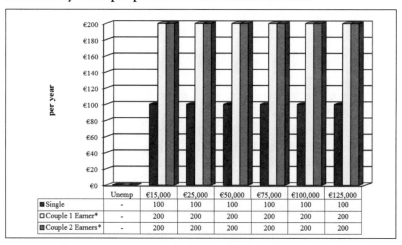

	Unemp	€15,000	€25,000	€50,000	€75,000	€100,000	€125,000
■ Single	-	100	100	100	100	100	100
□ Couple 1 Earner*	-	200	200	200	200	200	200
▨ Couple 2 Earners*	-	200	200	200	200	200	200

Note: * Except where unemployed, as there is no earner

During late 2010 *Social Justice Ireland* published a detailed study on the subject of refundable tax credits. Entitled '*Building a Fairer Tax System: The Working Poor and the Cost of Refundable Tax Credits*', the study identified that the proposed system would benefit 113,000 low-income individuals in an efficient and cost-effective manner.[54] When children and other adults in the household are taken into account the total number of beneficiaries would be 240,000. The cost of making this change would be €140m. The *Social Justice Ireland* proposal to make tax credits refundable would make Ireland's tax system fairer, address part of the working poor problem and improve the living standards of a substantial number of people in Ireland. The following is a summary of that proposal:

Making tax credits refundable: the benefits
- Would address the problem identified already in a straightforward and cost-effective manner.
- No administrative cost to the employer.
- Would incentivise employment over welfare as it would widen the gap between pay and welfare rates.
- Would be more appropriate for a 21st century system of tax and welfare.

Details of Social Justice Ireland proposal
- Unused portion of the Personal and PAYE tax credit (and only these) would be refunded.
- Eligibility criteria in the relevant year:
- Individuals must have unused personal and/or PAYE tax credits (by definition).
- Individuals must have been in paid employment.
- Individuals must be at least 23 years of age.
- Individuals must have earned a minimum annual income from employment of €4,000.
- Individuals must have accrued a minimum of 40 PRSI weeks.
- Individuals must not have earned an annual total income greater than €15,600.
- Married couples must not have earned a combined annual total income greater than €31,200.
- Payments would be made at the end of the tax year.

---

[54] The study is available from our website: www.socialjustice.ie

Cost of implementing the proposal

- The total cost of refunding unused tax credits to individuals satisfying all of the criteria mentioned in this proposal is estimated at €140.1m.

Major findings

- Almost 113,300 low income individuals would receive a refund and would see their disposable income increase as a result of the proposal.
- The majority of the refunds are valued at under €2,400 per annum, or €46 per week, with the most common value being individuals receiving a refund of between €800 to €1,000 per annum, or €15 to €19 per week.
- Considering that the individuals receiving these payments have incomes of less than €15,600 (or €299 per week), such payments are significant to them.
- Almost 40 per cent of refunds flow to people in low-income working poor households who live below the poverty line.
- A total of 91,056 men, women and children below the poverty threshold benefit either directly through a payment to themselves or indirectly through a payment to their household from a refundable tax credit.
- Of the 91,056 individuals living below the poverty line that benefit from refunds, most, over 71 per cent, receive refunds of more than €10 per week with 32 per cent receiving in excess of €20 per week.
- A total of 148,863 men, women and children above the poverty line benefit from refundable tax credits either directly through a payment to themselves or indirectly (through a payment to their household. Most of these beneficiaries have income less than €120 per week above the poverty line.
- Overall, some 240,000 individuals (91,056 + 148,863) living in low-income households would experience an increase in income as a result of the introduction of refundable tax credits, either directly through a refund to themselves or indirectly through a payment to their household.

Once adopted, a system of refundable tax credits as proposed in this study would result in all future changes in tax credits being equally experienced by all employees in Irish society. Such a reform would mark a significant step in the direction of building a fairer taxation system and represent a fairer way for Irish society to allocate its resources.

Reforming individualisation

Social Justice Ireland supports individualisation of the tax system. However, the process of individualisation followed to date has been deeply flawed and unfair. The cost to the exchequer of this transition has been in excess of €0.75 billion, and almost all of this money has gone to the richest 30 per cent of the population. A significantly fairer process would have been to introduce a basic income system that would have treated all people fairly and ensured that a windfall of this nature did not accrue to the best off in this society (see chapter 3).

Given the current form of individualisation, couples with one partner losing his/her job end up even worse off than they would have been had the current form of individualisation not been introduced. Before individualisation was introduced, the standard-rate income-tax band was €35,553 for all couples. After that they would start paying the higher rate of tax. Now, the standard-rate income-tax band for single-income couples is €32,800, while the band for dual-income couples is €41,800. If one spouse (of a couple previously earning two salaries) leaves a job voluntarily or through redundancy, the couple loses the value of the second tax band.

Making the taxation system simpler

Ireland's tax system is not simple. Bristow (2004) argued that "some features of it, notably VAT, are among the most complex in the world". The reasons given to justify this complexity vary but they are focused principally around the need to reward particular kinds of behaviour which is seen as desirable by legislators. This, in effect, is discrimination either in favour of one kind of activity or against another. There are many arguments against the present complexity and in favour of a simpler system.

Discriminatory tax concessions in favour of particular positions are often very inequitable, contributing far less to equity than might appear to be the case. In many circumstances they also fail to produce the economic or social outcomes which were being sought and sometimes they even generate very undesirable effects. At other times they may be a complete waste of money, since the outcomes they seek would have occurred without the introduction of a tax incentive. Having a complex system has other down-sides. It can, for example, have high compliance costs both for taxpayers and for the Revenue Commissioners.

For the most part, society at large gains little or nothing from the discrimination contained in the tax system. Mortgage interest relief, for example, and the absence of any residential or land-rent tax contributed to the rise in house prices up to 2007. Complexity makes taxes easier to evade, invites consultants to devise avoidance schemes and greatly increases the cost of collection. It is also inequitable because those who can afford professional advice are in a far better position to take advantage of that complexity than those who cannot. A simpler taxation system would better serve Irish society and all individuals within it, irrespective of their means.

Key Policy Priorities on Taxation

- *Social Justice Ireland* believes that Government should:
  - increase the overall tax take
  - adopt policies to broaden the tax base
  - develop a fairer taxation system

Policy priorities under each of these headings are listed below.

Increase the overall tax take

- Move towards increasing the total tax take to 34.9 per cent of GDP (i.e. a level below the low tax threshold identified by Eurostat). Provide additional tax revenue to cover the annual cost of servicing the banking element of Ireland's debt. As stated earlier a rough estimate of what the latter might require would be €2.5b extra per annum.

Broaden the tax base

- Continue to reform the area of tax expenditures and put in place procedures within the Department of Finance and the Revenue Commissioners to monitor on an on-going basis the cost and benefits of all current and new tax expenditures.

- Continue to increase the minimum effective tax rates on very high earners (those with incomes in excess of €125,000) so that these rates are consistent with the levels faced by PAYE workers.

- Move to negotiate an EU wide agreement on minimum corporate taxation rates (a rate of 17.5 per cent would seem fair in this situation).

- Introduce site-value tax to replace the €100 household charge.

- Impose charges so that those who construct or purchase second homes pay the full infrastructural costs of these dwellings.

- Retain the 80 per cent windfall tax on the profits generated from all land re-zonings.

- Collaborate with other EU member states to introduce a financial transactions tax (FTT) along the line proposed by the European Commission in 2011.

- Act with purpose to shift the burden of taxation from income tax to eco-taxes on the consumption of fuel and fertilisers, waste taxes and a land rent tax. In doing this, government should avoid any negative impact on people with low incomes.

Develop a fairer taxation system
- Apply standard rate of tax only to all discretionary tax expenditures.

- Adjust tax credits and the USC so that the minimum wage returns to being outside the tax net.

- Make tax credits refundable.

- Ensure that individualisation in the income tax system is done in a fair and equitable manner.

- Integrate the taxation and social welfare systems.

- Begin to monitor and report tax levels (personal and corporate) in terms of effective tax rates.

- Develop policies which allow taxation on wealth to be increased.

- Ensure that the distribution of all changes in indirect taxes discriminate positively in favour of those with lower incomes.

- Adopt policies to simplify the taxation system.

- Poverty-proof all budget tax packages to ensure that tax changes do not further widen the gap between those with low income and the better off.

5. WORK, UNEMPLOYMENT AND JOB CREATION

> ## CORE POLICY OBJECTIVE:
> ### WORK, UNEMPLOYMENT AND JOB CREATION
> **To ensure that all people have access to meaningful work**

The past five years have seen Ireland return to the phenomenon of widespread unemployment. Despite the attention given to the banking and fiscal collapse, the transition from near full employment to high unemployment has been the real characteristic of this recession. The implications for people, families, social cohesion and the exchequer's finances have been serious. CSO data and economic forecasts for the remainder of 2012 indicate that unemployment will stabilise at an annual rate of just over 14 per cent of the labour force for 2012, having been 4.6 per cent in 2007. There can be little doubt that we are in a very challenging period in which a high level of long-term unemployment has once again become a characteristic of Irish society.

This chapter reviews the evolution of this situation and considers the implications and challenges which arise for Government and society. It also looks at the impact on various sectors of the working-age population and outlines a series of proposals for responding to this unemployment crisis. To date, the response has been slow and limited. As the chapter shows, the scale and nature of our unemployment crisis deserves greater attention. This chapter concludes with some thoughts on the narrowness of how we consider and measure the concept of 'work'.

Labour force trends
The dramatic turnaround in the labour market after 2007 contrasts with the fact that one of the major achievements of the preceding 20 years had been the increase in employment and the reduction in unemployment, especially long-term unemployment. In 1992 there were 1,165,200 people employed in Ireland. That figure increased by almost one million to peak at 2,146,000 in mid-2007. During early 2006 the employment figure exceeded two million for the first time in the history of the state. Overall, the size of the Irish labour force has expanded significantly and today equals over 2.12 million people, almost one million more than in 1992 (see chart 5.1).

However, in the period since 2007 emigration has returned, resulting in a decline in the labour force. Initially this involved recently arrived migrants returning home but was then followed by the departure of native Irish. CSO figures indicate that during the first quarter of 2009 the numbers employed fell below two million and that since then they have continued to fall, reaching just over 1.8m in 2011 (see table 5.1).

Chart 5.1: The Numbers of People in the Labour Force and Employed in Ireland, 1991–2011.

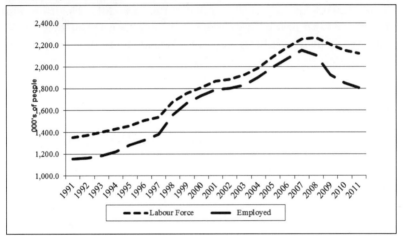

Source: CSO, QNHS various editions

When considering the term "unemployment" it is important to be as clear as possible about what we actually mean by it. Two measurement sources are often quoted, the *Quarterly National Household Survey* (QNHS) and the *Live Register*. The former is considered the official and most accurate measure of unemployment although, unlike the monthly live register data, it appears only four times a year.

The CSO's QNHS unemployment data use the definition of 'unemployment' supplied by the International Labour Office (ILO). It lists as unemployed only those people who, in the week before the survey, were unemployed *and* available to take up a job *and* had taken specific steps in the preceding four weeks to find employment. Any person who was employed for at least *one hour* is classed as employed. By contrast, the live register counts everybody 'signing-on' and includes part-time employees (those who are employed up to three days a week), those employed on short weeks, seasonal and casual employees entitled to Jobseekers Assistance or Benefit.[55]

As chart 5.2 shows, the period from 1993 was one of decline in unemployment. By mid-2001 Irish unemployment reached its lowest level in living memory at 3.6 per cent of the labour force. Since then the international recession and domestic economic crisis have brought about increases in the rate. During 2006 unemployment exceeded 100,000 for the first time since mid-1999 with a total of 102,600 people recorded as unemployed in mid-2006. As chart 5.2 shows, it exceeded 200,000 in early-2009 and 300,000 in early-2011. This chart also highlights the rapid growth in the number of long-term unemployed (those unemployed for more than 12 months). The CSO reports that there are now over 177,000 people in long-term unemployment and that this figure has increased five-fold since 2007. Quite simply, given the on-going economic crisis many of those who entered unemployment in 2007-2010 have remained unemployed for more than 12 months and have therefore become long-term unemployed.

Chart 5.2: The Numbers of Unemployed and Long-Term Unemployed in Ireland, 1991-2011.

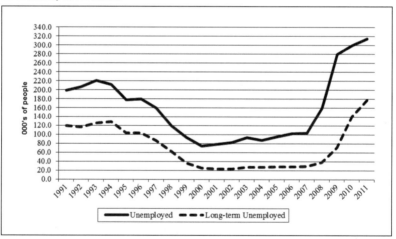

Source: CSO, QNHS various editions

---

[55] See Healy and Collins (2006) for a further explanation of measurement in the labour market.

The nature and scale of the recent transformation in Ireland's labour market is highlighted by the data in table 5.1. Over the five years from 2007-2011 the labour force decreased by almost 6 per cent, participation rates dropped, full-time employment fell by over 20 per cent, representing some 380,000 jobs, while part-time employment increased by over 9 per cent. By the third quarter of 2011 the number of underemployed people, defined as those employed part-time but wishing to work additional hours, had increased to 135,700 people – 6 per cent of the labour force. Over this period unemployment increased by over 210,000 people, bringing the unemployment rate up from 4.6 per cent to 14.8 per cent.

Table 5.1: Labour Force Data, 2007 - 2011

	2007	2010	2011	Change 07-11
Labour Force	2,253,100	2,150,500	2,120,300	-5.9%
LFPR %	64.6	61.2	60.4	-4.2%
Employment %	69.9	60.3	59.1	-10.8%
Employment	2,149,800	1,851,500	1,805,500	-16.0%
Full-time	1,764,000	1,436,800	1,383,700	-21.6%
Part-time	385,800	414,700	421,800	+9.3%
Underemployed	-	108,800	135,700	-
Unemployed %	4.6	13.9	14.8	+10.2%
Unemployed	103,300	299,000	314,700	+204.6%
LT Unemployed %	1.3	6.5	8.4	+7.1%
LT Unemployed	28,800	140,400	177,200	+515.3%

Source: CSO, QNHS on-line database.
Notes: All data is for quarter 3 of the reference year.
LFPR = Labour force participation rate and measures the percentage of the adult population who are in the labour market.
Underemployment measures people in part-time employment who indicate that they wish to work additional hours but these are not currently available.
Comparable underemployment data is not available for 2007.
LT = Long Term (12 months or more).

Recent trends in employment and unemployment

The transformation in the labour market has significantly altered the nature of employment in Ireland when compared to the pre-recession picture in 2007. Overall, employment fell 16 per cent between 2007-2011 and table 5.2 traces the impact of this fall across various sectors, groups and regions. Within the CSO's broadly defined employment sectors, industrial employment has seen the biggest fall of over 40 per cent while there have been sizeable, but smaller, falls in agriculture and services. Job losses have had a greater impact on males versus females with male employment down 21 per cent since 2007 while female employment decreased by 10 per cent. The proportional impact of the crisis has hit employment levels for employees and self-employed in much the same way; although there are many more of the former and the actual job losses among employees is significantly higher.

Table 5.2: Employment in Ireland, 2007 - 2011 (thousands of people)				
	2007	**2010**	**2011**	**Change 07-11**
Employment	2149.8	1851.5	1805.5	-16.0%
Sector				
Agriculture	111.7	89.5	82.5	-26.1%
Industry	573.8	355.7	341.1	-40.6%
Services	1464.3	1406.3	1382.0	-5.6%
Gender				
Male	1225.9	994.5	968.4	-21.0%
Female	923.9	857.0	837.2	-9.4%
Employment Status				
Employees	1781.9	1534.8	1504.1	-15.6%
Self Employed	350.3	304.5	291.6	-16.8%
Assisting relative	17.6	12.3	9.9	-43.8%
Region				
Border	222.8	188.1	182.4	-18.1%
Midlands	127.0	101.2	98.8	-22.2%
West	205.8	179.3	178.7	-13.2%
Dublin	626.9	531.5	507.6	-19.0%
Mid-East	257.2	234.1	235.2	-8.6%
Mid-West	172.4	151.1	152.3	-11.7%
South-East	225.1	194.0	186.5	-17.1%
South-West	312.6	272.2	264.0	-15.5%

Source: CSO, QNHS on-line database.

The consequence of all these job losses has been the sharp increase in unemployment and emigration described earlier. Dealing with unemployment, table 5.3 shows how it has changed between 2007 and 2011, a period when the numbers unemployed increased by over 200 per cent. As the table shows, male unemployment increased by over 140,000 people and female unemployment by more than 60,000. Most of the unemployed, who had been employed in 2007 and before it, are seeking to return to a full-time job and less than 11 per cent of those unemployed in 2011 are seeking part-time employment. The impact of the unemployment crisis was felt right across the age groups and it is only in the age-groups 15-19 years and 20-24 years than any recent decrease has been recorded – a phenomenon almost entirely explained by emigration.

Table 5.3:Unemployment in Ireland, 2007 - 2011 (thousands of people)				
	2007	2010	2011	Change 07-11
Unemployment	103.3	299.0	314.7	+204.6%
Gender				
Male	62.2	201.5	206.2	+231.5%
Female	41.1	97.5	108.6	+164.2%
Employment sought				
Seeking FT employment	87.7	274.9	281.4	+220.9%
Seeking PT employment	15.6	24.1	33.4	+114.1%
Age group				
15-19 years	11.5	20.1	19.2	+67.0%
20-24 years	21.9	47.0	44.9	+105.0%
25-34 years	31.4	95.1	106.2	+238.2%
35-64 years	38.1	136.0	144.2	+278.5%
Region				
Border	13.8	29.5	30.7	+122.5%
Midlands	4.9	21.1	23.1	+371.4%
West	10.0	32.8	33.4	+234.0%
Dublin	29.7	70.9	76.7	+158.2%
Mid-East	10.5	31.6	34.3	+226.7%
Mid-West	10.1	29.6	30.8	+205.0%
South-East	12.0	41.4	43.4	+261.7%
South-West	12.3	42.1	42.3	+243.9%
Duration				
Unemp. less than 1 yr	74.2	156.2	134.6	+81.4%
Unemp. more than 1 yr	28.8	140.4	177.2	+515.3%
LT Unemp. as % Unemp	27.9%	47.0%	56.3%	

Source: CSO, QNHS on-line database (see table 5.3)

The rapid growth in the number and rates of long-term unemployment are also highlighted in table 5.3 and in chart 5.3. The number of long-term unemployed was less than 30,000 in 2007 and has increased since to reach 177,200 in 2011. For the first time on record, the QNHS data for late 2010 indicated that long-term unemployment accounted for more than 50 per cent of the unemployed and by third quarter 2011 the long-term unemployed represented 56.3 per cent of the unemployed. The transition to these high levels has been rapid since 2007 – see chart 5.3. The experience of the 1980s showed the dangers and long-lasting implications of an unemployment crisis characterised by high long-term unemployment rates. It remains a major policy failure that Ireland's level of long-term unemployment has been allowed to increase so rapidly in recent years. Furthermore, it is of serious concern than Government policy has given limited attention to the issue.

Chart 5.3: The increased presence of long-term unemployed in Ireland, 2007-2011

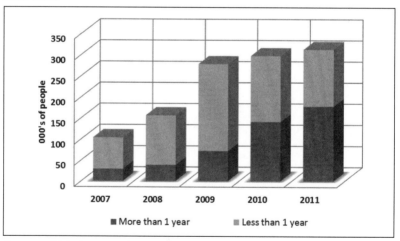

Source: CSO, QNHS on-line database.

Addressing a crisis such as this is a major challenge and we outline our suggestions for urgent policy action later in the chapter. However, as table 5.4 shows, it is clear that reskilling many of the unemployed, in particular those with low education levels, will be a key component of the response. In 2011 178,000 of the unemployed, almost 60 per cent, had no more than second level education with 95,000 not having completed more than lower secondary (equivalent to the junior certificate). At the other extreme, the scale and severity of the recession has resulted in high levels of third-level graduates being unemployed, with 12 per cent of all those unemployed having at least a degree or higher qualification. While Government should not ignore any group in its overdue attempts to address the unemployment crisis, major emphasis should be placed on those who are most likely to become trapped in long term unemployment – in particular those with the lowest education levels.

Previous experiences, in Ireland and elsewhere, have shown that many of those under 25 and many of those over 55 find it challenging to return to employment after a period of unemployment. This highlights the danger of these large increases in long-term unemployment and suggests a major commitment to retraining and re-skilling will be required. In the long-run Irish society can ill afford a return to the long-term unemployment problems of the 1980s. In the short-run the new-unemployed will add to the numbers living on low-income in Ireland and this, in turn, will have a negative impact on future poverty figures.

Table 5.4: Unemployment by highest education attained (thousands of people)		
	2010	**2011**
Primary or below	26.1	28.8
Lower secondary	64.1	66.2
Higher secondary	84.6	91.9
Post leaving cert	48.3	52.1
Third level non degree	30.3	29.2
Third level degree or above	35.8	38.7
Other	9.0	7.5
Total persons aged 15 to 64	**299.0**	**314.7**

Source: CSO, QNHS on-line database, table S9a.

The *Live Register*

While the live register is not an accurate measure of unemployment, it is a useful barometer of the nature and pace of change in employment and unemployment. Increases suggest a combination of more people unemployed, more people on reduced employment weeks and consequently reductions in the availability of employment hours to the labour force. Table 5.5 shows that the number of people signing on the live register increased rapidly since the onset of the economic crisis in 2007. By February 2012 the numbers signing-on the live register had increased more than 250,000 compared to four years earlier.

Year	Month	Males	Females	Total
2007	January	95,824	62,928	158,752
	September	98,015	62,637	160,652
2008	January	116,160	65,289	181,449
	September	156,055	84,162	240,217
2009	January	220,412	105,860	326,272
	September	278,003	141,851	419,854
2010	January	291,648	145,288	436,936
	September	289,798	152,619	442,417
2011	January	292,003	150,674	442,677
	September	281,988	155,453	437,441
2012	January	283,893	155,696	439,589
	February	283,450	155,972	439,422

Table 5.5: Numbers on the Live Register (unadjusted), Jan 2007 - 2012

Source: CSO Live Register on-line database.

Youth unemployment

While the increase in unemployment has been spread across people of all ages and sectors (see table 5.3), table 5.6 highlights the very rapid increase on the live register of those aged less than 25 years. The numbers in this group doubled between January 2008 and January 2009 and subsequently peaked at just over 89,000 in September 2010. Since then some decreases have occurred and, although we have no empirical knowledge of the reasons for these decreases, a large part of the decrease is likely explained by emigration.

Table 5.6: Persons under 25 yrs on the Live Register, Jan 2008 - Jan 2011

Month and Year	Numbers	Month and Year	Numbers
January 2008	36,945	September 2010	88,663
September 2008	53,666	January 2011	82,237
January 2009	70,268	September 2011	80,870
September 2009	89,810	January 2012	75,345
January 2010	85,910	February 2012	74,936

Source: CSO Live Register on-line database.

To complement the analysis in table 5.6, table 5.7 shows those on the live register by their last occupation and also examines the differences between those over and under 25 years. The figures once again highlight the need for targeted reskilling of people who hold skills in sectors of the economy that are unlikely to ever return to the employment levels of the early part of the last decade.

Table 5.7: Persons on Live Register by last occupation – February 2012			
Occupational group	**Overall**	**Under 25 yrs**	**Over 25 yrs**
Managers and administrators	16,911	657	16,254
Professional	23,695	1,947	21,748
Associate prof.& technical	12,247	1,441	10,806
Clerical and secretarial	41,955	4,037	37,918
Craft and related	106,234	13,381	92,853
Personal and protective service	52,722	10,289	42,433
Sales	46,972	13,575	33,397
Plant and machine operatives	71,035	10,085	60,950
Other occupation	49,698	10,919	38,779
Never employeded / not stated	17,953	8,605	9,348
Total	**439,422**	**74,936**	**364,486**

Source: CSO Live Register – February 2012 table 6.

Responding to the unemployment crisis

The scale of these increases is enormous and it is crucial that Government, commentators and society in general remember that each of these numbers represents people who are experiencing dramatic and, in many cases, unexpected turmoil in their lives and their families' lives. As Irish society comes to terms with the enormity of this issue, this perspective should remain central.

To date, the policy response to this crisis has been limited, comprising announcements of apprenticeship schemes, 'Job Initiative' reforms and the 'Pathways to Work' programme. Each of these has targeted small reforms and had limited success given the scale of the unemployment crisis. In responding to this situation *Social Justice Ireland* believes that the Government should:
- Launch a major investment programme focused on creating employment and prioritise initiatives that strengthen social infrastructure, such as the school building programme and the social housing programme.

- Resource the up-skilling of those who are unemployed and at risk of becoming unemployed through integrating training and labour market programmes.
- Maintain a sufficient number of active labour market programme places available to those who are unemployed.
- Adopt policies to address the worrying trend of youth unemployment. In particular, these should include education and literacy initiatives as well as retraining schemes.
- Recognise that many of the unemployed are skilled professionals who require appropriate support other than training.
- Resource a targeted re-training scheme for those previously employed in the construction industry, recognising that this industry is never likely to recover to the level of employment it had prior to 2007.
- Recognise the scale of the evolving long-term unemployment problem and adopt targeted policies to begin to address this.
- Ensure that the social welfare system is administered efficiently to minimise delays in paying the newly unemployed the social welfare benefits to which they are entitled.

It is clear that in addition to these measures Government needs to adopt a strategy of making large scale job-creation interventions into the labour market. Otherwise, the reality is that the current high levels of unemployment will only be eroded via emigration and the marginal impacts of the aforementioned recently announced schemes. *Social Justice Ireland* believes that the Governments current strategy is unlikely to see unemployment falling below 10 per cent of the labour force by 2015 (this is the Governments projection from Budget 2012) meaning that the prospect of Ireland persisting with a decade long unemployment crisis is very high. We propose that in addition to its current measures, Government makes two large-scale interventions which will significantly address the scale of the unemployment crisis and we outline the nature of these over the remainder of this section.

A Major Investment Programme

The depressed nature of the domestic economy and in particular domestic demand (see discussion in chapter 2) highlights the current dependency of Ireland's economic recovery and job creation prospects on external economic growth and exports. *Social Justice Ireland* believes that Government needs to adopt policies to stimulate the domestic economy given its current weakness and it should do so via the adoption of a major capital investment programme.

Such a multi-billion euro programme, structured over the next 3-4 years and focused on initiatives that strengthen social infrastructure such as a school building programme, a social housing programme, a nationwide high-speed broadband network, a water-system investment programme (e.g. pipes and meters), a green energy programme and a rural transport programme, would offer the prospect of simultaneously creating employment and addressing some of the socio-economic deficits that persist in Irish society.

A large-scale capital investment programme is attractive as it would stimulate the domestic economy by creating new economic activity and jobs, in particular jobs in the supressed construction sector. Furthermore, pursuing justifiable investment projects, which make good long-term socio-economic sense and is all the more appropriate given the economic and unemployment crisis we are in. We note that a commitment to a stimulus package along these lines was a commitment of both Fine Gael and Labour as they campaigned to be elected to Government in 2011.

Part Time Job Opportunities Programme

In a series of documents and briefings to Government, political parties and the Oireachtas over the past two years, *Social Justice Ireland* has outlined a proposal for a *Part Time Job Opportunities Programme* (PTJO). We proposed that the government introduce this programme to ensure real employment at the going hourly rate for the job is available to 100,000 people currently long-term unemployed. We believe that participation must be on a voluntary basis and that the scheme should be modelled on the *Part-Time Job Opportunities Programme* that was piloted in the 1994-1998 period.[56] Details of that pilot programme are outlined below.

The proposed programme would enable unemployed people to be employed on a part time basis by local authorities, the HSE, education authorities, voluntary and community organisations or groups; employed voluntarily and doing work of public or social value which is either not being done at all or is only being done partially at present; at the hourly 'going rate for the job'; for as many hours as would give them a net income equivalent to what they were receiving from jobseekers allowance plus an additional €20 a week, with participants employed for a minimum of 8 hours and a maximum of 19.5 hours per week; the person taking up the new position would lose none of his/her other social welfare entitlements; once the required number of hours had been worked, the person would be free to do whatever she/he wished for the remainder of the week; the money paid to the

---

[56] The current Directors of Social Justice Ireland led this pilot programme.

person filling the new position would be reallocated to the employing organisation by the Department for Social Protection; the employer would be encouraged to give extra hours to the worker who would be taxed accordingly; if the person received further income from another job, this income would be assessed for tax purposes in the normal way; and to protect against any 'deadweight effect', no position under the programme would be created if a person had been employed to do this particular work at any point during the previous two years.

The voluntary nature of the programme is considered very important from the point of view of the worker and the employer. It must not have any of the characteristics of 'workfare'.

- From the viewpoint of the worker, he/she must freely choose to come on the programme and must be free to leave if he/she chooses, subject only to normal requirements with regard to notice to the employer.
- From the point of view of the employer, there must be free choice in selecting workers from among those eligible for the programme. The employer should also be free to select the number of workers required. This ensures that the employment offered is real. The PTJO pilot programme showed that there would be more demand for these jobs than there were positions to accommodate them.

To protect the voluntary nature of the programme and to ensure that the employment is real the following would be expected:

- Positions should be advertised publicly by the employing body, through local media, or any other method used in the local area.
- A job description would be provided.
- Workers should be interviewed for the positions.
- Written job contracts should be provided.
- Employers would not be pressured to take more workers than they need.
- Leaving a particular job would not prejudice a worker seeking to participate in another project or training programme.
- Employers could replace workers immediately they left the programme.

Paying the 'going rate for the job' is an important concept in valuing the work done under the PTJO programme. It is the value which is placed on work in the market economy. In the pilot programme the programme's manager liaised with trade unions, professional organisations, employment agencies and personnel departments in an effort to arrive at a reasonable hourly rate for the various jobs created. In order to reflect incremental scales in many areas of employment, lower and higher level rates were provided in many instances, within which employers were free to negotiate the actual rate.

Social Justice Ireland estimates that 100,000 positions can be created using this PTJO approach – 10,000 places in the Community and Voluntary sector and 90,000 in the public sector. The total net additional cost of 100,000 places would be €150m; €90m for the 90,000 places in the public sector and €60m for the 10,000 places in the community and voluntary sector. Funding currently being spent on social welfare payments to participants on this programme would be switched to their new employers.

Part Time Job Opportunities (PTJO) Pilot Programme, 1994-98

The early 1990s saw high unemployment levels in Ireland and little prospect of jobs being available for some time to come, even though the economy was beginning to recover. Jobless growth was the reality. A proposal made by the current Directors of *Social Justice Ireland* was formally adopted by the Irish Government and announced in Budget 1994.

The proposal sought to create real part-time jobs in the community and voluntary sector principally. Long-term unemployed people could access these jobs on a voluntary basis. They were paid the going rate for the job and they worked the number of hours required to earn the equivalent of their social welfare payment with a small top up. The going rate for the job was agreed with the relevant trade unions and employers.

This programme was piloted in six very different areas: Finglas/Blanchardstown, Co. Laois, Waterford City, four towns in South Tipperary (Clonmel, Carrick-on-Suir, Cashel and Tipperary Town), North Kerry and the offshore islands.

The programme was taken on by 162 organisations and was extremely successful. Five hundred of the original 1,000 employees left during the course of the programme – almost all of these took up full-time employment. These were all replaced by others who fitted the criteria for participation.

The market economy is unable to provide anywhere near to the number of jobs required to reduce unemployment in the near future. This programme contributes to *Social Justice Ireland*'s view that public policy should change so that it recognises that people have a right to work; that unemployed people should not be forced to spend their lives doing nothing when traditional jobs do not exist; and that all meaningful work should be recognised.

Work and people with disabilities

The 2006 National Disability Survey (CSO, 2008 and 2010) and Census 2006 clearly show the scale and nature of disability in Ireland. Census 2006 found that 9.3 per cent of the population, some 393,785 people, had a disability while the National Disability Survey recording a slightly lower rate (CSO, 2007:13). Both these reports reflect the findings of a more detailed labour market examination of the disabled as part of a 2004 QNHS special module on disability. It found that of all those indicating that they had a longstanding health problem or disability only 37 per cent (110,800) were in employment. This is a figure considerably below the participation rate of the overall population, which at the times was over 60 per cent. Furthermore, of those employed approximately one-quarter worked part-time while the remaining three-quarters were in full-time employment.

This low rate of employment among people with a disability is of concern. Apart from restricting their participation in society it also ties them into state dependent low-income situations. Therefore, it is not surprising that Ireland's poverty figures reveal that people who are ill or have a disability are part of a group at high risk of poverty (see chapter 3). *Social Justice Ireland* believes that further efforts should be made to reduce the impediments faced by people with a disability to obtain employment. In particular, consideration should be given to reforming the current situation in which many such people face losing their benefits, in particular their medical card, when they take up employment. This situation ignores the additional costs faced by people with a disability in pursuing their day-to-day lives. For many people with disabilities the opportunity to take up employment is denied to them and they are trapped in unemployment, poverty or both.

Some progress was made in Budget 2005 to increase supports intended to help people with disabilities access employment. However, sufficient progress has not been made and recent Budgets have begun to reduce these services. New policies, including that outlined above, need to be adopted if this issue is to be addressed successfully. It is even more relevant today, given the growing employment challenges of the past few years.

Asylum seekers and work

Social Justice Ireland is very disappointed that the government continues to reject any proposal that the right to work of asylum seekers should be recognised. Along with others, we have consistently advocated that where government fails to meet its own stated objective of processing asylum applications in six months, the right to work should be automatically granted to asylum seekers. Detaining people for an unnecessarily prolonged period in such an excluded state is completely unacceptable. Recognising asylum seekers' right to work would assist in alleviating poverty and social exclusion in one of Ireland's most vulnerable groups.[57]

The need to recognise all work

A major question raised by the current labour-market situation concerns assumptions underpinning culture and policy making in this area. The priority given to paid employment over other forms of work is one such assumption. Most people recognise that a person can be working very hard outside a conventionally accepted "job". Much of the work carried out in the community and in the voluntary sector comes under this heading. So too does much of the work done in the home. *Social Justice Ireland*'s support for the introduction of a basic income system comes, in part, because it believes that all work should be recognised and supported (see chapter 3).

The need to recognise voluntary work has been acknowledged in the Government White Paper, *Supporting Voluntary Activity* (Department of Social, Community and Family Affairs, 2000). The report was prepared to mark the UN International Year of the Volunteer 2001 by Government and representatives of numerous voluntary organisations in Ireland. The report made a series of recommendations to assist in the future development and recognition of voluntary activity throughout Ireland. A 2005 report presented to the Joint Oireachtas Committee on Arts, Sport, Tourism, Community, Rural and Gaeltacht Affairs also provided an insight into this issue. It established that the cost to the state of replacing the 475,000 volunteers working for charitable organisations would be at least €205 million and could be as high as €485 million per year.

Social Justice Ireland believes that government should recognise in a more formal way all forms of work. We believe that everyone has a right to work, to contribute to his or her own development and that of the community and the wider society. However, we believe that policy making in this area should not be exclusively focused on job creation. Policy should recognise that work and a *job* are not always the same thing.

---

[57] We examine this issue in further detail in chapter 10.

The Work of Carers

The work of Ireland's carers receives minimal recognition despite the essential role their work plays in society. According to the Carers Association, people caring full-time for the elderly and people with disabilities save the state approximately €2.5 billion a year in costs which it would otherwise have to bear. In its Pre-Budget Submission in 2010 the Carers Association calculated there were 160,917 carers in Ireland providing 3,724,434 hours of care, which it valued at more than €2.5bn.

Results from the 2006 Census give similar indications (comparable results of the 2011 Census are not yet available). It found that 4.8 per cent of the population aged over 15 provided some care for sick or disabled family members or friends on an unpaid basis. This figure equates to almost 161,000 people. The dominant caring role played by women was highlighted by the fact that 100,214 (62.25 per cent) of these care providers were female.[58] When assessed by length of time, the census found that almost 41,000 people provide unpaid help to ill or disabled family members and friends for 43 hours a week or more, a working week considerably in excess of the standard working week for paid workers (CSO, 2007: 119-121).

Social Justice Ireland welcomed a commitment in *Towards 2016,* and more recently in the Fine Gael/Labour Party *Programme for Government* (2011), to develop a National Carers Strategy. However, progress has been slow and despite significant work on this strategy in 2008 the commitment to complete and publish such a strategy has been lacking. We strongly urge the Government to complete and publish this strategy ahead of the forthcoming data from Census 2011, which will almost certainly once again underscore the importance of carers and their work to Irish society. It is crucial that policy reforms be introduced to reduce the financial and emotional pressures on carers. In particular, these should focus on addressing the poverty experienced by many carers and their families alongside increasing the provision of respite care for carers and for those for whom they care. In this context, the 24 hour responsibilities of carers contrast with the improvements over recent years in employment legislation setting limits on working-hours of people in paid employment.

Key policy priorities on work, unemployment and job creation

- Adopt the following policy positions in responding to the recent rapid increase in unemployment:

---

[58] A CSO QNHS special module on carers (CSO, 2010) and a 2008 ESRI study entitled 'Gender Inequalities in Time Use' reached similar conclusions (McGinnity and Russell, 2008:36, 70).

- Launch a major investment programme focused on creating employment and prioritise initiatives that strengthen social infrastructure, such as the school building programme and the social housing programme.
- Resource the up-skilling of those who are unemployed and at risk of becoming unemployed through integrating training and labour market programmes.
- Maintain a sufficient number of active labour market programme places available to those who are unemployed.
- Adopt policies to address the worrying trend of youth unemployment. In particular, these should include education and literacy initiatives as well as retraining schemes.
- Recognise that many of the unemployed are skilled professionals who require appropriate support other than training.
- Resource a targeted re-training scheme for those previously unemployed in the construction industry, recognising that this industry is never likely to recover to the level of employment it had prior to 2007.
- Recognise the scale of the evolving long-term unemployment problem and adopt targeted policies to begin to address this.
- Ensure that the social welfare system is administered such that there is minimal delays in paying the newly unemployed the social welfare benefits to which they are entitled.

- Introduce a *Part Time Job Opportunities Programme* to create 100,000 positions for unemployed people.

- Funded programmes supporting the community should be expanded to meet the growing pressures arising from the current economic downturn.

- A new programme should be put in place targeting those who are very long-term unemployed (i.e. 5+ years).

- Seek at all times to ensure that new jobs have reasonable pay rates and adequately resource the inspectorate.

- As part of the process of addressing the working poor issue, reform the taxation system to make tax credits refundable.

- Develop employment-friendly income-tax policies which ensure that no unemployment traps exist. Policies should ease the transition from unemployment to employment.

- Adopt policies to address the obstacles facing women when they return to the labour force. These should focus on care initiatives, employment flexibility and the provision of information and training.

- Reduce the impediments faced by people with a disability in achieving employment. In particular, address the current situation in which many face losing their benefits when they take up employment.

- Recognise the right to work of all asylum seekers whose application for asylum is at least six months old and who are not entitled to take up employment.

- Recognise that the term "work" that is not synonymous with the concept of "paid employment". Everybody has a right to work, i.e. to contribute to his or her own development and that of the community and the wider society. This, however, should not be confined to job creation. *Work* and a *job* are not the same thing.

- Request the CSO to conduct an annual survey to discover the value of all unpaid work in the country (including community and voluntary work and work in the home). Publish the results of this survey as soon as they become available.

- Give greater recognition to the work carried out by carers in Ireland and introduce policy reforms to reduce the financial and emotional pressures on carers. In particular, these should focus on addressing the poverty experienced by many carers and their families as well as on increasing the provision of respite opportunities to carers and to those for whom they care.

6. PUBLIC SERVICES

CORE POLICY OBJECTIVE: PUBLIC SERVICES

To ensure the provision of, and access to, a level of public services regarded as acceptable by Irish society generally.

This chapter looks at a range of public services not addressed elsewhere in this Review[59]. It is important in this context to note that public services are not identical with the public sector. While the public sector does deliver a wide spectrum of public services, such services are also delivered by the community and voluntary sector and by the business sector in a variety of combinations with the public sector.

We noted in chapter 2 that public services and infrastructure have been eroded since the crisis of 2008. At both national and local level social services and related initiatives have been cut jat rthe very time that demand for these services is increasing. We also noted that particular budgetary decisions may provide a short-term gain or saving for Government but have huge negative long-term consequences. *Social Justice Ireland* is very concerned that many decisions made during the current series of crises are set to have such negative effects. Government's continuing insistence on making cuts of €2 for every €1 increase in taxation in Ireland's low-tax economy has serious implications for public services and affects Ireland's low and middle-income individuals and households in a negative way.

Many public services are provided by community and voluntary organisations. These have come under huge pressure in recent years as the recession has forced an ever growing number of people to seek their help. We will return to this issue in chapter 11.

Increasingly Ireland is being identified as a country whose public services are underdeveloped. Because poorer people rely on public services more than those who are better off, it is they who are most acutely affected by this shortage.

---

[59] Other chapters address issues such as housing and accommodation, healthcare and education.

This issue was examined by the National Economic and Social Forum (NESF). It recommended a series of developments in its report Improving *the Delivery of Quality Public Services,* (2006:112-117). *Social Justice Ireland* believes that Government should implement the approach for the delivery of public services outlined in this report.

This chapter assesses public transport, library services, financial services, information and communications technology, telecommunications, free legal aid, sports facilities and regulation.

Public transport

Public transport is a significant component of both health social inclusion issues. "The provision of adequate and affordable public transport will not only address the needs of those who are isolated from services or employment, it will contribute to reduced traffic and environmental pollution and better public health" (Farrell et al. 2008: 44). According to Farrell et al (2008), increased car dependency compounds issues relating to social isolation, increasing obesity, health hazards connected to heavy traffic and environmental pollution. As well as this, access in terms of transport, to jobs, health services, education and other facilities, is a major factor in ensuring social inclusion (Lucas, et al, 2001; Wilkinson,& Mormot, 2003; Considine & Dukelow, 2009).

"Over the last 20 years, the percentage of total journeys undertaken by public transport has declined and public transport also accounts for a declining share of overall transport" (Department of Transport 2009: 40). Car dependency has been on the increase, which suggests that public transport provision in Ireland is not adequate.

As part of the consultation for *A Sustainable Transport Future a New Transport Policy for Ireland 2009 – 2020,* such issues as the availability and quality of public transport in Ireland, lack of integration, lack of capacity, overcrowding poor availability and design of routes, were highlighted. According to a report carried out by the EPA (2011), one of the most significant barriers to achieving sustainable transport in Ireland is the "lack of reliable and efficient public transport and cycling facilities, particularly in low-density rural areas and residential neighbourhoods" (Browne et al. 2011: vii).

The Department of Transport (2009) acknowledges the need to ensure that alternatives to car transport are available in creating a sustainable transport system.

Improved public transport systems, along with investment in cycling and walking, are a central means by which this will be achieved. "Public transport has to gain a higher share than today in the transport mix, become easily accessible for everyone and fully integrated with non-motorised modes" (European Commission, 2011:24).

However, in 2012, as a result of 8 per cent reductions in the subsidies for public transport, there were fare increases across all public transport operators – Dublin Bus, Iarnród Éireann, Bus Éireann and Luas. Reducing the affordability of public transport does little to encourage people to use this form of transport and ultimately achieve a more sustainable transport system. With continuing reductions envisaged, it is essential that affordability is maintained.

While it has been necessary to re-schedule some public transport initiatives that had been planned as part of the National Development Plan, it is crucial that Government continue to give priority to public transport over private transport in allocating capital funding. In light of the discussion relating to the role public transport plays in undermining social exclusion it is also essential that continued support is provided for the development and maintenance of the rural transport programme[60]. It should also be recognised that public transport in Ireland generally has a long way to go before it reaches the levels usually associated with a developed society.

Library services

Libraries play an important role in Irish society. They perform a valuable community service, ensuring access to reading, information and learning. "They provide a focal point for community and intergenerational contact, and enable access to learning and an ever-expanding range of information for a wide constituency through an increasingly broad and varied range of media" (Mc Grath et al, 2010: 6).

Statistics for 2010 show the important function that libraries play in Ireland. In that year registered membership of libraries was virtually unchanged on the previous year at 809,169Just over 19 per cent of the population were registered as members of the public library service Children's library membership in 2010 increased by 1.6 per cent in 2010 to 311,625 but adult membership declined by 1per cent to 492,369. Visits to full-time branches over the same period rose by 1per cent to 14,702,901, while visits to all branches increased by 1.4 per cent to 16.3 million. (An Chomhairle Leabharlanna 2010).

---

[60] Issues specifically related to the provision of public services in rural areas area addressed in chapter 13.

However, in its annual report for 2010 An Chomhairle Leabharlanna expressed concern about the increase in annual charges being levied on adult users of the service. The agency says that fees are a serious barrier to users and that he benefits of free access outweigh the value of the money gained. This is a particularly important point in the current economic climate and local authorities are urged to reconsider this measure.

Investment in public libraries is being reduced as a result of the current economic climate resulting in the book funds down by 19 per cent on the previous year. Total local authority operational expenditure on libraries in 2010, both recurrent and capital, fell by 16per cent from €144.5m o €121.5mWhen the service support charges are included, the decrease was 12per cent (An Chomhairle Leabharlann, 2010).

Clearly, public libraries play a critical role in Irish society. *Social Justice Ireland* believes that as part of our commitment to providing a continuum of education throughout the life-cycle, Ireland needs to recognise the value that the library service provides. This requires ready availability and easy access to information, including easy access to modern means of communication. Libraries are obvious centres with the potential to support these objectives. To play this potential role, however, continued support for and expansion of the library service is essential.

Financial services
Financial exclusion refers to a household's difficulty accessing and using financial services. This has particular implications for people as we move towards an increasingly cashless society in which groups already financially excluded will become more marginalised. A 2011 study by the ESRI examined four dimensions of financial exclusion: access to a bank current account, access to credit, ability to save, and access to housing insurance (Russell et al, 2011). Of these, access to a bank current account was considered the most fundamental, as exclusion from basic banking services means that households can experience difficulties carrying out everyday transactions such as paying bills, receiving earnings or welfare benefits, transferring funds and purchasing goods and services.

The results of this research highlighted some serious deficiencies in the ability of Irish households to access these basic financial services. In 2008 it was found that 20 per cent of Irish households did not have a bank current account - a figure that is almost three times higher than the average for the EU15. The proportion without a bank current account rose to 40 per cent among those with low education qualifications, 38 per cent in households in the bottom 20 per cent of the income distribution, 50 per cent among local authority tenants, 52 per cent among those who are ill or disabled and 27 per cent among those aged over 55 years (Russell et al 2011:126-127).

The *Strategy for Financial Inclusion* published in 2011 indicates that a binding requirement on banks in other EU countries to address the issues faced by people who are financially excluded yielded dividends. "As a significant first step in this direction, a binding requirement to support the provision of a BPA (basic payment account) was introduced for Allied Irish Banks and Bank of Ireland in 2009 as part of the recapitalisation of those banks. This commitment was extended to the remainder of the domestic banking sector in a package of sector-wide commitments which was agreed with the European Commission in 2010 as part of its Decision on the Bank of Ireland Restructuring Plan" (Steering Group on Financial Inclusion, 2011: 7).

While the provision of a basic payment account will not address all elements of financial exclusion it is considered to be the essential first step. The steering group has advised that the roll-out on a pilot basis of a basic payment account should be progressed in the early stages of 2012. The potential role for post offices in providing an access point has also been emphasised as an effective tool in addressing financial exclusion.

Information and communications technology

In 2011, an estimated 81 per cent of households had a home computer. This was an increase of 16 percentage points since 2007. Internet and broadband connection has also increased substantially over this period, with an estimated 78 per cent now connected to the internet compared with 72 per cent in 2010 and 57 per cent in 2007. Further to this, the CSO figures also show that in 2010 27per cent of adults never used the internet. This was reduced to 21 per cent in 2011. (CSO, 2011). These figures underscore the increasingly important role which ICT plays in modern society and also the level of progress made in accessing digital technology in Ireland.

"Digital literacy is increasingly becoming an essential life competence and the inability to access or use ICT has effectively become a barrier to social integration and personal development. Those without sufficient ICT skills are disadvantaged in the labour market and have less access to information to empower themselves as consumers, or as citizens saving time and money in offline activities and using online public services" (European Commission, 2008: 4). Digital competence is also highlighted was identified as one of the key competencies required for lifelong learning by the European Commission in 2006. Factors such as disability, age, and social disadvantage play significant roles in increasing digital exclusion. Digital exclusion has major consequences for those who experience it, including reduced consumer choice, reduced employability, exclusion from popular forms of social interaction and exclusion from online public services and the associated advantages such as convenience and time saving. Apart from the impact on the individual, there are also losses to the business community and the economy at large. (McDaid & Cullen, 2008).

According to the European Commission's scorecard, 63.5 per cent of the Irish population in 2010 were regular internet users. But this was just 47.3 per cent for disadvantaged members of the population[61]. Ireland is still performing below the EU 27 average in these areas, albeit only marginally lower. (European Commission, 2010). So, while progress is being made, the Government needs to show sustained commitment to counteract the issue of digital exclusion in particular for the more vulnerable sectors of society. A continued commitment of resources is required in this area.

Telecommunications

Two issues are of note in this section. Firstly, Com Reg has put in place a system to ensure that a basic set of telecommunications services is available to all consumers throughout the country. This is known as Universal Service Obligation. The services to be provided include: meeting reasonable requests for connections at a fixed location to the public communications network and access to publicly available telephone service; provision of directory services and maintenance of the national directory database; public telephone provision; specific services for disabled users; affordability of tariffs and options for consumers to control expenditure (Commission for Communications Regulation, 2011: 13). Eircom is the designated Universal Service Provider (USP) and has a number of obligations regarding the supply of these services. We welcome the fact that to date, Com Reg has been particularly vigilant in maintaining the quality of the service provided under this obligation, taking into account any negative impacts which would be potentially incurred by disadvantaged members of the community were these obligations not to be met.

---

[61] Disadvantaged people are defined as individuals having at least one of the following characteristics: aged 55-74, those with a low level of education (ISCED 0-2) and/or out of the labour market (unemployed, inactive or retired). Regular use is defined as having used the internet at least once a week, in the last three months. Figures are calculated based on available microdata.

Secondly, as part of the Digital Agenda for Europe, the European Commission has set targets of ensuring access to 30mbps broadband for all citizens and 100mbps for 50per cent of citizens by 2020. We believe that the use of technological advances offers a real method of addressing many of the inequities that exist in the allocation of, and access to, information and telecommunications resources. While progress has been made in regard to the provision of basic broadband services (see section on Information and Communications Technology), Ireland is performing badly in relation to the roll out and take up of advance broadband services. "Given the weak telecommunications investment climate in Ireland, our dispersed population patterns and the recession, there is a strong risk, if appropriate action is not taken, that Ireland is likely to fall even further behind as other countries are moving ahead to deploy advanced telecoms networks" (Forfas, 2011:27). In June 2011, the Government convened a Task Force on High Speed Broad Band. This taskforce is due to conclude its work in early 2012. It is essential that consideration be given to the cost of broadband provision in Ireland in order to ensure it is accessible to all.

Free legal aid

Citizens depend on the law and associated institutions to defend their rights and civic entitlements. A central element of this system, particularly for those with limited incomes, is the free legal aid system. The Legal Aid Board provides civic legal aid to people with incomes of less than €18,000 per annum; recipients contribute a nominal sum. *Social Justice Ireland* believes that free legal aid is an important public service. In the current economic climate of rising unemployment and decreasing income the demands on the Legal Aid Board are continuing to grow. Most notably, there has been an increase in demand for services regarding debt issues.

"In the four years since 2006 the number of applications is up by more than 70 per cent and the upwards trajectory of demand has continued into 2011. In 2010 alone there was an increase in applications to law centres alone of almost 22 per cent" (Legal Aid Board, 2010: 13). In 2010 Exchequer funding for the civil legal aid service was cut by 8 per cent to €24.22 million. There is increasing pressure on the service due to decreasing resources. The waiting time for a full appointment with a solicitor has increased beyond four months in more than half of the centres. The provision of, and adequate support for, this service is a basic requirement of governance. Considering the increasing pressure on this service it is vital that it is adequately resourced and supported by the government.

Sports

An increase in the proportion of adults (aged 16 and over) who actively participate in sport is a welcome trend. The Irish Sports Monitor (2009), found such participation rose from 30.8p er cent in 2008 to 33.5 per cent in 2009 (Lunn and Layte, 2009). Sport provides significant direct health benefits to participants and also significant social benefits to the wider community. A report carried out by Indecon International Economic Consultants (2010) highlighted the contribution provided by sport to the Irish economy. It also showed the vital role played by sport in assisting the development of social capital and in contributing to the health and quality of life of the population.

It is of concern, therefore, that the level of voluntary activity related to sport fell g from 8.2per cent in 2007 to 6.8p per cent in 2009 (Lunn and Layte, 2009). The 2010 Indecon study conservatively estimated that over 270,000 people participate in some form of sport-related voluntary activity. The Irish Sports Council Strategic Plan (2009) estimated that the number was closer to 400,000. The estimated value of volunteering is between €321 million and €582 million per annum (Indecon, 2010). The Government needs to continue to support policies aimed at encouraging participation through volunteerism.

Special consideration also needs to be given to disadvantaged areas. People who are socially disadvantaged are less likely to participate in sport and, therefore, less likely to obtain the health benefits of physical activity. The National Sports Council has developed a creative initiative of local sports partnerships. Some of these are working effectively and attempting to address this problem. Further funding for local sports partnerships should be made available. Given their huge potential, such funding would be most worthwhile. These local sports partnerships could also go some way towards addressing the considerable level of fall off in sport-related volunteerism.

The national agreement, *Towards 2016*, contained a number of initiatives relating to sport and sports facilities which the Government should implement. These include commitments to:

- increasing support for sports infrastructure and sporting organisations, recognising that sport has the potential to be a driver for social change and that targeting specific groups can address issues of exclusion and inequality;
- promoting sport in education settings; and

- achieving the Irish Sport Council target of increase the number of children taking part in sport by 3 per cent.

Social Justice Ireland supports each of these commitments and looks forwards to implementation of various initiatives aimed at fulfilling them.

As sports policy is developed against the background of increasingly scarce public expenditure resources, *Social Justice Ireland* believes that more in-depth consideration needs to be given to how we maximise the returns of these investments. Income and time are both major barriers to sports participation and policy makers need to be aware of this in developing sports policy (Lunn and Layte, 2009). In many cases simple schemes to encourage participation and use of existing sports facilities are required.

Regulation

Regulatory policy in Ireland has failed in many areas and requires significant reform over the next few years. This has been clearly demonstrated by the problems that have emerged in the financial services sector. While some of the required reforms have been put in place, a serious re-think is required to ensure that regulation plays a stronger and far more effective role to ensure there is no repetition of the huge failures of the past decade.

Central to our opinion on how regulation should develop is the view that all regulators, be they currently in existence or established in the future, should be required to consider the societal impact of any reforms they propose before they are implemented. They should also have the capacity to monitor what is happening and to act effectively and quickly when negative events occur.

A range of impacts flow from decisions taken by people in the various areas in which regulation applies. Regulation should be judged on how it affects social, cultural and sustainability issues in society as well as on the economy. Implementing regulation with this as its central aim would certainly achieve better regulation for all. It would also ensure consistently better outcomes for consumers. Such an approach would have prevented the failure of the regulatory process in the current banking crisis.

We also believe that there should be solid and justifiable reasons for introducing regulation. It should not be introduced just to create choice or competition within a market. For example, to achieve competition in the electricity market the electricity regulator increased the price of electricity. While this may achieve competition we question the benefit to people. Furthermore, assessment mechanisms should be established to allow an analysis of regulation before and after its implementation. Examination of its societal impacts should be central to such an assessment procedure. We also believe that, as part of the assessment procedure, inputs should be sought from interested parties, including the community and voluntary sector.

A further important aspect is the need to consider the impact of regulation on regional policy. Cross-subsidisation issues, in postal or electrical services, are important to retain equity between rural and urban dwellers. A further challenge for regulatory authorities must be to retain this inter-regional equity.

Regulation and regulatory law has profoundly failed Ireland in recent years. It should be framed to ensure that it is effective, timely, accessible and interpretable. Currently regulatory law is complex and in many cases requires those being regulated to divert a considerable quantity of resources to keep up with it. Complex regulation also makes it difficult for interested parties to participate in the pre and post-regulation assessment mechanisms. *Social Justice Ireland* believes it is important that whenever regulation is judged to have failed, government should reform it at the earliest opportunity.

Key policy priorities for public services
- Focus policy on ensuring that there is provision of, and access to, a level of public services regarded as acceptable by Irish society generally.
- Ensure equality of access across all public services.
- Target funding strategies to ensure that far greater priority is given to providing an easy-access, affordable, integrated and high-quality public transport system. This should include adequate support for the Rural Transport Initiative which improves significantly the quality of life of those living in remote rural areas, particularly older people and women.
- Support the further development of library services throughout the country, including provision of open-access information technology.
- Ensure that financial institutions provide people with easy to access and affordable basic bank accounts and financial facilities as per the Strategy for Financial Inclusion (2011).
- Give more in-depth consideration to how public funds are used to encourage sport and sporting activity. In many cases simple schemes to encourage participation and use of existing sports facilities are required.

- Adopt further information-technology programmes to increase the skills of disadvantaged members of society.
- Take action to address the huge failures identified in the regulatory process, as clearly demonstrated by the crisis in banking and financial services. This process should ensure that all types of regulation are judged against how they affect social, cultural and sustainability issues within society as well as on the economy.

7. HOUSING AND ACCOMMODATION

CORE POLICY OBJECTIVE:
HOUSING & ACCOMMODATION

To ensure that adequate and appropriate accommodation is available for all people and to develop an equitable system for allocating resources within the housing sector.

Housing and accommodation policy

Issues relating to housing and accommodation have held a very prominent role in policy debates in Ireland over recent years. Most of that discussion, however, has been concerned with the provision and cost of privately owned accommodation. More recently the issues associated with housing in Ireland have included challenges involving the large surplus housing stock, negative equity, high levels of mortgage arrears, unfinished developments and increasing social housing need.

Initially the massive increase in housing was a response to increasing demand, as a result of a sustained growth in the population, low interest rates and increasing income per capita. As noted in chapter 2, this situation changed and construction was promoted and supported as an end in itself because it appeared to generate economic growth. During the boom years Ireland experienced an astonishing growth in property construction and house prices. Construction became a major element in and driver of the Irish economy. However, housing construction increased at a rate which was not supported by demand. The result was a housing bubble which has contributed to the current economic crisis. Poor financial and planning regulations along with tax incentives served to support this negative phenomenon (Kitchin et.al 2010).

Housing Tenure in Ireland

There are three main models of housing provision in Europe: an owner-occupier sector, a rental sector and a social housing sector. Table 7.1 shows how Irish tenure patterns have changed over time using data from various Censuses of Population. In 2006, 77.2 per cent of households were owner-occupiers, one of the highest rates of owner occupancy in the EU (CSO, 2009:61; 2003:55). Ireland's level of home

---

ownership reflects the high value Irish people place on owning their own homes. It also flows from Irish housing policy which supported owner occupation and placed little value on other forms of housing tenure.

Policies which favoured investment in residential development, combined with policies of mortgage-interest tax relief and very favourable tenant purchase schemes, have resulted in an extremely high level of home ownership. Owner-occupiers make up 77.2 per cent of Irish households. This is considerably higher than the EU average of 63.4 per cent. Government housing policy over many years produced a housing system that is not tenure neutral and which led to the residualisation of the rental sector, both public and private.

Since the 1970s it has been the policy of successive Irish governments to subsidise owner occupation. This has been achieved by the abolition of local rates on residential property and the subsequent failure to implement a system of residential property tax. This is being addressed to some extent by the current government through the introduction of a property tax. Such a tax is necessary in some form for the development of a fairer system of taxation. As indicated in chapter 4, this needs to be implemented as a matter of urgency. It should also be noted that for decades people in social housing had the option of purchasing their house and many did. In practice this produced a transfer of wealth to the purchaser as these houses were available for far less than their real market value.

Table 7.1: Nature of Occupancy of Private Households, Ireland 1961-2006

Year	Owner-occupied	Rented	Other
1961	59.8%	35.6%	4.6%
1971	68.8%	28.9%	2.3%
1981	74.7%	22.6%	2.6%
1991	80.0%	17.9%	2.1%
2002	79.8%	18.5%	1.7%
2006	77.2%	21.3%	1.5%

Source: CSO, 2009:61

In its recent housing policy statement the Government has acknowledged the issues associated with this hierarchical structure in home ownership by indicating that "This structure and the value judgement that underlies it – which implicitly holds that the tenure which must ultimately be aspired to is homeownership – has had a considerable role in leading the Irish housing sector, Irish economy, and the wider Irish society to where they are today" (Department of the Environment, Community and Local Government, 2011b).

With this in mind, Government has indicated that its vision for the housing sector is one which will be based on "choice, fairness, and equity across tenures and on delivering quality outcomes for the resources invested" (ibid).

Housing: a new philosophy

A series of publications by the economist Professor PJ Drudy of Trinity College offered an interesting new approach to how Irish society might view housing. Drudy has outlined these views in a paper delivered at a 2005 Social Policy Conference, in a book, *Out of Reach* (2005) co-authored with Michael Punch and in a chapter in the book *Social Policy in Ireland* book (Drudy, 2006).

Drudy's proposal is that housing should be regarded as a home rather than as a market commodity. In his conference paper Drudy stated that we should "place the emphasis on housing as a home – shelter, a place to stay, to feel secure, to build a base, find an identity and participate in a community and society". Therefore, he continued, "housing thus becomes a central feature of 'development' – a process not simply comprising increases in economic growth, but containing positive actions to improve the quality of life and wellbeing for all" (2005: 44).

Drudy has suggested that Irish society now needs to address "a fundamental philosophical question: is it the purpose of a housing system to provide investment, speculative or capital gains for those with the necessary resources or should the critical aim be to provide a home as a right for all citizens?" (2004: 46). In his view it is time for Ireland to regard housing as a social requirement like health services or education.

Social Justice Ireland strongly welcomes and endorses these views. Had society adopted this approach over the past decade the Irish economy, and many Irish families, would not have fallen into its present precarious financial position. It is time that we formally incorporate this approach into our national housing policy.

Total housing stock

Housing numbers (dwellings) increased more rapidly than total population between 2006 and 2011. There was a 13.3 per cent increase in dwellings over this period compared with an 8.1 per cent in the population. The number of dwellings increased by 234,562 from 1,769,613 in 2006 to 2,004,175 in 2011 – an annual average increase of 46,912.The largest percentage increase in households occurred in Laois (21.2%). Cavan, Donegal, Leitrim and Longford all showed increases above 19 per cent (CSO, 2011).

"House building in Ireland has run counter to what one would expect given the vacancy rate. Those counties that had the highest rates of vacant stock in 2006 subsequently increased their housing stock by the greatest percentage in the following years, and those counties with low vacancy, increased their stock the least" (Kitchin, et.al. 2010: 25).

House completions
Table 7.2 shows the rate of house completions in the various sectors between 1993 and 2011. Completions peaked in 2006 at over 93,000 units. Since then the rate of dwelling completion has rapidly declined.The number of completions in 2010 was 14,602 and this fell further to 10, 480 in 2011.

In 2009 the vast majority of new houses (80 per cent) were built by the private sector, down from 91 per cent in 2007. Local authorities built 3,362 new homes in 2009. However, the Government has indicated that a return to large scale building of Local Authority housing is unlikely and has instead decided to focus resources in the area of social leasing initiatives and the rental accommodation scheme (RAS) in order to ensure social housing provision. However, *Social Justice Ireland* still contends that the government should ensure some continued investment in social housing acquisition in order to maintain a stock of Local Authority houses. Major scaling back in the provision of new Local Authority stock will have long term consequences for people in housing need.

The figures for 2009 also reveal a further growth in the levels of voluntary/non-profit and co-op housing. These organisations built 2,011 dwellings during that year and they now account for over a third of all publicly assisted housing completions. This trend is very welcome and underscores the growing role this sector is playing in Irish society. *Social Justice Ireland* believes this sector has the capacity to make an even greater contribution to addressing the current housing crisis and that government must provide further assistance to facilitate its continued growth.

Table 7.2: House Completions, 1993 – 2011

Year	Local Authority Housing	Voluntary/Non Profit Housing	Private Housing	Total
1993	1,200	890	19,301	21,391
1994	2,374	901	23,588	26,863
1995	2,960	1,011	26,604	30,575
1996	2,676	917	30,132	33,725
1997	2,632	756	35,454	38,842
1998	2,771	485	39,093	42,349
1999	2,909	579	43,024	46,512
2000	2,204	951	46,657	49,812
2001	3,622	1,253	47,727	52,602
2002	4,403	1,360	51,932	57,695
2003	4,516	1,617	62,686	68,819
2004	3,539	1,607	71,808	76,954
2005	4,209	1,350	75,398	80,957
2006	3,968	1,240	88,211	93,419
2007	4,986	1,685	71,356	78,027
2008	4,905	1,896	44,923	51,724
2009	3,362	2,011	21,076	26,240
2010	–	–	–	14,602
2011	–	–	–	10,480

Source: Department of Environment, Heritage and Local Government, Housing Statistics Bulletins (various editions).

Vacant Dwellings

In the absence of a residential property tax Local Authorities adopted a model of funding which derived income from development levies. This was supported by central Government through tax incentive schemes and poor regulation of local planning. This has resulted in vacant housing stock in areas where there is the least demand, as well as the phenomenon of unfinished estates and developments across the country (Kitchen et.al 2010).

With increasing housing need in Ireland the preliminary findings from Census 2011 revealed a fascinating aspect of the Irish housing sector. The 2006 Census showed that 15.0 per cent of all housing was vacant in April 2006. The preliminary results from Census 2011 showed that the total number of vacant dwellings in 2011 had increased by 27,880 since 2006 to 294,202. As the total housing stock has also increased since 2006 by 13.3 per cent – higher than the 10.5 per cent increase in vacant dwellings – the percentage of dwellings that are vacant has fallen slightly to 14.7 per cent. The vacancy rate varies across the country, with Leitrim recording the highest vacancy rate at 30.4%. The vacancy rate in Dublin at the time of the census indicated one in every 10 dwellings were vacant (CSO, 2011).

Unfinished estates

Many local authorities disregarded good planning guidelines and consideration was not given to "regional and national objectives; sensible demographic profiling of potential demand; and the fact that much of the land zoned lacks essential services such as water and sewerage treatment plants, energy supply, public transport or roads" (Kitchin, et.al. 2010: 28). A recent report indicates that from a total of 2,876 housing development sites of two or more dwellings, there are 2,066 unfinished housing developments in the country. Of these 2,066 sites, 1,822 were predominantly inactive at the time of inspection and only 245 active (Department of Environment, Community and Local Government, 2011a).

In its report the Advisory Group on Unfinished Housing Developments (2011) indicated that critical issues relating to public safety should be addressed as a matter of priority by local authorities in the absence or failure of the developer to implement a site resolution plan. This would require appropriate state funding. Further to this there are social and economic implications for house owners, often in negative equity, residing in poorly finished estates which in some instances have few neighbours, no street lighting, paths, green areas and are located a good distance away from amenities or services (Kitchin et.al.2010).

Mortgage arrears

Central Bank figures (Table 7.3) on mortgage arrears show that at the end of December 2011, there were 768,917 private residential mortgage accounts held in the Republic of Ireland. Of these, 70,911, or 9.2%, were in arrears of more than 90 days. This compares with 62,970 accounts (8.1% of total) that were in arrears of more than 90 days at end September 2011.

Table 7.3 Mortgage Arrears 2011

	March 2011	June 2011	Sept 2011	Dec 2011
Total amount of residential mortgage loans outstanding at end of quarter	782,429	777,321	773,420	768,917
In arrears 91-180 days- at end of quarter	14,268	15,723	16,599	17,825
In arrears over 180 days- at end of quarter	35,341	40,040	46,371	53,086
Total arrears cases over 90 days	49,609	55,763	62,970	70,911
outstanding (no. and %)	6.3%	7.2%	8.1%	9.2%

Source: Central Bank 2012

The report of the Inter-Departmental Mortgage Arrears Working Group (2011) made a range of recommendations, including, new bankruptcy legislation, non-judicial debt settlement options and further mortgage restructuring solutions. They also emphasised the need for the establishment of a mortgage support and advice service, recommending that this should be linked to MABS and that the expense of providing this service should be borne by the mortgage lenders.

In addition, it recommended the establishment of two state sponsored mortgage-to-rent schemes to help protect the most distressed mortgage holders. The schemes will allow certain struggling mortgage holders to remain in the family home as social housing tenants. Eligibility criteria are as follows: the mortgage position should be deemed unsustainable under a Mortgage Arrears Resolution Process; agree to voluntary repossession; must qualify for social housing support from the relevant Local Authority and make an application for social housing support; the house must be valued at less than €220,000 and must be suitable for the applicant's needs.

In the first scheme the property is bought by an approved housing body (housing association or co-operative) at current market value and the household becomes a social housing tenant of the housing body. The purchase of the house is partly financed by a loan and partly from the Exchequer under the Capital Advance Leasing Facility (CALF).

In the second scheme the mortgage lender becomes the long-term owner of the property and the household becomes a social housing tenant of the Local Authority. The Local Authority leases the property from the mortgage lender. These schemes are in the pilot stage and will be rolled out more widely at a later date so it is still too early to assess their effectiveness.

Housing needs assessment: Waiting lists – how many and how long?

Social housing support "is broadly defined as accommodation provided, or arranged, by housing authorities or approved housing bodies for households who are unable to provide for their accommodation needs from their own resources" (Department of Environment, Community and Local Government, 2011c, pg.48). The most recent assessment of housing needs took place in March 2011. This provides a national picture of the level of housing need across the country. It must be noted that the approach used in the collection of the data in 2011 differs from that employed in previous years, so the figures are not strictly comparable (Housing Agency, 2011).

Net need refers to "the number of households in need of housing support who are not currently receiving social housing support (those already in Local Authority, voluntary cooperative or RAS accommodation are excluded)" (Housing Agency, 2011:1). Table 7.4 presents a measure of the numbers of households who cannot be accommodated through the current stock available to housing authorities.

The net need figure for 2008 shows that 56,249 households were in need of social housing support at 31st March 2008. This was an increase of some 31% on the level of need in 2005. While it is already acknowledged that the data from 2008 and 2011 are not strictly comparable, it is still alarming to see that the increase reported in net need from 2008 to 2011 amounts to 42,069 households – an increase of 74.8% increase over the period (see Table 7.4).

In 2008 the largest category of households on the lists was those labelled as being not able to meet costs of existing accommodation. This group accounted for 53 per cent of the waiting list, or 29,583 households. The largest category of need in 2011 was again those people who are unable to meet the cost of accommodation. This category accounted for almost two thirds of all households, or 65,643 households.

The next largest categories in 2011 were medical or compassion reasons (9.7%) and involuntarily sharing (8.7 per cent). Overcrowding and unfit accommodation accounted for 4.7 per cent and 1.7 per cent respectively.

The household structure of those on the waiting list in 2011 shows that 48,748, or 49.6 per cent of households, were single adult households while 24,819 (25.2%) were family households with one child. Households with 2 children account for 12 per cent (11,792), households with 3 children accounted for 4.5 per cent and households with 4+ children accounted for 2.6 per cent. Overall, 44 per cent of households in need of housing support consisted of households with children.

Table 7.4 Breakdown of the Local Authority Waiting List by Major Categories of Need 2005, 2008 and 2011

Category of need	2005	as % of net need 2005	2008	as % of net need 2008	2011	as % of net need 2011
Homeless	1,987	4.5	1,394	3	2,348	2.4
Traveller	1,004	2	1,317	2	1,824	1.9
Accommodation unfit	1,719	4	1,757	3	1,708	1.7
Accommodation overcrowded	4,073	10	4,805	9	4,594	4.7
Involuntary sharing	3,371	8	4,965	9	8,534	8.7
Young persons leaving care	256	.5	715	1	538	.5
Medical or compassion	3,504	8	8,059	14	9,548	9.7
Older Persons	1,658	4	2,499	4	2,266	2.3
People with a disability	455	1	1,155	2	1,315	1.3
Unable to meet Accommodation Cost	24,919	58	29,583	53	65,643	66.8
Total	42,946	100	56,249	100	98,318	100

Source: Department of the Environment, Heritage and Local Government, Annual Housing Statistics Bulletin 2008 & Housing Agency, 2011.

The age profile of those in need of housing support shows that the majority are under 40 years of age (69%), with the largest category occurring in the age range of 31–40 years (30.5 per cent).

The citizenship of households in need of housing support shows that the majority of households had Irish citizenship (70.5%) and 20.2 per cent (19,855 households) were EU citizens. The final 9.3 per cent, or 9,162, were categorised as having refugee status, permission to remain in the state or subsidiary protection status.

There is a clear association between being in housing need and low income. According to the OECD (2011), people with low incomes are more likely to face poorer basic housing conditions and are also less likely to be satisfied with their housing arrangements. Table 7.5 shows gross household income (unadjusted for household composition). It reveals that over three quarters (78.5 per cent) of households in need of social housing had incomes below €15,000. The majority of these households had gross incomes between €10,000 and €15,000. Overall, 89.6 per cent (88,064 households) had incomes below €20,000. Larger households are likely to have larger incomes coupled but also larger living expenses. That said, only 3.6 per cent of households had income levels above €25,000.

Table 7.5 Breakdown of Local Authority Housing Waiting List by Gross Household Income 2011		
Income Band	**No. of Households**	**%**
Below	€ 10,000 27,065	27.5
€ 10,001 - € 15,000	50,118	51
€ 15,001 - € 20,000	10,881	11.1
€ 20,001 - €25,000	6,736	6.8
€25,001 - € 30,000	2,159	2.2
Over €30,000	1,359	1.4
Total	**98,318**	**100**

Source: Housing Agency, 2011.

The length of time spent by households on waiting lists once they have applied for social housing support is another area which deserves attention. In 2011, 22.5 per cent of households had applied to the Local Authority for housing less than one year previously. Of these, 31,286 (31.8%) households had been waiting for between two and four years. Almost a quarter (24.6%), or 24,138, households had been more than four years waiting for social housing. There is clearly a high level of housing need in Ireland which appears to be increasing at a substantial rate. These numbers represent the most vulnerable people in Irish society. It is apparent that significant action is required to address this situation.

Opportunities to address social housing need

The current situation provides opportunities for addressing social housing need. In December 2011 Minister Hogan and NAMA agreed that 2,000 housing units would be made available in 2012 to people on social housing lists through leasing agreements with Local Authorities and voluntary housing associations. However, it remains to be seen how many of these houses will be suitable for the provision of social housing. Further to this, the Irish Council for Social Housing and the National Association of Building Cooperatives indicated that "opportunities exist for the voluntary and cooperative sector to have an impact on the issue of unfinished housing developments by working in partnership with Local Authorities to serve local social housing need" (Advisory Group on Unfinished Housing Developments, 2011:12).

The private rented sector

Traditionally the private rented sector was the residual sector of the Irish housing system. The private rented sector is the "tenure of last resort for those unable to obtain Local Authority housing or not yet ready to enter owner-occupation" (McCashin, 2000:43). It was characterised by poor-quality accommodation and non-secure tenure at the lower end of the housing market. Today, this sector is highly differentiated, with high-quality housing and relatively secure tenure at the upper end, and low-quality housing and insecurity of tenure at the lower end of the market.

Table 7.6: Percentage distribution of housing units by occupancy status,   1961-2006.

Occupancy Status	1961	1971	1981	1991	2002	2006
LA Rented	18.4	15.9	12.7	9.7	6.9	7.5
Private Rented	17.2	10.9	8.1	7.0	11.1	10.3
Owner Occupied	53.6	60.7	67.9	80.2	77.4	77.2
Other	10.8	12.5	11.2	3.0	4.6	5.0
Total	**100**	**100**	**100**	**100**	**100**	**100**

Source: CSO (2003:28) and calculated from CSO (2007:48).

The percentage of the population dependent on this sector to meet their housing needs declined from 17.2 per cent in 1961 to 7 per cent in 1991 (see table 7.6). This compares with an EU average of 21 per cent. The results of Census 2006 indicate that the composition of the sector has changed dramatically. A combination of a growing population, changing household structure, and the increasing cost of owner-occupation has resulted in the number of households in the private rented sector increasing by almost 50 per cent. As table 7.6 shows, the private rented sector now accounts for 10 per cent of households. In total in 2006 there were 145,317 households living in the private rented sector. Of these 16,621 rented unfurnished dwellings and 128,696 rented furnished or part-furnished dwellings (CSO, 2006).

According to the rental agency Daft (2012) the national average rent in 2011 was €821 a month, down from a peak of €1,100 in early 2008. There is a gap between the costs of renting in urban and rural centres with rents in cities 1.5 per cent higher in January 2012 than a year previously. However, rents elsewhere in the country fell by 1.3 per cent. Overall the national average rent for the year 2010 to 2011 fell by 0.7 per cent.

The task of ensuring that the standard of accommodation offered by this sector is at an appropriate level falls to the Private Residences Tenancy Board (PRTB) and local councils. Despite legal requirements and the linking of tax deductions to registration, many privately rented residences are still not registered with the PRTB. The total number of tenancies registered with the Board at the end of 2010 was 231,818 (Private Residential Tenancy Board, 2010).

The Housing Statistics also report on the level and geographical distribution of inspections of these registered properties. The data indicates that in some areas inspections are common while in others they are less so. The numbers of inspections carried out have been increasing on a yearly basis. In 2007, 14,008 inspections were carried out. This rose to 17,186 in 2008 and 19,801 in 2009. Of the inspections carried out in 2009, 4,306 did not meet regulatory requirements. Social Justice Ireland believes that as this sector continues to expand the government must take steps to ensure that all local authorities carry out a reasonable number of inspections. Implementing such a policy would further enhance recent progress towards increasing standards in this sector. We also believe that it is important that further efforts are made to ensure official registration of all private rented properties.

Rent Supplement and RAS

Rent supplement is supposed to be an interim support to assist people to meet their immediate accommodation needs. There has been a massive increase in participation in this programme over the period from 2002 to 2011 and a consequent increase in its cost (see table 7.7). Increasingly people are in receipt of this support for long periods of time, as timely progression to Rental Accommodation Scheme and social housing has not occurred in line with demand.

Table 7.7 Rent Supplement Recipients and Expenditure		
Year	Expenditure	€m Recipients
2002	252	54,210
2007	391	59,720
2009	511	93,030
2011 (Estimate)	465	98,200

Source: Department of Social Protection 2011

The rent limits for this scheme have been decreased while the minimum contribution was increased in 2011. Reducing the support provided, while at the same time failing to address the long term housing need of people in receipt of rent supplement, places such people in a very vulnerable position. In December 2010 there were 48,073 households in receipt of rent supplement for a period of 18 months or longer. These are the target group for the Rental Accommodation Scheme (RAS) referred to above.

The government has indicated that it will attempt to reduce reliance on rent supplement by increasing the supply of accommodation available under RAS. Unlike Rent Supplement, which is considered to be a short term response to housing need, RAS provides a longer term contract. This has the effect of ensuring that people have increased security of tenure and better quality accommodation. Clearly, with the numbers of households requiring social housing increasing, it is imperative that the Government address this issue swiftly by making more accommodation available through RAS.

Homelessness

People experiencing homelessness are not a homogenous group and there is a range of causes associated with people who find themselves homeless. "Structural explanations locate the reasons for homelessness in social and economic structures and cite poverty, negative labour market forces, cuts and restrictions in social welfare payments and reductions or shortfalls in the supply of affordable housing as the leading causes. Individualistic accounts, on the other hand, focus on the personal characteristics and behaviours of homeless people and suggest that homelessness is the consequence of personal problems, such as mental illness and addiction" (O'Sullivan, 2008:21). In addressing homelessness there needs to be a focus on both the structural and individualistic causes of homelessness.

Spending cuts which occurred in Budget 2012 would seem to undermine the hope of addressing both causes of homelessness. There has been a decrease in funding for homeless services, placing severe pressure on these services at a time when many service providers have reported a significant increase in demand. Coupled with this, according to the Irish Council for Social Housing the reduction in the capital funding budget in Budget 2012, as well as reductions in provisions for leasing and an increase in the minimum contribution that single tenants make towards their rent and other welfare cuts, may have unintended consequences of increasing homelessness.

Gaining an accurate measure of the numbers of people experiencing homelessness is extremely difficult. This is due to the complexity of issues surrounding homelessness and the level to which, by its very nature, it is a hidden problem.

According to the Irish housing charity Focus Ireland (2011) there are no reliable national figures for the number of people experiencing homelessness. There is a gap between the administrative data (Local Authority Needs Assessment) held and the numbers of people accessing homeless services. To overcome this difficulty a survey called "-Counted In" was carried out. 'Counted In' is 'a point in time' survey method of identifying the numbers of people accessing homeless services. Although there was an overlap between households with homeless priority and those in homeless services surveyed as part of 'Counted In' in 2008, a substantial number of potentially qualifying households had not registered with the Local Authorities. A comparison between the Local Authorities' needs assessments in 2008 and 'Counted In' 2008 illustrates the variance in numbers identified as homeless[62].

"2,144 households were in homeless services during the week of the 'Counted In' survey in March 2008 (Data for the Dublin Area only). This represents a definite minimum number of households that were either resident in homeless accommodation, resident in long-term supported accommodation for people who were previously homeless, or else sleeping rough during the week of the survey" (Homeless Agency, 2008:4). At the same time the numbers of people identified as homeless in the Local Authority Needs Assessment for 2008 across the country showed 1,394 households as homeless. Further to this, the trends recorded in both surveys also conflict. Data from the needs assessments indicated that the level of homelessness across the country had fallen to 1,394 in 2008 from 1,987 in 2005[63]. However, 'Counted In' indicated an increase of 4% from 2005(in the Dublin area) of people resident in homeless accommodation, long-term supported accommodation or sleeping rough.

---

[62] It is not possible to carry out a comparison between the 2011 needs assessment and 'Counted In' as no 'Counted In' survey was carried out in 2011 as homelessness was included in the census which occurred in April 2011

[63] These figures are different from those reported in the 2005 Housing Needs Assessment because an adjustment was made to the 2005 figures for comparison purposes with the 2results of the 2008 Housing Statistics Bulletin which was released by the Department of the Environment Heritage and Local Government.

The 2011 needs assessment identified 2,348 households as homeless, an increase of almost 1,000 households on 2008 (although as previously stated, these numbers are not strictly comparable). While this is probably a more accurate number than those for earlier years, it is also likely that this figure does not represent all the households experiencing homelessness nationally. According to the Dublin Region Homeless Executive, changes have been implemented in the way that homelessness is counted and a more comprehensive assessment is due for release in 2012.

The Homelessness Strategy, *The Way Home A Strategy to Address Adult Homelessness in Ireland 2008 - 2013,* identified 2010 as the year in which long-term homelessness would be ended. This has yet to be achieved "From 2010, long term homelessness (i.e. the occupation of emergency accommodation for longer than 6 months) and the need for people to sleep rough will be eliminated throughout Ireland)" (Department of the Environment Heritage and Local Government, 2008: 7). In order to show a renewed commitment to addressing the issue of homelessness in Ireland, the government should restate this target and indicate a new deadline for its achievement.

Traveller accommodation

As part of the All-Ireland Traveller Health Study (2010), a census of the Traveller community in Ireland was undertaken in 2008. According to this count the estimated Traveller population in the Republic of Ireland is 36,224. This study indicated that most Travellers now live in houses (73.3%), followed by trailer/mobile home or caravan (18.2%). 92.9% of homes had central heating and 94.4% had both hot and cold running water. While the majority of Traveller families have basic household amenities (flush toilet, running water, waste disposal), there are still a disproportionately greater amount of Traveller families without these amenities than in the general population. Significant numbers of families in group housing or sites reported lack of footpaths, public lighting, fire hydrants and safe play areas. 24.4% of Traveller families in the Republic of Ireland considered where they lived to be unhealthy or very unhealthy and again significant numbers (26.4%) considered their place of residence unsafe. The increase in Travellers living in unauthorised sites from 422 in 2009 to 444 in 2010 is a cause of concern highlighted by the National Traveller Accommodation Consultative Committee, (2010). The Committee believes this should be monitored in case it marks the beginning of a trend.

"Traveller accommodation is inextricably linked to almost all other aspects of Travellers' lives – their traditions, health, education, employment prospects and any number of other issues" (Coates et.al. 2008, pg.81). Despite many legislative and policy changes and increased support for Traveller specific accommodation, there is widespread consensus that in practice Traveller accommodation is a challenging area to address. According to Coates et al (2008), politicians, policy makers, Local Authorities as well as Traveller organisations and members of both the Traveller and settled community are dissatisfied with the existing situation in regard to Traveller accommodation in Ireland. It would seem that reform in this area is long overdue. According to Pavee Point (2011,) there is a need for the government to ensure that Local Authorities fulfil their obligations in relation to Traveller accommodation.

Housing and people with disabilities

"The housing options available to people with disabilities generally fall far short of those available to the general population. Limited understanding of disability and the needs and aspirations of people with disabilities on the part of society generally may result in inadequate policy responses to the housing needs of people with disabilities" (Browne, 2007: iv).

A feature of having a disability is additional housing costs. Primarily these costs are for adjustments to residences to ensure access and continued use. Expenditure for these grants has been reduced over recent years. This is a worrying development as the social and economic benefits of assisting people to remain in their own homes are well documented.

The "National Housing Strategy for People with a Disability 2011-2016" sets out a framework for delivering housing to people with disabilities through mainstream housing policy. The vision underpinning this strategy is "To facilitate access, for people with disabilities, to the appropriate range of housing and related support services, delivered in an integrated and sustainable manner, which promotes equality of opportunity, individual choice and independent living" (Department of the Environment, Community and Local Government, 2011c: 34). This represents a most welcome policy framework aimed at ensuring that the rights of people with disability are upheld. The Government should ensure implementation of this framework.

Housing and children

Factors which affect child well-being and development are varied and interconnected. The OECD (2011), highlight that housing conditions and child development outcomes are strongly linked because children spend the largest proportion of their time indoors. Poor housing affects children at different stages of their life. For example, lack of affordable housing may have an impact during early childhood because it weakens the family's ability to meet basic needs. Furthermore, associations between poor housing conditions and child development are difficult, if not impossible, to reverse in later life. One of the objectives of the National Children's Strategy is to ensure that "Children will have access to accommodation appropriate to their needs" (Department of Health and Children, 2000, pg. 65). One of the ways in which this was to be achieved was through the prioritisation of families with children for accommodation under the new streams of housing to become available under the Local Authority and Voluntary Housing Programmes.

However, the number of households with children in need of social housing increased between 2005 and 2008. In 2008, 27,704 households with children were identified as being in need of social housing. In 2005 this figure had been 22,335 (Office of Minister for Children and Youth Affairs, 2010). As already indicated, figures from 2008 and 2011 are not strictly comparable therefore it is difficult to assess the extent to which this trend may have continued. However, in 2011, 44 per cent of households or, in numerical terms, 43,578 households, which were in need of social housing support included children.

As already highlighted, low income and low accommodation standards are associated with poor health levels and poor future educational and life opportunities. *Social Justice Ireland* believes that urgent action is needed in respect of children and housing.

Key policy priorities on housing and accommodation

- The high level of housing need in Ireland, which is increasing at a substantial rate, requires immediate and significant action. The government should ensure the supply of social housing, including co-op and voluntary/non-profit housing, on the scale required to eliminate Local Authority housing waiting lists.

- Any sale or transfer of housing to the voluntary, cooperative sector or Local Authority for social housing use must be considered within the context of sustainable communities and mixed tenure.

- With major reductions in capital funding for housing, it is important that the government ensure prompt delivery and adequate resources to the delivery of alternatives such as the Rental Accommodation Scheme (RAS).

- Sufficient resources should be made available to all Local Authorities for them to address any current outstanding public safety issues arising on unfinished housing estates.

- As per the recommendations from the Inter-Departmental Mortgage Arrears Working Group (2011), Government should implement programmes to assist the most distressed mortgage holders as a matter of priority.

- Government should implement a new target for the elimination of long-term homelessness.

- Local Authorities need to fulfil their obligations in respect of Traveller accommodation.

- Sufficient funding is required to ensure the on-going implementation and monitoring of the *National Housing Strategy for People with Disability 2011-2016.*

- Social Justice Ireland believes that the area of children and housing requires urgent action. Adequate resources should be allocated to this area.

8. HEALTHCARE

CORE POLICY OBJECTIVE: HEALTHCARE
To provide an adequate healthcare service focused on enabling people to attain the World Health Organisation's definition of health as a *state of complete physical, mental and social well-being and not merely the absence of disease or infirmity.*

Healthcare is a social right that every person should enjoy. People should be assured that care in their times of vulnerability is guaranteed. The standard of care is dependent to a great degree on the resources made available, which in turn are dependent on the expectations of the society. The obligation to provide healthcare as a social right rests on all people. In a democratic society this obligation is transferred through the taxation and insurance systems to government and other bodies which assume/contract this responsibility. These are very important considerations at this particular moment as Government proposes fundamental changes in Ireland's healthcare system. This chapter outlines some of the major considerations *Social Justice Ireland* believes Government should bring to bear on its decision-making on these issues.

Social determinants of health
At the outset it should be noted that health is not just about healthcare. For a number of years the World Health Organisation (WHO) has been concerned with what it terms the "social determinants of health". The WHO Commission established to study this topic produced their final report in 2008. This Commission found that health is influenced by factors such as poverty, food security, social exclusion and discrimination, poor housing, unhealthy early childhood conditions, poor educational status and low occupational status. These are important determinants of most diseases, deaths and health inequalities between and within countries. A follow up conference was held in Brazil in October 2011. At the end of the conference the Heads of Government "expressed their determination to achieve social and health equity through action on the social determinants of health and well-being by a comprehensive inter-sectoral approach."(WHO 2011: no. 1)

They noted that: "Health inequities arise from the societal conditions in which people are born, grow, live, work and age, referred to as social determinants of health. These include early years' experiences, education, economic status, employment and decent work, housing and environment, and effective systems of preventing and treating ill health." They continued, "We are convinced that action on these determinants, both for vulnerable groups and the entire population, is essential to create inclusive, equitable, economically productive and healthy societies. Positioning human health and well-being as one of the key features of what constitutes a successful, inclusive and fair society in the 21st century is consistent with our commitment to human rights at national and international levels." (WHO 2011: no.6)

The reflections and outcomes of the conference are very relevant to the situation in Ireland at this time.

Health inequalities in Ireland

A very welcome insight into the extent of health inequalities in Ireland has been provided by the Public Health Alliance of the Island of Ireland (PHAI). This group is a north-south alliance of non-governmental organisations, statutory bodies, community and voluntary groups, advocacy bodies and individuals who are committed to work together for a healthier society by improving health and tackling health inequalities. It has published two detailed reports in the past decade: *Health in Ireland – An Unequal State* (2004) and *Health Inequalities on the island of Ireland: the facts, the causes, the remedies* (2007). These reports gather together the baseline information on health inequalities in Ireland and their findings are worthy of serious attention. These include:

- Between 1989 and 1998 the death rates for all causes of death were over three times higher in the lowest occupational class than in the highest.
- The death rates for all cancers among the lowest occupational class is over twice as high for the highest class; it is nearly three times higher for strokes, four times higher for lung cancer, six times for accidents.
- Perinatal mortality is three times higher in poorer families than in richer families.
- Women in the unemployed socio-economic group are more than twice as likely to give birth to low birth weight children as women in the higher professional group.
- The incidence of chronic physical illness has been found to be two and a half times higher for poor people than for the wealthy.

- Men in unskilled jobs were four times more likely to be admitted to hospital for schizophrenia than higher professional workers.
- The rate of hospitalisation for mental illness is more than six times higher for people in the lower socio-economic groups than for those in the higher groups.
- The incidence of male suicide is far higher in the lower socio-economic groups than for those in the higher groups.
- The most recent Survey of Lifestyle, Attitudes and Nutrition (SLAN) found that poorer people are more likely to smoke cigarettes, drink alcohol excessively, take less exercise and eat less fruit and vegetables than richer people. Poorer people's lifestyle and behavioural choices are directly limited by their economic and social circumstances.

The reports also found that some groups experience particularly extreme health inequalities. These include:

- Members of the Traveller community live between 10 and 12 years less than the population as a whole.[64]
- The rate of sudden infant deaths among Travellers is 12 times higher than for the general population.
- Many expectant mothers among asylum seekers in direct provision suffer malnutrition, babies in these communities suffer ill-health because of diet, many adults experience hunger.
- Homeless people experience high incidence of ill-health – a 1997 report found that 40 per cent of hostel dwellers had a serious psychiatric illness, 42 per cent had problems of alcohol dependency, and 18 per cent had other physical problems.
- The incidence of injecting drug use is almost entirely confined to people from the lower socio-economic groups.

The PHAI also compared the health of people in Ireland to that of the 14 other EU states (pre-EU enlargement). It found that Irish people compare badly with the experience of citizens in other EU counties. These findings included:

---

[64] For much greater detail on age-specific mortality rates among Travellers and a range of other Traveller health statistics cf. *All Ireland Traveller Health Study: Our Geels,* September 2010, published by the All Ireland Traveller Health Study Team, School of Public Health, Physiotherapy and Population Science, University College Dublin.

- Mortality rates in Ireland are worse than the EU average for a range of illnesses, particularly diseases of the circulatory system, breast cancer and death from smoking related illnesses.
- Irish women have almost twice the rate of death from heart disease as the average European woman.
- The incidences of mortality for Irish women for cancers of the breast, colon, larynx and oesophagus and for ischaemic heart disease are among the highest in the EU.
- At the age of 65 Irish men have the lowest life expectancy in the EU. (PHAI, 2004:3-4).

In its 2007 study the PHAI summarised what the international research literature highlights as the most important influences on health and the causes of health inequalities. These are the economic, social and political environments in which people live including:

- level of income;
- early life experience;
- access to education and employment;
- food and nutrition;
- work opportunities;
- housing and environmental conditions; and levels of stress and social support.

Furthermore, it noted that "research has also established that the greatest determinant of health is the level of income equality in society. Societies with more equal distribution of income across the population have higher average life expectancies and better health outcomes than less equal societies" (PHAI, 2007:8). It is the nature of these inequalities and the fact that they are so interconnected with the social, economic and political environment of Ireland that places this issue as central to the agenda of *Social Justice Ireland*.

Poverty and healthcare exclusion
As shown in the studies noted above, the link between poverty and ill health has been well established by international and national research. The poor get sick more often and die younger than those in the higher socio-economic groups. Poverty directly affects the incidence of ill health; it limits access to affordable healthcare and reduces the opportunity for those living in poverty to adopt healthy lifestyles. A recent survey by the CSO measuring the economic downturn (CSO 2012), showing that more than half of all households have cut back their spending on groceries, is of particular concern.

Life expectancy

In 2010 Irish males had life expectancies of 76.8 years while Irish females were expected to live 4.8 years longer, reaching 81.6 years. Based on these figures, Ireland's life expectancy performance is similar to the European average; the EU average, however, is dragged down by low life expectancies among men in Estonia, Latvia and Lithuania among others (see table 8.1). Relative to the older member states of the EU, the Irish figures are less impressive. The story behind Ireland's life expectancy figures incorporates many of the findings of the PHAI reports and the earlier poverty figures (see Chapter 3). Ireland's poverty problem has serious implications for health in light of the fact that there is a clear link between poverty and ill health, a relationship that has been well supported by international research. Thus, those in lower socio-economic groups have a higher percentage of both acute and chronic illnesses.

Access to Healthcare: Medical Cards and Health Insurance

Recent CSO statistics (August 2011) showed that 47 per cent of adults over 18 years had private health insurance. 30 per cent reported they had a medical card only while 23 per cent indicated they had neither a medical card nor private health insurance. A Department of Health fact sheet (October 2010) indicated that 1,578,613 persons had a medical card and 110,297 persons had a GP visit card.

The process for obtaining a medical card has been centralised recently. While this development is seen as progressive, transparent and efficient for some, it has given rise to serious concerns for others. Among these concerns are the following:

- The system does not allow for discretionary measures regarding eligibility. People on similar incomes do not necessarily have similar healthcare needs.
- The online facility is very helpful for many people. However there are many people who do not have easy access to the technology or the capacity to use it. The system should provide designated people to assist in these situations.
- Renewal of medical cards. The 14 days allowed for response is not user-friendly. People who may have moved home or have literacy difficulties are being deprived of their medical card. In the past GPs showed great tolerance in these situations and took care of their patients in lieu of the medical card being restored. Because of long delays, difficulties in getting the medical card restored and general cutbacks, GPs are less likely to take the risk of incurring expense that may not be recouped.

The length of waiting lists remains a cause of major concern in the Irish healthcare system. The CSO study showed that in the third quarter of 2010 8 per cent of the adult population (aged18 and over) were on a hospital waiting list, compared to 6 per cent in 2007.

Table 8.1: EU–27 life expectancy at birth by sex in 2009, in years.

Country	Males	Females	Difference
Spain	78.6	84.6	6.0
France	77.8	84.5	6.7
Italy	78.9	84.1	5.2
Sweden	79.4	83.4	4.0
Finland	76.5	83.1	6.6
Austria	77.4	82.9	5.5
Greece	77.7	82.8	5.1
Luxembourg	77.6	82.7	5.1
Netherlands	78.5	82.7	4.2
Germany	77.4	82.6	5.2
Belgium	77.2	82.4	5.2
Cyprus	77.9	82.4	4.5
EU 27	**76.4**	**82.4**	**6.0**
Slovenia	75.8	82.3	6.5
Malta	77.7	82.2	4.5
United Kingdom	78.1	82.1	4.0
Portugal	75.8	81.8	6.0
IRELAND	**76.8**	**81.6**	**4.8**
Denmark	76.5	80.8	4.3
Czech Republic	74.2	80.1	5.9
Estonia	69.8	80.1	10.3
Poland	71.5	80.1	8.6
Slovakia	71.3	78.7	7.4
Lithuania	67.5	78.6	11.1
Latvia	68.3	78.1	9.8
Hungary	70.1	77.9	7.8
Bulgaria	69.9	77.1	7.2
Romania	69.7	77.1	7.4

Source: CSO 2011:54

Full medical card coverage is necessary for all people in Ireland who are vulnerable. The current income threshold for obtaining a medical card is well below the poverty line. This in effect creates an employment trap as parents are often afraid to take up a job and, consequently, lose their medical card even though their income remains low. The 'doctor visit only' cards are an improvement on the previous situation only if they are upgraded to full medical cards in due course. At present they create new problems because many people are in the unenviable situation of knowing what is wrong with them but not having the resources to purchase the medicines they need to be treated.

Health expenditure

Healthcare is a social right for everyone. For this right to be upheld governments must provide the funding needed to ensure that the relevant services and care are available when required. Comparative statistics are available for total expenditure on health (i.e. public plus private). Table 8.2 shows that Ireland spends 8.7 per cent of GDP on healthcare, a little below the EU-27 average of 9.0 per cent. In Gross National Income (GNI) terms this expenditure translates into a figure of 10.0 per cent.[65] In comparison France spends 11.1 per cent; Germany spends 10.4 per cent and Austria 10.1 per cent. Ireland is ranked twelfth on this basis among EU counties and this ranking has been improving over time. This data, for 2008, is the most recent comparative data available and Ireland's ranking may have changed since then. Healthcare costs tend to be higher in countries which have a higher old age dependency ratio. This is not yet a significant issue for Ireland as the old age dependency ratio is low (11.1 per cent are aged 65 years and over) compared to the much higher EU average.

An open and transparent debate on funding of healthcare services is needed. Ireland must decide what services are expected and how these should be funded. Despite expenditure of 8.7 per cent of GDP going to fund healthcare there are major problems in areas such as waiting lists, bed closures, shortage of staff and long-term care requirements. However, this debate must acknowledge the enormous financial expenditure on healthcare. The budget allocation for gross public expenditure on healthcare in Ireland in 2012 is €14.034bn which is 25 per cent of all projected government expenditure. (Comprehensive Expenditure Review 2012-2014 p.130)

---

[65] GNI is similar to the concept of GNP and has a similar value.

Table 8.2: EU-27 health expenditure as a percentage of GDP, 2008			
Country	%	Country	%
France	11.1	Slovakia	7.8
Germany	10.4	**IRELAND (% GDP)**	**8.7**
Austria	10.1	Malta	7.5
Portugal	10.1	Hungary	7.4
IRELAND (% GNI)	**10.0**	Bulgaria	7.3
Denmark	9.9	Luxembourg	7.2
Belgium	9.7	Czech Republic	6.8
Greece	9.7	Cyprus	6.7
Netherlands	9.1	Poland	6.6
Sweden	9.1	Latvia	6.5
Italy	9.0	Lithuania	6.2
United Kingdom	9.0	Estonia	5.9
Spain	8.7	Romania	4.7
Finland	8.4		
Slovenia	7.8	**EU 27**	**9.0**

Source: CSO 2011:53

Public healthcare expenditure grew rapidly over the ten year period 2000 to 2010, from €5.334bn to €14.165bn. This was, an increase of 160 per cent over a period in which inflation increased by 33 per cent. The difference is attributed in part to improved and expanded services and in part to 'medical inflation'.

Home-helps, for example, became members of staff and were paid full salaries etc. However, the issue of medical inflation needs to be addressed. Clearly there are significant efficiencies to be gained in restructuring the healthcare system. Obtaining value for money is essential. However these efforts should be targeted at areas where efficiencies can be delivered without compromising the quality of the service. *Social Justice Ireland* continues to argue that there is a need to be specific about the efficiencies that are needed and how they are to be delivered.

As well as a debate on the overall budget for healthcare, there should be discussion and transparency on the allocation to each of the services. Currently about 60 per cent of the budget is allocated to Primary, Community and Continuing Care, which includes the medical card services schemes. (Department of Health, Key Trends 2011, table 6.2). *Social Justice Ireland* recommends an increase in this percentage and greater clarity about the budget lines.

The model of healthcare

Community-based health and social services require a model of care that:

- is accessible and acceptable to the community they serve;
- is responsive to the local community and its particular set of needs and requirements;
- is supportive of local communities in their efforts to build social cohesion; and accepts primary care as the key component of the model of care and gives it priority over acute services as the place where health and social care options are accessed by the community.

Action is required in four key areas if the basic model of care that is to underpin the health services is not to be undermined. There areas are:

> *Older people's services*
> *Primary care, primary care teams and primary care networks*
> *Children and family services*
> *Disability and mental health*

Older people's services

If the health of older people is to be addressed appropriately it is essential that there be support for older people to live at home as long as possible by providing community-based services to meet their needs. This approach needs to be complemented by ensuring that access to acute services is available in an appropriate manner when required. If this approach is to be followed there is an urgent need to address the specific deficits in infrastructure that exist across the country. There should be an emphasis on replacement and/or refurbishment of facilities. If this is not done the inappropriate admission of older people to acute care facilities will continue, along with the consequent negative impacts on acute services and unnecessary stress on older people.

Social Justice Ireland acknowledges the work done to date to develop services for older people. The introduction of '*A Fair Deal – The Nursing Home Care Support Scheme 2008*'was a step in the right direction. However recent cut-backs have resulted in long waiting lists, even after people are assessed and deemed in need of care. This inevitably leads to patients remaining in inappropriate care facilities such as acute hospitals. This outcome is not in the best interests of either the person or the hospital. At the same time nursing home beds may be available but funding is not committed.

It is crucial that funding be released in a timely manner when a person is deemed in need of a 'Fair Deal' bed and that sufficient capital investment is provided to ensure that sufficient residential care beds are available to meet the growing demand for them. The focus on the development of community based services to support older people in their own homes/communities for as long as possible is welcome. However, this is only aspirational if funding is not provided for home help services, day care centres and home care packages – each area that have received serious and unwelcome cuts in recent Budgets. One possible outcome of these cuts is that the service would become nothing more than a 'Bed and Breakfast' facility. This would be a travesty of what was intended and, more importantly, of what is required.

Social Justice Ireland believes that a total investment of €500m over five years, i.e. €100m each year, is needed to meet this growing need. This would enable 12-15 community nursing facilities with about 50 beds each to be replaced or refurbished each year. This proposal in addition to supporting the needs of older people will also to beneficial to stimulating economic activity and increased employment across many local communities during the construction period.

Primary care, primary care teams and primary care networks

Primary care has been recognised as one of the cornerstones of the health system. This was acknowledged in the strategy document y *Primary Care – A New Direction* (2001). Between 90 and 95 per cent of the population are treated by the primary care system. The model of a primary care team presented in the document must be viewed in its most flexible form so that it can respond to the local needs assessment. The principle underlining this model should be a social model of health. This is in keeping with the World Health Organisation's definition on health outlined above. Universal access is needed to ensure that a social model of health can become a reality. For the strategies outlined in *Primary Care – A New Direction* to be implemented there is a clear need for an increase in the proportion of the total healthcare budget being allocated to primary care.

Paying attention to local people's own perspective on their health and understanding the impact of the conditions of their lives on their health is essential to community development and to community orientated approaches to primary care. A community development approach is needed to ensure that the community can define its own health needs, work out collectively how these needs can best be met and decide on a course of action to achieve this in partnership with service providers. This will ensure greater control over the social, political, economic and environmental factors that determine the health status of any community.

The Primary Care Strategy acknowledges the need for "community involvement" as a key factor in addressing health issues and recognises the need for partnership in both the planning and evaluation of all services. Community participation is an "essential component of a more responsive and appropriate care system which is truly people-centred" (Chief Medical Officers Report 2002).

The decision by Government to appoint a Minister of State with specific responsibility for primary care is welcome. Government must ensure this appointment is matched with tangible progress in the development and delivery of such care over the next few years.

Primary care teams and primary care networks

Ireland's healthcare system has struggled to provide an effective and efficient response to the health needs of its population. Despite a huge increase in investment in recent years great problems persist. The development of primary care teams across the country would make a substantial positive impact on reducing these problems.

Primary care teams draw the health professionals in an area together to provide a local one-stop shop, avoiding unnecessary presentations at acute hospital Emergency Departments.

The HSE is committed to developing primary care teams and primary care networks as the basic 'building blocks' of local public health care provision. The Primary Care Team (PCT) is intended to be a team of health professionals catering for a catchment of 7,000 to 10,000 people who work closely together and with the local community to meet the needs of people living in that community. These professionals include GPs and Practice Nurses, community nursing i.e. public health nurses and community RGNs, physiotherapists, occupational therapists and home-care staff. They provide the first point of contact when individuals need to access the health system. When fully developed, it is expected that 519 primary care teams could cover the whole country. These are to be supported by 134 Health and Social Care Networks. PCTs are expected to link in with other community-based disciplines to ensure that health and social needs are addressed. These include: speech & language therapists, dieticians, area medical officers, community welfare officers, addiction counsellors, community mental health nursing, consultant psychiatrists, etc. PCTs provide a single point of contact between the person and the health system. They facilitate navigation 'in', 'around' and 'out' of the health system. According to the HSE, there were 393 PCTs in place by the end of

September 2011. The work done on these teams is very welcome but much more is needed to ensure they command the confidence and trust of local communities.

In this context the recent Government proposal to introduce a new system of seven directorates to run the health system is of concern. This development is likely to obstruct the delivery of an integrated healthcare system for service users at local level. There are real concerns that the proposed new approach will increase rather than reduce costs and bureaucracy. Instead of an integrated system based on primary care teams at local level seven 'silos' could emerge, competing for resources and producing a splintered system that is neither effective, sustainable nor viable in the long term.

Social Justice Ireland believes that reform of the healthcare system is necessary but is seriously concerned that the proposed new structure will see each directorate establish its own bureaucracy at national, regional and local levels.

Children and family services
There is a need to focus on health and social care provision to children and families in tandem with the development of primary care team services. The obligation on the State to develop and provide services and facilities to support vulnerable and at risk children has been highlighted recently. The standard of care, as monitored by the Health Information and Quality Authority (HIQA), and the challenges posed for care providers by young people with complex needs have proven difficult for both public and private service providers.

Many community and voluntary services are being provided in facilities badly in need of refurbishment or rebuilding. Despite poor infrastructure, these services are the heart of local communities, providing vital services that are locally 'owned'. There is a great need to support this activity and in particular meet its infrastructural requirements.

Social Justice Ireland believes that a total of €250 m is required over a five-year period to address the infrastructural deficit in Children and Family Services. This amounts to €27m per area for each of the nine Children Services Committee areas and a national investment of €7m in Residential and Special Care.

Social Justice Ireland welcomes the appointment of a Minister for Children and Youth Affairs. This is an area with a substantial agenda that could, however, be addressed effectively in a relatively short period of time if the political will to do so were present. As well as the Children's Rights Referendum and the issue of Child

Safeguarding that have been highlighted by the Government, we believe the key issues for the new Department are the second National Children's Strategy, policy on early childhood care and education, child poverty, youth homelessness, disability among young people and the issue of young carers.

Disability

We welcome the 2011 *Programme for Government* commitment to complete a consultation to establish "a realistic implementation plan for the National Disability Strategy". There are many areas within the Disability Sector in need of further development and core funding. These areas need to be supported.[66] *Social Justice Ireland* is particularly concerned about the further 2 per cent "efficiency" cut to services to people with disabilities made in Budget 2012. This is an across the board cut which means some services will experience greater cuts. This reduction has been made without consideration of the Value for Money Review which has not yet been published.

Mental health

The National Health Strategy entitled *Quality and Fairness* (2001) identified mental health as an area needing to be developed. The Expert Group on Mental Health Policy published a report entitled *A Vision for Change - Report of the Expert Group on Mental Health Policy* (2006). This report offered many worthwhile pathways to adequately address mental health issues in Irish society. Unfortunately, to date little has been implemented to achieve this vision.

There is an urgent need to address this whole area in the light of the World Health Report (2001) *Mental Health: New Understanding, New Hope*. This estimated that in 1990 mental and neurological disorders accounted for 10 per cent of the total Disability-Adjusted Life Years (DALYs) lost due to all diseases and injuries. This estimate increased to 12 per cent in 2000. By 2020, it is projected that these disorders will have increased to 15 per cent. This has serious implications for services in all countries in the coming years. In June 2011 the Institute for Public Health published a study of the impact of the recession on men's health, especially mental health. Entitled *Facing the Challenge: The Impact of Recession and Unemployment on Men's Health in Ireland, the* study showed that employment status was the most important predicator of psychological distress, with 30.4 per cent of those unemployed reporting mental health problems.

---

[66] Other Disability related issues are addressed throughout this review.

Commitments in the 2011 *Programme for Government* offer hope that progress in this area will be made over the next few years. We welcomed the appointment of a Minister of State with responsibility in this area and the allocation of €35m in Budget 2012 for the development of Community Mental Health Teams. It is hoped that these teams will reduce the stigma of mental health and improve access to facilities and services for assisting those with mental health problems.

Areas of concern in mental health

There is a need for effective outreach and follow-up programmes for people who have been in-patients in institutions upon their discharge into the wider community. These should provide:

- sheltered housing (high, medium and low supported housing); monitoring of medication; retraining and rehabilitation; and assistance with integration into community.

In the development of mental health teams there should be a particular focus on people with an intellectual disability and other vulnerable groups including children, the homeless, prisoners, Travellers, asylum seekers, refugees and other minority groups. People in these and related categories have a right to a specialist service to provide for their often complex needs. A great deal remains to be done before this right could be acknowledged as being recognised and honoured in the healthcare system.

The connection between those who are disadvantage and ill health when the social determinants of health (housing, income, childcare support, education etc.) are not met is well documented. This is also true in respect of mental health issues.

Suicide – a mental health issue

Suicide is a problem related to mental health. For many years the topic of suicide was rarely discussed in Irish society and, as a consequence, the healthcare and policy implications of its existence were limited. The number of suicides in Ireland has climbed over the last decade and the current recession has accelerated this increase. In 1993 327 suicides were recorded. By 2009 the number had increased to 527. Provisional data for 2010 indicates 486 deaths by suicide, of which 386 were male and 100 female. This represents a welcome decrease of 8 per cent on the previous year. Over time Ireland's suicide rate has risen significantly, from 6.4 suicides per 100,000 people in 1980 to a peak of 13.9 in 1998 to 11.7 suicides per 100,000 people in 2008 (OECD, 2005 and National Office of Suicide Prevention, 2010:23).

Table 8.3 provides details on the levels and gender distribution of suicides in Ireland since 2003. It shows that suicide is predominantly a male phenomenon with 80 per cent of suicide victims being male. Young people, young males in particular, are the groups most at risk. In the period 2003-2007 young males aged between 20-24 years had a suicide rate of 30.7 per 100,000 in the population – almost three times the national average. Among this age-group, suicide is one of the largest causes of death (2010:24 -25).

Table 8.3: Suicides in Ireland 2003-2010						
	Overall		**Males**		**Females**	
Year★★	**No.**	**Rate**	**No.**	**Rate**	**No.**	**Rate**
2003	497	12.5	386	19.5	111	5.5
2004	493	12.2	406	20.2	87	4.3
2005	481	11.6	382	18.5	99	4.8
2006	460	10.8	379	17.9	81	3.8
2007	458	10.6	362	16.7	96	4.4
2008	506	11.4	386	17.5	82	3.8
2009★	527	11.7	422	19.0	105	4.7
2010★	486	10.9	386	17.4	100	4.4

Source: National Office of Suicide Prevention (2010:23-24)
Notes: ★ Provisional figures
★★Annual data is by year of occurrence (2003 to 2008) and by year of registration (2009 and 2010).
Rate is rate per 100,000 of the population.

The slight decrease in the number of suicides in the past year is welcome. However the sustained high level of suicides in Ireland is a significant healthcare and societal problem. Of course the statistics in table 8.3 only tell one part of the story. Behind each of these victims are families and communities devastated by these tragedies. Likewise, behind each of the figures is a personal story which leads to victims taking their own life. *Social Justice Ireland* believes that further attention and resources need to be given to addressing and researching Ireland's suicide problem.

Older people and mental health
Mental health issues affect all groups in society. Older people with dement are a particularly vulnerable group because they often "fall between two stools" (i.e. between mental health services and general medical care). A co-ordinated service needs to be provided for this group. It is important that this be needs-based and

service-user led and should be in keeping with the principles set out in the World Health Organisation's 2001 annual report.

Research and development in all areas of mental health is needed to ensure a quality service is delivered. Providing good mental health services should not be viewed as a cost but rather as an investment in the future. Public awareness needs to be raised to ensure a clearer understanding of mental illness so that the rights of those with mental illness are recognised.

Future healthcare needs

A number of the factors highlighted elsewhere in this review will have implications for the future of our healthcare system. The projected increases in population forecast by the CSO imply that there will be more people living in Ireland in 10-15 years' time. One clear implication of this will be additional demand for healthcare services and facilities. In the context of our past mistakes it is important that Ireland begin to plan for this additional demand and begin to train staff and construct the needed facilities.

We look forward to the publication of the Government 2012-2020 strategy on public health. We share the concerns of Council for Justice and Peace of the Irish Episcopal Conference (2012) about the lack of focus on outcomes. We agree that the "public health strategy should therefore not only spell out goals for public health but also set out the role that each major field of intervention is expected to perform in achieving those goals, the implications for resource allocation that arise from such roles and the mechanisms that will be used to ensure that spending actually goes to the areas where it will achieve greatest benefit."

Key policy priorities on healthcare
- Recognise the considerable health inequalities present within the Irish healthcare system, develop strategies and provide sufficient resources to tackle them.

- Give far greater priority to community care and restructure the healthcare budget accordingly. Care should be taken to ensure that the increased allocation does not go to the GMS or the drug subsidy scheme.

- Resource and continue the roll out of the 519 primary care teams.

- Increase the proportion of the health budget allocated to health promotion and education in partnership with all relevant stakeholders.

- Focus on obtaining better value for money in the health budget.

- Provide the childcare services with the additional resources necessary to effectively implement the Child Care Act.

- Provide additional respite care and long stay care for elderly people and people with disabilities.

- Promote equality of access and outcomes to services within the Irish healthcare system.

- Ensure that structural and systematic reform of the health system reflects the key principles of the Health Strategy aimed at achieving high performance, person centred, quality of care and value for money in the health service.

- Develop and resource mental health services, and recognise that they will be a key factor in determining the health status of the population.

- Continue to facilitate and fund a campaign to give greater attention to the issue of suicide in Irish society. In particular, focus resources on educating young people about suicide.

- Enhance the process of planning and investment so that the healthcare system can cope with the increase and diversity in population and the ageing of the population projected for the next few decades.

- Ensure the new healthcare structure is fit for purpose.

9. EDUCATION AND EDUCATIONAL DISADVANTAGE

CORE POLICY OBJECTIVE: EDUCATION AND
EDUCATIONAL DISADVANTAGE
To provide relevant education for all people throughout their lives, so
that they can participate fully and meaningfully in developing
themselves, their community and the wider society.

Education can be an agent for social transformation. *Social Justice Ireland* believes that
education can be a powerful force in counteracting inequality and poverty while
recognising that, in many ways, the present education system has quite the opposite
effect. Recent studies confirm the persistence of social class inequalities which are
seemingly ingrained in the system. Even in the context of the increased
participation and economic expansion of much of the last decade, the education
system continues to mediate the vicious cycle of disadvantage and social exclusion
between generations. While there are a number of programmes and initiatives to
tackle educational disadvantage, many of these initiatives simply involve providing
additional resources for disadvantaged schools.

Education in Ireland – the numbers
There are just over one million full-time students in the formal Irish education
system. Of these, 510,460 are at primary level, 354,235 at second level and 164,843
at third level. The sector accounts for 22 per cent of the population and with recent
increases in the birth rate, the figures have continued to grow over the last decade
(CSO 2011:96).

Ireland's expenditure on education equalled 5.6 per cent of GDP in 2008 (CSO
2011: 48), the latest year for which comparable EU-wide data is available. This
compares to an EU-27 average of 5.1 per cent of GDP in that year. Over much of
the last decade, as national income has increased the share allocated to education
has slowly increased. This is something we greatly welcome. Table 9.1 (CSO 2011:
47) details how real current public expenditure on education per student rose
steadily until 2009 when it reduced across all categories due to budgetary measures.

The increases in expenditure until 2009 can be partly attributed to increased pay. However they can also be partly explained by an increase in student numbers at all levels. Between 2000/01 and 2009/10 the numbers of students in Ireland grew by 14.7 per cent at first level and by 1.4 per cent at second level. Over the same period, the number of third level students increased by around 30 per cent (CSO 2011: 96). It should also be noted, however, that Ireland's young population as a proportion of total population is large by EU standards and, consequently, a higher than average spend on education might be expected.

Table 9.1: Ireland: Real current public expenditure on education, 2001-212			
Year	First Level★ €	Second Level★ €	Third Level★ €	Real Current Public Expenditure★★ €m
2001	4,342	6,624	10,264	5,674
2002	4,768	7,041	10,352	6,064
2003	5,219	7,576	10,204	6,474
2004	5,617	7,673	10,017	6,682
2005	5,718	8,010	10,364	6,916
2006	5,916	8,360	10,872	7,268
2007	6,058	8,811	10,789	7,586
2008	6,174	8,935	10,665	7,823
2009	6,428	9,057	10,160	8,119
2010	6,409	8,828	9,415	8,065

★€ per student at 2010 prices   ★★€m at 2010 prices
Source: Department of Education and Skills, CSO (CSO 2010:47)

Real expenditure per student in Ireland increased over the period 2001-2010 by 47.6% at first level and by a third at second level. At third level there was a decrease of 8.3% over the same period. When viewed in an international context, the most striking feature of investment in education in Ireland relative to international norms in other OECD countries is our comparative under-investment in primary education. Irish investment in third-level education, which is widely regarded as inadequate (and declining as detailed in table 9.1), is approximately at the OECD average. Issues regarding third level funding are discussed later in this chapter. However, our public investment at second level and, in particular, at primary level is substantially below the OECD average and is among the lowest of all OECD countries. When expenditure is standardised as a percentage of GDP Ireland is ranked 27th out of 31 countries. Our public investment in early childhood education is also far from adequate.

The importance of investment in education is widely acknowledged, and for individuals the rewards from education are clear. The European Commission reports Europe's future will be based on smart, sustainable and inclusive growth and that improving the quality and effectiveness of education systems is essential to this (European Commission, 2011). To achieve this growth, and to honour the educational commitments outlined in the Programme for Government and National Recovery, there must be significant and strategic investment in early childhood education and lifelong learning and a policy making process that has long-term planning at its core.

Planning for future education needs

There is a history of minimal long-term strategic planning by the Department of Education in respect of investment in facilities at primary and second level. *Social Justice Ireland* has been proposing for the past decade that the Department of Education use the population projections by the CSO based on the census results to plan for future education needs, timing and spatial distribution.[67] Using CSO figures, the Department projects the following possible increases in enrolment across the system:

- an additional 45,050 places will be needed at primary level between 2012 and 2018;
- an additional 24,900 places will be needed at second level between 2012 and 2017 and a further 40,800 places will be needed between 2017 and 2024;
- at third level the number of students is expected to rise by 40,300 to 213,500 by 2017/18.[68]

---

[67] The preliminary results of Census 2011 are available, a more comprehensive analysis and projection will be available later in 2012.

[68] http://www.education.ie/robots/view.jsp?pcategory=10861&language=EN&ecategory=10876&link=link001&doc=55526

The Department of Education has published a capital works programme amounting to €2.2 billion between 2012 and 2016 to address this issue and to increase the number of places available through a five year School Building Programme. *Social Justice Ireland* believes it is critically important that Government, and in particular the Department of Education and Skills, pay attention to the population projection by the CSO for the years to come in order to adequately plan and provide for the increased places needed within the education system in the coming decades.

Literacy and adult literacy

The issue of literacy has been contentious in recent times. In 1997 an OECD survey found that a quarter of Ireland's adult population performed at the very lowest level of literacy.[69] More recently, results from the OECD's PISA study found that Ireland's fifteen-year olds rank 17th for reading levels among 34 OECD countries. They also highlighted that average reading levels have been decreasing across all ability levels over time in Ireland and that 17 per cent of students in Ireland are low-achieving in reading. This means that they are "below the basic level needed to participate effectively in society and in future learning" (OECD, 2010). Worryingly, the study also found that almost a quarter of all male students achieved a score which is considered to be below the level of literacy needed to participate effectively in society. This means they may lack the skills needed to function in today's labour market and can be at risk of leaving school early and struggling to find a job. Numeracy levels display a similar pattern with Ireland's ranking 26th in mathematics out of the 34 countries.

The OECD's findings suggest that while reading levels among the school-going population are better than the population generally, this difference is much smaller than should be expected. However, there is something fundamentally wrong with an education system in which one in every six students has difficulty reading at the most basic level. It is clear that fundamental reforms are needed to Ireland's education system[70] to address this problem. Left unresolved, it will store up continuous socio-economic problems for decades to come. *Social Justice Ireland* therefore welcomes the national strategy to improve literacy and numeracy in schools. '*Literacy and Numeracy for Learning and Life*' sets out national targets and a range of significant measures to improve literacy and numeracy in early childhood

---

[69] Ireland is currently participating in the OECD PIAAC study of adult skills with results due to be published in 2013, a sixteen year gap since the IALS survey in 1997.

[70] A discussion paper by Áine Hyland for the HEA summer School 2011 suggests that the emphasis on rote learning at second level might have affected our results as the PISA test is based on the application of prior knowledge.

education and in primary and post-primary schools. These measures include improving the performance of children and young people in PISA literacy and numeracy tests at all levels, fundamental changes to teacher education and the curriculum in schools and radical improvements in the assessment and reporting of student progress at student, school and national level. Progress on this issue is overdue and budgetary and economic constraints must not be permitted to impede the implementation of the strategy.

The Programme for Government and National Recovery states that the government will address the widespread and persistent problem of adult literacy through the integration of literacy in vocational training and through community education. No updated targets have been given and nor has a strategy been outlined or developed. It is reasonable to assume, therefore, that the Government is committing itself to the target already outlined in the 2007 NAP inclusion document. This target for adult literacy policy states that "the proportion of the population aged 16-64 with restricted literacy will be reduced to between 10%-15% by 2016, from the level of 25% found in 1997" where "restricted literacy" is defined as level 1 on the International Adult Literacy Scale. People at this level of literacy are considered to possess "very poor skills, where the individual may, for example, be unable to determine the correct amount of medicine to give a child from information printed on the package" (OECD). As table 9.2 shows, in numerical terms this implies that the aim of government policy is to have "only" 301,960 adults of labour force age with serious literacy difficulties in Ireland by 2016. In the opinion of *Social Justice Ireland* this target is simply unacceptable.

Table 9.2: Irish Government Adult Literacy Target for 2016	
Adult population (under 65 yrs) in 2016	3,019,600
10% "restricted literacy" target	301,960
15% "restricted literacy" target	452,940

Source: Calculated from CSO (2008:27) using the lowest CSO population projection for 2016 – The MOF2 population projection assumption

How can policy aim to be so unambitious? How will these people with serious literacy problems function effectively in the economy and society that is emerging in Ireland? How can they get meaningful jobs? In reality, achieving this target could only be interpreted as representing substantial and sustained failure. With the latest PISA results showing that 23.2% of all male students aged 15 have a reading level below Level 1a the need for a comprehensive strategy to tackle adult literacy has never been more pressing.

Overall, *Social Justice Ireland* believes that the Government's literacy target is illogical, unambitious and indicative of a complete lack of interest in addressing this problem in a serious way. The lack of focus on this issue was further underscored by Budget 2012's decision to reduce funding for adult literacy programmes by 2 per cent. By 2015, funding for adult literacy will have been reduced by 11%.[71] The current target on literacy should be revised downwards dramatically and the necessary resources committed to ensuring that the revised target is met. *Social Justice Ireland* believes that the government should adopt a new and more ambitious target of reducing the proportion of the population aged 16-64 with restricted literacy to 5 per cent by 2016 and to 3 per cent by 2020. This will still leave approximately 150,000 adults without basic literacy levels in 2016. However, this target is more ambitious and realistic in the context of the future social and economic development of Ireland.

Key issues: Early school leaving and unemployment

One in ten 18-24 year olds are early school leavers (CSO 2011): 7). Early school leaving not only presents problems for the young people; it also has economic and social consequences for society. Education is the most efficient way of safeguarding against unemployment. The risk of unemployment increases considerably the lower the level of education. Early school leavers are:
- At higher risk of poverty and social exclusion;
- Confronted with limited opportunities to develop culturally, personally and socially;

and
- Face a cyclical effect associated with early school leaving, resulting in the children of early school leavers experiencing reduced success in education (European Commission, 2011).

In Ireland in 2010 the rate of early school leavers from education and training stood at 10.5%. This rate has been decreasing steadily since 2002-. While this is a very positive trend, early school leaving remains a serious issue in Ireland and the Irish Government has committed to reducing this to 8% (Department of An Taoiseach,

---

[71] Department of Public Expenditure and Reform 2011 (Budget 2011 reduced capitation grants for adult and further education courses by 5%, a 2% reduction in Budget 2012, 2% in 2013 and 1% in 2014 and 2015).

2011). The unemployment rate for early school leavers is 37% – almost twice that for other people in the same 18-24 age cohort. They also had an employment rate that was half that of their peers (21% compared to 42%) (CSO 2011: 7). Government has invested heavily in trying to secure a school-based solution to this problem through, for example, the work of the National Educational Welfare Board (NEWB). In the current situation early school leaving presents a major challenge for government that needs a long-term policy response. 79% of early school leavers are either unemployed or classified as economically inactive, a situation that is simply unacceptable and cannot be allowed to continue. It may well be time to try alternative approaches aimed at ensuring that people in this cohort attain the skills required to progress in the future and participate in society.

Key issues: Early childhood education

Through the Department of Children and Youth Affairs, Ireland provides one universal pre-school year to all children at a cost of €180m.[72] In Budget 2012, the capitation rate for this pre-school year was reduced by 3 per cent and the staff to child ratio was increased to 1:11. Early childhood education and care is the essential foundation for successful lifelong learning, social integration, personal development and later employability (European Commission, 2011), yet Ireland continues to under-invest in this area. Ireland invested €180m in early childhood education in 2012 and €3 billion in primary level and second level education. The Heckman curve below illustrates that the highest return from investment in education is obtained between the ages of 0 to 5years. This is the point in the developmental curve at which differences in early health, cognitive and non-cognitive skills, which are costly causes of inequality, can be addressed most effectively.

It is important that adequate resources are invested in early childhood education as this plays a crucial role in providing young people a chance to develop their potential to the fullest possible extent. Early childhood is also the time when education can most effectively influence the development of children and help reverse disadvantage (European Commission, 2011). It has the potential to both reduce the incidence of early school leaving and to increase the equity of educational outcomes. Therefore, early childhood education and investment in this area must be given prominence within the policy development process.

---

[72] Budget 2012 estimate

Figure 9.1: The Heckman Curve

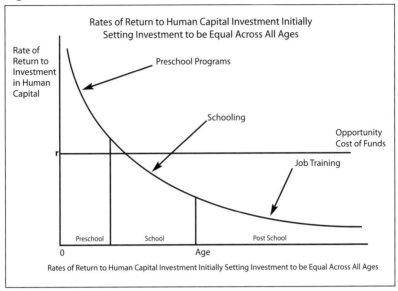

Source: Carneiro and Heckman, 2003

Key issues: Lifelong learning

Equality of status as people is one of the basic principles that should underpin lifelong learning. Access in adult life to desirable employment and choices is closely linked to the level of educational attainment. Equal political rights cannot exist if some people are socially excluded and educationally disadvantaged. The lifelong opportunities of those who are educationally disadvantaged are in sharp contrast to the opportunities for meaningful participation of those who have completed a second or third level education. Therefore, lifelong education should be regarded as a basic need. Second chance education and continuing education are vitally important and require on-going support.

Table 9.3 clearly highlights the link between educational attainment and employment. Those aged 25-64 with only primary level qualification are three times more likely to be unemployed than those with a third level qualification (24per cent versus 7 per cent). This gap has increased 10 percentage points since 2009 which shows the difficulties faced by government in helping those with low levels of educational attainment to upskill and improve their prospects of getting a job. The Programme for Government refers to lifelong learning as a high priority for jobseekers. However, labour market activation cannot be the sole factor defining the lifelong learning agenda and education and training curricula. Many reports identify generic skills and competences as a core element of the lifelong learning framework. The Forfás Report "*Sharing our future: Ireland 2025*" (Forfás 2009), for example, highlights the increasing range of generic skills that individuals require to operate within society and the economy. These include basic skills such as literacy, numeracy, use of technology, language skills, people related and conceptual skills. The report of the Expert Group on Future Skills Needs "*Tomorrow's Skills – Towards a National Skills Strategy*" (2007) indicates that there is substantial evidence to show that employers regard generic skills as equal to, if not more important than, technical or job specific skills.

Table 9.3: Summary of educational attainment and labour force participation 25-64 year olds, April 2011

Highest education level attained	%	Labour force participation rate	Employment rate	Unemployment rate
Primary or below	10	46	35	24
Lower secondary	15	67	54	21
Higher secondary	24	76	65	14
Post leaving cert	13	78	64	18
Third Level	38	87	81	7
Total persons aged 25 to 64	**100**	**76**	**66**	**13**

Source: CSO 2011:1

The report by the Council of Europe and the European Parliament (2006) "*Key Competences for Lifelong Learning*" identified eight key competences for lifelong learning:
- communication in the mother tongue (reading, writing, etc.);
- communication in foreign languages;
- mathematical and basic competences in science and technology;
- digital competence;
- Learning to learn;
- social and civic competences;
- sense of initiative and entrepreneurship; and
- cultural awareness and expression.

These key competences are interdependent, with an emphasis in each case on critical thinking, creativity, initiative, problem solving, risk assessment and decision taking. They also provide the framework for community education and training programmes within the European Education and Training 2010 work programme and the Strategic Framework for European cooperation in education and training (ET 2020) (European Commission, 2011).

Access to educational opportunity and meaningful participation in the system, together with access to successful outcomes, is central to the democratic delivery of education. Resources should be made available to support people who wish to engage in lifelong learning, in particular those people who completed second level education but who chose not to progress to third level education at that time. The right to equality of educational opportunity has long been accepted by both individuals and by the state. This concept implies equality of educational funding by the state for its citizens. Such funding is, in fact, an issue of rights, of equality, of social inclusion and of citizenship. It should be additional to funding for educationally disadvantaged, socially excluded and marginalised people. It should also be additional to funding provided to respond to educational disadvantage through the home and the community. Unfortunately, recent policy decisions have moved away from, rather than towards, these objectives. Budget 2012 reduced funding for the School Completion Programme, Youthreach, Adult Literacy and Community Education by 2 per cent in each case, and reduced overall programme funding by 7 per cent over two years.[73] These programmes provide training and skills to those at risk. Again, poor and vulnerable people will not be provided with the skills to participate fully in Ireland's recovery and the cycle of disadvantage and social exclusion will continue.

Key issues: contributing to higher education

There are strong arguments from an equity perspective that those who benefit from higher education, and who can afford to contribute to the costs of their higher education, should do so. This principle is well established internationally and is an important component of funding strategies for many of the better higher education systems across the world. Third-level graduates in employment in Ireland earn on average 64 per cent more than those with a leaving certificate only (OECD, 2011), and 81 per cent of people aged 25-64 with a third-level qualification are employed, compared with 35 per cent of those with a primary level qualification only. Ireland

---

[73] Budget 2011 reduced funding to these programme by 5%.

is the highest ranking country in the EU in terms of higher education attainment, with 48 per cent of all 25-34 year olds having a third-level qualification. At present third-level students do not pay fees but incur a student contribution charge at the beginning of each academic year. This student charge has risen significantly from £150 (€191) in 1995/96 to €2,250 in 2012/13. There are a number of difficulties with this charge:

- there is no definition of what services the 'student charge' covers;
- it does not adequately cover the cost of providing 'student services' (HEA, 2010); and
- Upfront charges and payments such as the student charge act as a significant barrier to students from lower socio-economic backgrounds.

Social Justice Ireland believes that Government should introduce a system in which fees are paid by all participants in third-level education. However, an income-contingent loan facility should also be put in place to ensure that all participants who need to do so can borrow to pay their fees and cover their living costs. The amount borrowed would be repaid when their income rose above a specified level. In this system:

- all students would be treated on the same basis insofar as both tuition and living cost loans would be available on a deferred repayment basis;
- all students would be treated on the same basis as repayment is based on their own future income rather than on current parental income; and inclusion of all part-time students would reduce the present disparity between full-time and part-time students.

Social Justice Ireland calculates that the gain to the Exchequer from such a scheme would be €445m on a full-year basis (2011 estimates). It proposes that €120m of this should go towards early childhood education, primary level and adult literacy programmes.

Resources required and challenges for our education system

The Irish public has consistently favoured a situation where government meets all the costs of first and second level education. There is also strong support for additional funding for developing early childhood education, supporting children with learning difficulties and supporting lifelong learning and alternative pathways to education for adult learners. However the education budget has been consistently reduced since 2009 and further cuts are anticipated. While the cuts to

DEIS schools are under review as this chapter is written the impact of many other cuts are being felt across the system. These are:

- 100 posts will be lost in small rural primary schools in 2012 due to the increase in pupil threshold, a further 150 posts will be lost in these schools in 2013;
- 500 language support posts will have been removed from the system by 2015;
- since 2011 capitation grants, which support the day-to-day running of schools, community education, adult literacy, Youthreach and other programmes, has been cut by 7 per cent; and
- since 2011 the student maintenance grant for third-level has been cut by 7 per cent and the student contribution has increased by €750 and will be increased by a further €750 by 2015. [74]

Education is widely recognised as crucial to the achievement of our national objectives of economic competitiveness, social inclusion and active citizenship. However, the overall levels of public funding for education in Ireland are out of step with these aspirations. This under-funding is most severe in early childhood education and in the areas of lifelong learning and second chance education – the very areas that are most vital in terms of the promotion of greater equity and fairness.

Key policy priorities on education and educational disadvantage
- Invest in universal, quality early childhood education.
- Increase resources available to lifelong learning and alternative pathways to education.
- Adopt a new, more ambitious adult literacy target and significantly increase the funding provided to address adult literacy problems, including the funding provided to the National Adult Literacy Agency.
- Introduce an income-contingent loan facility for all third-level students and develop a system in which fees are paid by all participants in third-level education.

---

[74] Department of Public Expenditure and Reform, 2011 (The student contribution is projected to increase by €250 each year in 2013, 2014 and 2015.)

10. MIGRATION AND INTERCULTURAL ISSUES

CORE POLICY OBJECTIVE:
MIGRATION & INTERCULTURAL ISSUES

To ensure that all citizens have the opportunity to stay in Ireland and contribute to Ireland's future, and to ensure that Ireland is open to welcoming people from different cultures and traditions in a way that is consistent with our history, our obligations as world citizens and with our economic status.

Migration issues of various kinds, both inwards and outwards, present important challenges for Government. The circumstances that generate involuntary emigration must be addressed in an open, honest and transparent manner. For many migrants immigration is not temporary. They will remain in Ireland and make it their home. Irish society needs to adapt to this reality. Ireland is now a multi-racial country and Government policies should promote and encourage the creation of an inclusive and integrated society in which respect for and recognition of their culture is an important right for all people.

The key challenge of integration

The rapid internationalisation of the Irish population in recent years presents Ireland with the key challenge of avoiding mistakes made by many other countries. The focus should be on integration rather than on isolating new migrant communities. While the scale of this internationalisation has declined during the current recession, immigrants make up approximately 12 per cent of the labour force (CSO, 2011) and that figure is unlikely to change significantly over the next few years even, when allowance is made for emigration levels. The detailed results of the 2011 Census will provide more detailed information on the immigrant population in Ireland when it is published. These results should be analysed and used by Government to inform the policy agenda in this area.

Although this chapter focuses principally on the problems facing refugees, asylum-seekers and migrants, it is important to recognise that other groups, such as Travellers, also require their culture to be respected as a right. In the Programme for Government and National Recovery 2011-2016 the Government commits to promoting "greater coordination and integration of delivery services to the Traveller communities across Government, using available resources more effectively to deliver on principles of social inclusion particularly in the area of Traveller education"(Government of Ireland 2011: 53).While the structures recommended by the Task Force on Travelling People have been established, it is very important to ensure that the recommendations of the report are fully implemented.

Migrant Workers

Ireland has had one of the largest declines in foreign-born working population in the EU 27 states – a fall of 105,000 between 2008 and 2010 (Eurofound, 2011).The latest figures are presented in Table 10.1.They show that there was an overall decrease of 3.5 per cent in the number of non-Irish nationals in employment in 2011.

Table 10.1: Estimated number of persons aged 15 years and over in employment and classified by nationality 2008-2011						
Year	Irish	UK	EU 15*	EU 15/27**	Other	Total
			000			
2011	1,584.3	29.4	21.1	114.3	58.7	1,807.8
2010	1,603.2	34.1	22.9	107.8	55.3	1,823.2
2009	1,632.5	44.9	28.5	114.0	67.8	1,887.7
2008	1,781.4	54.0	34.1	169.2	85.4	2,124.1

Source: CSO QNHS Series (2011:25 2010:25 2009:28)
*excluding Ireland and UK   **EU15 to EU27 states

There has been criticism of Irish immigration policy and legislation due to the lack of support for the integration of immigrants and a lack of adequate recognition of the permanency of immigration.Two significant areas of concern are:

- work permits are issued to employers, not to employees, which ties the employee to a specific employer, increasing their vulnerability to exploitation and reducing their labour market mobility; and
- the Irish asylum process can take many years and most refugees coming onto the Irish labour market are *de facto* long-term unemployed. A process for training and education asylum seekers is needed so that they can retain and gain skills (ECRI, 2006 & Employers Diversity Network, 2009).

Refugees and Asylum Seekers

Until recently the number of refugees forced to flee from their own countries in order to escape war, persecution and abuses of human rights had been declining worldwide over many years. In its most recent report, however, the United Nations High Commission for Refugees (UNHCR) signalled a sizeable reversal of this positive trend. At the end of 2010 the total population of concern to UNHCR was estimated at 33.9 million people, including 10.5 million refugees; 850,200 asylum seekers (a drop of 10 per cent compared to 2009); 223,000 refugees who had repatriated in 2010; 14.7 million internally displaced persons and an estimated number of 12 million stateless people worldwide (UNHCR 2011).

Irish people have had a long tradition of solidarity with people facing oppression within their own countries, but that tradition is not reflected in our policies towards refugees and asylum-seekers. *Social Justice Ireland* believes that Ireland should use its position in international forums to highlight the causes of displacement of peoples. In particular, Ireland should use these forums to challenge the production, sale and free access to arms and the implements of torture.

Despite this tradition of solidarity with peoples facing oppression, racism is an everyday reality for many migrants in Ireland. A recent report published by the Immigrant Council of Ireland (Immigrant Council of Ireland, 2011) highlights this and the lack of leadership in dealing with the issue. An integrated policy response is needed to address the root causes of racism within communities; political and institutional responses are required to address this problem in order to prevent it deteriorating.

The establishment of Citizenship Ceremonies by the Minister for Justice, Equality and Defence and the reforms to the procedure of assessing and processing citizenship applications are welcome and have the potential to promote inclusiveness and integration. However, *Social Justice Ireland* has significant concerns over the Minister's plans to offer residency visas in return for investment of €2m on Irish bonds and €1m in an Irish company or spend €1m on Irish property.[75] The inducement of residency in return for cash investment sends out the wrong message about Irish residency and there is potential for abuse of the programme if not monitored carefully.

Table 10.2 shows the number of applications for asylum in Ireland between 2000 and 2011. In 2011 Ireland experienced reduction in applications of almost 40 per

---

[75] Immigrant Investor Programme and Start-up Entrepreneur programme see
http://www.inis.gov.ie/en/INIS/Pages/PR12000003

cent. This is in spite of the numbers seeking asylum in the EU 27 increasing by almost 25 per cent in 2011[76] and this is the smallest number of applications for asylum that the state has received in recent years. Almost 4,000 people were deported from the State in 2011.

Table 10.2: Applications for Asylum in Ireland 2000 – 2011			
Year	**Number**	**Year**	**Number**
2000	10,938	**2006**	4,314
2001	10,325	**2007**	3,985
2002	11,634	**2008**	3,866
2003	7,900	**2009**	2,689
2004	4,766	**2010**	1,939
2005	4,323	**2011**	1,290

Source: Office of the Refugee Applications Commissioner (2012) *Statistical Report January 2012*

The European Commission against Racism and Intolerance (ECRI) has identified difficulties in gaining recognition for professional qualifications as a major challenge facing refugees and asylum-seekers when they have been granted leave to stay in Ireland. It means refugees are often unable to find employment commensurate with their qualifications and experience, impeding their full integration into society. It also means their valuable skills, which could contribute to the Irish economy, are unused or underused (ECRI, 2006). *Social Justice Ireland* proposes that asylum-seekers who currently are not entitled to take up employment should be allowed to do so with immediate effect and that structures are established to recognise professional qualifications. Any recommendations to this effect contained in the forthcoming ECRI fourth report on Ireland, due in late 2012 should be implemented.

While asylum-seekers are assigned initial accommodation in Dublin, most are subsequently allocated accommodation at locations outside Dublin, pending the completion of the asylum-seeking process. The Reception and Integration Agency (RIA) was established to perform this task. The latest statistics from the RIA (RIA, 2011) show that it has 46 accommodation centres throughout the country accommodating 6,107 people. The policy for "direct provision" employed in almost

---

[76] http://www.emn.ie/emn/statistics

all of these centres results in these asylum-seekers receiving accommodation and board, together with €19.10 direct provision per week per adult and €9.60 per child. Over time this sum has remained unchanged and its value has therefore been eroded by inflation. Between 2002 and 2010 the buying power of these payments has been decreased by almost 19 per cent. This situation, combined with the fact that asylum-seekers are denied access to employment, means that asylum-seekers are among the most excluded and marginalised groups in Ireland.

Social Justice Ireland proposes that asylum-seekers who currently are not entitled to take up employment should be allowed to do so with immediate effect and that the direct provision payments should be increased immediately to at least €65 per week for an adult and €38 per week for a child. Removing employment restrictions and increased the direct provision allocation would cost €12.5m per annum and provide noticeable improvements in the subsistence life being led by these asylum-seekers.

Emigration

Emigration among Irish nationals, particularly young Irish, has continued to increase dramatically. An estimated 27,000 Irish nationals left Ireland between April 2009 and April 2010. A further 40,200 left in the following 12 months. Overall, emigration of all nationalities is estimated to have reached 76,400 in the year to April 2011, an increase of 16.9 per cent from April 2010 when 65,300 left. Table 10.3 below outlines the numbers of people leaving the country between 2006 and 2011, both Irish and non-national.

Table 10.3: Estimated Emigration by Nationality, 2006 – 2011						
Year	Irish	UK	EU 13★	EU 10/12★★	Rest of World	Total
			'000			
2011	40.2	3.8	9.1	15.2	8.2	76.4
2010	27.7	2.6	7.8	19.1	8.1	65.3
2009	18.4	2.9	5.5	30.1	8.3	65.1
2008	13.4	2.4	4.2	18.8	6.4	45.3
2007	13.1	2.3	6.9	14.4	5.5	42.2
2006	15.3	2.2	5.1	7.2	6.2	36.0

Source: CSO 2011, Population and Migration Estimates
★ EU 15 excluding UK and Ireland ★★ EU MS that joined in 2004 and 2007

The rate of emigration of Irish nationals has tripled since 2008. This demonstrates the lack of opportunities available for people in Ireland, especially for those seeking employment in the 15-44 age group. The austerity programme is contributing to Ireland's loss of young people, the implications of which are stark as this loss will pose significant problems for economic recovery. Emigration from Ireland to Britain rose by 25 per cent in 2010 and the vast majority of those who emigrated were between the ages of 19 and 34.

According to a report by the UK Department for Work and Pensions, 6,130 Irish citizens between the ages of 18 and 24 and 5,730 Irish citizens between the ages of 25 and 34 registered for a National Insurance Number in the UK in 2010 (UK Statistics Authority, 2011). The number has risen steadily from 9,510 in 2006 to 11,050 in 2009. This emigration 'brain drain', which in some quarters is perversely being heralded as a 'safety valve', is in fact a serious problem for Ireland. It may well result in a significant skills deficit in the long-term and hamper Ireland's recovery. In 2011 the Minister for Jobs, Enterprise and Innovation stated that *"emigration is now draining our country and our economy of some of our best and brightest people and we must do everything we can to create opportunities for them to stay here and contribute to our recovery."*[78] However Government has done little to stem the tide of emigration thus far and in its own projections for 2012 (Department of Finance, 2011) sees emigration and a reduction in labour force participation as the two main factors that will contribute to a reduction in unemployment in the coming year. It is of concern that Government also projects that unemployment will remain high, at 11.6 per cent in 2015.

Youth unemployment

The latest Eurostat figures show that youth unemployment in Ireland now stands at 29.9 per cent, 8 per cent above the EU 27 average.[79] This is a rise of almost 17 per cent in Ireland since 2007. The OECD expects the youth unemployment rate to stay at this high level for the next two years and many unemployed young people are likely to experience a prolonged period of joblessness.[80] Addressing the issue of youth unemployment and its link to high emigration rates among young people must be a core policy priority for Government. Radical initiatives to create jobs are urgently required.

---

[78] http://www.merrionstreet.ie/index.php/2011/06/minister-bruton-comments-on-unemployment-figures/

[79] http://epp.eurostat.ec.europa.eu/statistics_explained/index.php?title=File:Youth_unemployment_rates,_2008-2011Q3,_%28%25%29.png&filetimestamp=20120127135533

[80] http://www.oecd.org/dataoecd/9/14/48679203.pdf

The most recent figures released by the Higher Education Authority (HEA) show that graduates in 2008 with an honours degree had a 10 per cent unemployment rate, those with a postgraduate degree had a 12 per cent unemployment rate and those with a Masters or PhD had a 16 per cent unemployment rate. In 2007 the figures were 3 per cent and 5 per cent respectively. In 2008 almost 15 per cent of honours degree graduates and 17 per cent of PhD graduates were in employment overseas while 34 per cent were engaged in further studies. Ireland is relying on the "smart economy" as the foundation of economic recovery. The latest emigration and graduate employment statistics raise serious questions about the sustainability of such reliance.

Key policy priorities on migration and intercultural issues

- Address involuntary emigration and the long-term policy problems it presents the State.
- Promote integration and an inclusive society, giving priority to recognising the right of all refugees and asylum-seekers to work.
- Immediately increase the weekly allowance allocated to asylum-seekers on 'direct provision' to at least €65 per week for an adult and €38 for a child.

11. PARTICIPATION

CORE POLICY OBJECTIVE: PARTICIPATION

To ensure that all people have a genuine voice in shaping the decisions that affect them and to ensure that all people can contribute to the development of society.

The changing nature of democracy has raised many questions for policy-makers and others concerned about the issue of participation. Decisions often appear to be made without any real engagement with the people directly affected by those decisions. The background to the 2011 general election dissipated some of the voter apathy that had been widespread over previous years. Indeed the election also reminded voters of the importance of governance and decision making in democratic societies. But as chart 11.1 shows up to then voter turnout had been falling over time, reaching a low point of 62.6 per cent in 2002. The 2011 turnout, at 70.9 per cent, was an improvement on previous elections and brought Ireland's turnout above the European average for the first time since the 1980s. The EU-27 average turnout is 69.7 per cent (CSO, 2010:44).[81] However there is a gender imbalance among Ireland's elected representatives which averages at 25% (McGing, 2012).

The most recent in-depth analysis of voter participation over recent years was done in 2011 by the CSO. In a quarterly national household survey the CSO examined participation in the February 2011 general election. It found that the turnout of young people had increased considerably since the previous survey, undertaken in 2003. Just over 62 per cent of those aged 18-24 voted in the 2011 general election. This contrasts with participation figures of 92 per cent for voters aged 55-64 years, (CSO 2011: 3).

The survey also examined why people did not participate in the election and found that over one-third of those who did not vote were not registered to vote. Eleven per cent of non-voters said they had "no interest", 10 per cent were "disillusioned"

---

[81] The 2006 review of the accuracy of the electoral register may suggest that the official figures for 2002 and 2007 are somewhat understated.

with politics, 11 per cent had difficulty getting to the polling station (particularly common among non-voters aged 55 and over). (CSO, 2011:4) The survey also found that those educated to primary level or below were most likely to say they did not vote because they were disillusioned with politics. This highlights the need for Government to engage with civil society in a deliberative democracy process.

Chart 11.1: Percentage turnout in Irish General Elections, 1973-2011

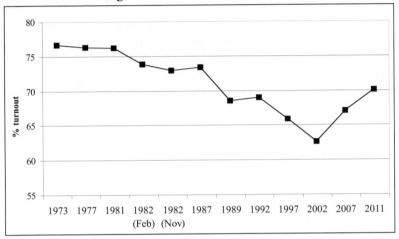

Source: CSO (2011:87) and Department of Environment, Heritage and Local Government (2011).

The implications of these findings suggest that many people, especially young people and those who have lower educational attainment levels, have little confidence in the political process. They have been disillusioned because the political process fails to involve them in any real way, while also failing to address many of their core concerns. Transparency and accountability are demanded but rarely delivered. Many of the developments of recent years will simply have added to the disillusionment of many people. A new approach is clearly needed to address this issue.

The need for an agreed forum and structure for discussion of issues on which people disagree is becoming increasingly obvious as political and mass communication systems develop. Most people are not involved in the processes that produce plans and decisions which affect their lives. They know that they are being presented with a *fait accompli*. More critically, they realise that they and their families will be forced to live with the consequences of the decisions taken. This is particularly relevant in Ireland in 2012 as people are living with the consequences of the bailout programme and repaying the debts of European Banks through a programme of austerity and upward redistribution of resources. A lack of structures and systems to involve people in the decision-making process results in the exclusion and alienation of large sections of society. It causes and maintains inequality.

Any exclusion of people from debate on the issues that affect them is suspect. Such exclusion leaves those responsible for it open to charges of arbitrary use of power. Some of the decision-making structures of our society and of our world allow people to be represented in the decision-making process. However, almost all these structures fail to provide genuine participation for most people affected by their decisions. Our society and the world in which we live need decision-making structures that enable participation. A process of deliberative democracy is required which would enable discussion and debate to take place without any imposition of power differentials. It would allow issues and positions to be discussed on the basis of the available evidence rather than on the basis of assertions by those who are powerful and/or unwilling to consider the evidence. Deliberative democracy produces evidence-based policy.

Deliberative democracy
Deliberative participation by all is essential if society is to develop and, in practice, to maintain principles guaranteeing satisfaction of basic needs, respect for others as equals, economic equality and religious, social, sexual and ethnic equality. Modern means of communication and information make it relatively easy to involve people in dialogue and decision-making. It is a question of political will - will the groups who have the power share it with others?

Some progress has been made over the past decade. At local government level the development of Community Forums, Strategic Policy Committees and County/City Development Boards are moves in the right direction. So also are some of the developments in social dialogue at national level, most importantly the creation of the Community and Voluntary Pillar and the Environmental Pillar. However, these initiatives failed to develop real deliberative processes. In practice, power differentials have been used to undermine the validity of evidence-based policy proposals. As long as evidence-based proposals can be undermined in this way, the issue of real participation has some distance to go before the rhetoric of participation is matched by reality.

In September 2011 the Department of Environment, Community and Local Government established a steering group to consider an alignment process for local government and local and community development. This group published the *Interim Report of the Local Government Local Development Alignment Steering Group* in December 2011. Among the recommendations were (Department of Environment, Community and Local Government 2011):

- A more co-ordinated and integrated approach to local service provision is required, based on an enhanced role for local government in planning, decision-making, oversight and, where appropriate delivery of local development programmes within agreed structures.
- Meaningful community engagement and involvement will be essential in identifying local needs and agreeing services to be delivered.
- A bottom-up approach, with a focus on targeting those most in need and facilitating meaningful citizen participation, should be an integral part of the planning and decision making process and in the delivery of services.
- There should be greater flexibility at local level to customise programmes and policy initiatives to local needs and priorities. Policy making at national level should be informed by delivery and practice at local level.

Social Justice Ireland believes a deliberative democracy process, in which all stakeholders would address the evidence collectively, would go some way towards ensuring that local issues are addressed and would also ensure a high level of accountability among stakeholders. This process could be implemented under the framework of the Council of Europe's *Charter on Shared Social Responsibilities*[82]. The Charter states that shared social responsibility in terms of local government requires that local government *'frame local policies which acknowledge and take into account the contribution made by everyone to strengthening social protection and social cohesion, the fair allocation of common goods, the formation of the principles of social, environmental and intergenerational justice and which also ensure that all stakeholders have a negotiation and decision-making power'* (Council of Europe, 2011). We believe these guidelines can be adapted to the Irish context and are a very useful tool for devising a policy to promote greater alignment between local government and the community and voluntary sector in promoting participation at local level. This would involve:

---

[82] The Charter of Shared Social Responsibilities is also discussed in chapter 2.

- Local government, the community and voluntary sector and the local community working together to ensure the design and efficient delivery of services for local communities that cater to the need of that local community.
- Highlighting the key role of social citizenship in creating vibrant, participative and inclusive communities.
- Direct involvement of local communities, local authorities, state bodies and local entrepreneurs in the policy making and decision making processes.
- Ensuring all voices are heard (especially those who are on the margins) in the decision making process.
- Reform of current local government structures to better involve local communities in the governance and decision making of their local area.
- An increased sense of 'ownership' over local government by the local community. This will only come with increased participation; the community and voluntary sector has a key role to play in this regard.

Social Justice Ireland believes that these guidelines would be highly relevant in the Irish context. They could provide a key part of the framework aimed at creating a truly participatory and inclusive system of local governance that involves all of the stakeholders equally. These guidelines would also provide a framework to achieve the high level objective for a strong, democratic, participative and responsive local government providing services to socially inclusive and sustainable communities (Department of Environment, Heritage and Local Government, 2008).

A forum for dialogue on civil society issues

The range of civil society issues that are of major concern to large numbers of people but are rarely discussed contributes to disillusionment with the political process.

The development of a new forum within which a civil society debate could be conducted would be a welcome addition to the political landscape in Ireland. Such a forum could make a major contribution to improving participation by a wide range of groups in Irish society.

Social Justice Ireland proposes that government authorise and resource an initiative to identify how a civil society debate could be developed and sustained in Ireland and to examine how it might connect to the growing debate at European level around civil society issues.

There are many issues such a forum could address, such as the issue of citizenship, its rights, responsibilities, possibilities and limitations in the21st century and he shape of the social model Ireland wishes to develop in the decades ahead. The issues a civil society forum could address are many and varied. Ireland would benefit immensely from having such a forum.[83]

Impact on the democratic process

Would a civil society forum and a new social contract against exclusion detract from the democratic process? The very nature of democracy is that people participate in shaping the decisions that affect them most closely. What we have, in practice, is a highly centralised government in which we are 'represented' by professional politicians. The more powerful a political party becomes, the more distant it seems to become from the electorate. Party policies on a range of major issues are often difficult to discern. Backbenchers have little control over, or influence on, government ministers, opposition spokespersons or shadow cabinets. Even within the cabinet some ministers seem to be able to ignore their cabinet colleagues.

The democratic process has certainly benefited from the participation of various sectors in different arenas. It would also benefit from taking up the proposals to develop a new social contract against exclusion and a new forum for dialogue on civil society issues.

The decline in participation is exacerbated by the primacy given to the market by so many analysts, commentators, policy-makers and politicians. Many people feel that their views or comments are ignored or patronised, while the views of those who see the market as solving most if not all of society's problems are treated with the greatest respect. This situation seems to be persisting despite the total failure of market mechanisms in recent years during which these very mechanisms combined to produce Ireland's range of current crises – and the linked EU-level crises that are not currently being recognised by most decision-makers.

Markets have a major role to play but they produce very mixed results when left to their own devices. Recent experience has shown clearly that in terms of many policy goals, markets are extremely limited. Consequently, other mechanisms are required to ensure that some re-balancing, at least, is achieved. The mechanisms proposed here simply aim to be positive in improving participation in a 21st century society.

---

[83] For a further discussion of this issue see Healy and Reynolds (2003:191-197).

Supporting the community and voluntary sector

The issue of governance is of major importance for Government and for society at large. It is an especially crucial issue for the community and voluntary sector. There is a substantial role for civil society in addressing both the causes and the consequences of the multi-faceted crises Ireland currently faces (economic, banking, fiscal, social and reputational as outlined in chapter 2). All communities are different and not every community has the capacity or the infrastructure to engage meaningfully with and participate in local government. This is where the community and voluntary sector has a key role to play in informing, engaging with and providing the local communities with the skills to participate in and contribute to local government. In light of the recommendations contained in the interim report of the Steering Group on Local Government and Local Development Alignment Process, it is important that the community and voluntary sector is supported in promoting deliberative democracy processes and participation at local level.

The community and voluntary sector plays a major role in responding to both the causes and the consequences of these crises. Support for this work is crucial and it should not be left to the welcome but very limited charity of philanthropists. Funding is required by the sector and has been provided over many years by Government. In recent years much of that funding has been reduced with obvious consequences for those depending on the sector. It is crucial that Government appropriately resource this sector into the future and that it remains committed to the principle of providing multi-annual statutory funding.

Social dialogue is a critically important component of effective decision-making in a modern democracy. The Community and Voluntary Pillar provides a mechanism for social dialogue around a range of important policy issues. Social dialogue contributes to both transparency and accountability and we believe governance along these lines can and should be developed in Ireland.

Key policy priorities on participation
- Incorporate the shared social responsibility and deliberative democracy frameworks into the local government and local development process.
- Strengthen the mechanisms of engagement between the state and the C&V sector.
- Establish and resource a forum for dialogue on civil society issues. This initiative should identify how a civil society debate could be developed and

sustained in Ireland and explore how it might connect to the growing debate at European level around civil society issues.

- Significantly increase the funding to C&V sector organisations providing services, facilitating participation at national and local level and addressing both the causes and the consequences of Ireland's current series of crises.

12. SUSTAINABILITY

> ## CORE POLICY OBJECTIVE: SUSTAINABILITY
> To ensure that all development is socially, economically and environmentally sustainable.

The search for a humane, sustainable model of development has gained momentum in recent times. After years of people believing that markets and market forces would produce a better life for everyone, major problems such as resource depletion and pollution have raised questions and doubts. There is a growing awareness that sustainability must be a constant factor in all development, be it social, economic or environmental. Sustainability is about ensuring that all development is socially, economically and environmentally sustainable. This understanding underpins all the other chapters in this review. This chapter focuses in more detail first promoting sustainable development and on reviewing environmental issues.

Promoting sustainable development
Sustainable development is defined as *'development which meets the needs of the present, without compromising the ability of future generations to meet their needs (World Commission on Environment and Development, 1987)*. It encompasses the three pillars: environment, society and economy. All three pillars must be addressed in a balanced manner if development is to be sustainable. Maintaining this balance is crucial to the long-term development of a sustainable, resource-efficient future for Ireland. While growth and economic competitiveness are important, they are not the only issues to be considered and cannot be given precedence over others. They must be dealt with using a framework for sustainable development which ensures equal consideration is given to the environmental, social and economic pillars. It is also important to note that although economic growth is seen as the key to resolving many aspects of the current crisis across the EU, this very growth may be damaging the possibility of securing sustainable development in the Global South.

Sustainable development is our only means of creating a long term future for Ireland in which the environment, growth and social needs are met in a balanced manner with consideration for the needs of future generations. Sustainability and the adoption of a sustainable development model presents a significant policy challenge. It requires environmental policy decisions with varying distributional consequences to be made in a timely manner while also ensuring that a disproportionate burden is not imposed on certain groups, for example, low income families or rural dwellers This policy challenge highlights the need for an evidence-based policy process involving all stakeholders. The costs and benefits of all policies must be assessed and considered on the basis of evidence only. This is essential in order to avoid the policy debate being influenced by hearsay or vested interests or the inconsiderate exercise of power.

The need for shadow national accounts

Realisation of the need to move away from money-measured growth must be central to any model of development which has sustainability at its core. Our present national accounts, which are based on GNP/GDP as scorecards of wealth and progress, miss fundamentals such as environmental sustainability and, the value of unpaid work. Paradoxically, while environmental depletion is ignored, the environmental costs of dealing with the effects of economic growth, such as cleaning up pollution or coping with the felling of rainforests, are regarded as an addition to GNP/GDP. It is widely acknowledged that GDP is "*an inadequate metric to gauge well-being over time particularly in its economic, environmental, and social dimensions, some aspects of which are often referred to as sustainability*" (Stiglitz Commission 2009: 8). A new scorecard or metric model is needed which measures the impacts of policy decisions on people's lives, which spans all policy areas and which measures the environmental, social and economic costs and benefits of policies.

The development of "satellite" or "shadow" national accounts should be a central initiative in this. Already a number of alternative scorecards exist, such as the United Nations' Human Development Index (HDI), former World Bank economist Herman Daly's Index of Sustainable Economic Welfare (ISEW) and Hazel Henderson's Country Futures Index (CFI). A 2002 study by Wackernagel et al presented the first systematic attempt to calculate how human demands on the environment are matched by its capacity to cope. It found that the world currently uses 120 per cent of what the earth can provide sustainably each year.

In the environmental context it is crucial that dominant economic models are challenged on, among other things, their assumptions that nature's capital of clean air, water and environment, are essentially free and inexhaustible, that scarce resources can always be substituted and that the planet can continue absorbing human and industrial wastes. Shadow national accounts would help to make sustainability and 'green' procurement mandatory considerations in the decision and policy making process. They would also go some way towards driving a civil society awareness campaign to help decouple economic growth from consumption. *Social Justice Ireland* welcomes the publication by the Department of Environment, Community and Local Government of its *Action Plan on Green Public Procurement*[84] as a step on the road towards making green procurement mandatory in public sector procurement decisions.

Some governments and international agencies have picked up on these issues, especially in the environmental area. They have begun to develop "satellite" or "shadow" national accounts, which include items not traditionally measured. Our 2009 publication *Beyond GDP: What is prosperity and how should it be measured?* explored many of these new developments. It also proposed a series of policy developments which would assist in achieving similar progress in Ireland. There has been some progress in this area, including commitments to better data collection and broader assessment of well-being and progress by the CSO, ESRI and EPA. However, much remains to be achieved and *Social Justice Ireland* strongly urges government to adopt this broader perspective and commit to producing these accounts alongside other indicators of progress. Measures of economic performance must reflect their environmental cost and a price must be put on the use of our natural capital.

The OECD Global Project on measuring the progress of society recommends that sets of key environmental, social and economic indicators be developed and that these should be used to inform evidence-based decision making across all sectors (Morrone, 2009: 23).

Social Justice Ireland recommends that government commit to producing shadow national accounts and that these accounts include indicators that measure the following:

- the use of energy and materials to produce goods;
- the generation of pollution and waste;
- the amount of money spent by industry, government and households to protect the environment or manage natural resources;

---

[84] For more information see
http://www.environ.ie/en/Environment/SustainableDevelopment/GreenPublicProcurement/News/MainBody,29206,en.htm

- natural resource asset accounts measuring the quantity and quality of a country's natural resources;
- sustainability of the growth being generated vis a vis our social and natural capital;
- natural resource depletion and degradation as a cost to society;
- the output of waste and pollution as a result of commercial activity as a cost within the satellite national accounts;
- the measures of the GPI (Genuine Progress Indicator) which measure and deduct for income inequality, environmental degradation, cost of crime amongst other items. By measuring and differentiating between activity which diminishes natural and social capital and activity that enhances our natural and social capital we can ensure that our economic welfare is sustainable (Daly & Cobb, 1987).

Stakeholder involvement

One of the key indicators of sustainability is how a country runs stakeholder involvement. Sustainable Development Councils (SDCs) are a model for multi-stakeholder bodies which are composed of members from all major groups, including public, private, community, civil society and academic, engaged in evidence-based discussion.[85] The EU-wide experience has been that SDC's are crucial to maintaining a medium and long-term vision for a sustainable future whilst concurrently working to ensure that sustainable development policies are embedded into socio-economic strategies and budgetary processes.

Ireland established its sustainable development council (Comhar) in 1999 and disbanded it in 2011, transferring its functions to NESC (National Economic and Social Council). While it is admirable that government wishes to place sustainable development at the core of policy making and has asked NESC to ensure it gives sustainable development major consideration in all it does, it is also important to note that NESC is not in a position to do the detailed work done previously by Comhar. There is need for a deliberative democracy arena within which all stakeholders can discuss evidence without power differentials impeding outcomes.

---

[85] For more information see http://www.eeac.eu/images/doucments/eeac-statement-backgr2011_rio_final_144dpi.pdf

Principles to underpin sustainable development

Principles to underpin sustainable development were proposed in a report for the European Commission prepared by James Robertson in May 1997. Entitled *The New Economics of Sustainable Development*, the report argued that these principles would include the following:

- systematic empowerment of people (as opposed to making and keeping them dependent) as the basis for people-centred development;
- systematic conservation of resources and environment as the basis for environmentally sustainable development;
- evolution from a "wealth of nations" model of economic life to a "one-world" economic system;
- evolution from today's international economy to an ecologically sustainable, decentralising, multi-level one-world economic system;
- restoration of political and ethical factors to a central place in economic life and thought;
- respect for qualitative values, not just quantitative values; and
- respect for feminine values, not just masculine ones.

At first glance, these might not appear to be the concrete guidelines that policy-makers so often prefer. Yet they are principles that are relevant to every area of economic life. They also apply to every level of life, ranging from personal and household to global issues. They have an impact on lifestyle choices and organisational goals. If these principles were applied to every area, level and feature of economic life they would provide a comprehensive checklist for a systematic policy review.

It is also important that any programme for sustainable development should take a realistic view of human nature, recognising that people are altruistic and selfish, co-operative and competitive. Consequently it is important to develop the economic system to reward activities that are socially and environmentally benign (and not the reverse, as at present). This in turn would make it easier for people and organisations to make choices that are socially and environmentally responsible. A simple example is the tax on plastic bags. It shows how quickly people can and will change. In just one week some retail outlets were reporting a 90 per cent reduction in the use of plastic bags. Overall the Department of Environment, Community and Local Government estimated that usage had declined by 95 per cent (approximately one billion bags) in 2002. Since then there has been some increase in usage despite an increase in the levy. This highlights the need to sustain the effort required in relevant areas to ensure that the need for sustainable development is recognised and pursued.

Any programme for sustainable development has implications for public spending. In addressing this issue it must be understood that public expenditure programmes and taxes provide a framework which helps to shape market prices, rewards some kinds of activities and penalises others. Within this framework there are other areas which are not supported by public expenditure or are not taxed. This framework should be developed to ,encourage economic efficiency and enterprise, social equity and environmental sustainability. Systematic reviews should be carried out and published on the sustainability effects of all public subsidies and other relevant public expenditure and tax differentials. This could lead to the elimination of subsidies that favour unsustainable development.

Systematic reviews should also be carried out and published on the possibilities for re- orientating public spending programmes, with the aim of preventing and reducing social and environmental problems. *Social Justice Ireland* welcomes the publication of a draft *Framework for a Sustainable Development for Ireland* which is a late, but positive step on the road towards a sustainable development model. The failure to implement the previous sustainability strategies (2000 & 2007) and the lack of quantitative and qualitative targets contained in the draft framework in its present form are both causes of concern. *Social Justice Ireland* proposes that responsibility for the framework should lie with the Department of An Taoiseach to ensure the sustainable development is at the heart of policy making in all government departments.

Monitoring sustainable development

Many studies have highlighted the lack of socio-economic and environmental data in Ireland required to assess trends in sustainable development. A chapter by Carrie in the Feasta review (2005) focused on the lack of long-run socio-economic data on issues such as education participation, crime and healthcare. Another paper by Scott (ESRI, 2005) outlined the empirical and methodological gaps which continue to impede the incorporation of sustainable development issues into public policy making and assessment. It is only through a sustained commitment to data collection in all of these areas that these deficiencies will be addressed. We welcome recent developments in this area, particularly at the CSO, and look forward to all of these data impediments being removed in the years to come.

Comhar undertook a lot of work developing indicators to set targets and quantitative means of measuring the progress of sustainable development. *Social Justice Ireland* proposes that the work done by Comhar[86] be adopted by NESC and consultation take place with the CSO to ensure that these indicators are immediately put in place and the necessary data are collected. In a study of national strategies towards sustainable development in 2005 (Niestroy, 2005: 185) Ireland's sustainability strategy was criticised on the following issues in terms of targets:

- no systematic monitoring system;
- no general timetable; and
- a lack of quantitative national targets.

Implementation, targets and monitoring will be crucial to the success of sustainable development. It is important that these targets and indicators and the mechanisms for monitoring, tracking and reviewing them are developed and clearly explained to ensure that responsibility is taken across all departments and all stakeholders for its implementation.

Environmental issues

Maintaining a healthy environment remains one of the greatest global challenges. Without concerted and rapid collective action to curb and decouple resource depletion and the generation of pollution from economic growth, human activities may destroy the very environment that supports economies and sustains life (UNEP 2011: II).

Our environment is a priceless asset. It is also finite, a fact often ignored in current debates. Protection and conservation of our environment is of major importance as the environment is not just for our use alone, it is also the natural capital of future generations.

Ireland: some key environmental facts (CSO 2011, CSO 2010, EPA 2010)

- Ireland's greenhouse gas emissions decreased by 1.1 per cent in 2010 to 61.64 million tonnes. Emissions from the transport sector decreased by 10 per cent. However emissions from agriculture, energy, industry, residential and waste sectors all increased in 2010.

---

[86] For a detailed list of these indicators see: http://www.comharsustainableindicators.ie/explore-the-indicators/comhar-indicators.aspx

- Agriculture and transport are the largest contributors to Irelands' greenhouse gas emissions, making up 30.4 per cent and 19.1 per cent of total emissions respectively.
- Ireland is likely to breach its EU 2020 target and obligations on emissions from 2016 onwards (EPA, 2012).
- The percentage of waste recovered in Ireland rose to 42 per cent in 2010, and 45 per cent of waste was landfilled, a reduction of 13 per cent from the previous year.
- The proportion of Irish rivers classified as being unpolluted has declined from 77.3 per cent in 1987-1990 to 68.9 per cent in 1997-2009. The percentage of slightly polluted river water has increased steadily from 12 per cent in 1987-1990 to 20.7 per cent in the period 2007-2009.
- The total number of registered vehicles has increased by 134 per cent over the period 1990-2009. Related CO_2 emissions increased by 168 per cent in the same period.
- Road transport accounted for 99.4 per cent of total inland freight transport in Ireland in 2009, compared with an EU average of 77.5 per cent.
- 46 per cent of the State's sewage treatment plants in urban areas fail to meet EU standards (EPA 2012).

Table 12.1: Irish River Water Quality 1987 - 2009

Quality	Unpolluted	Slightly polluted	Moderately polluted	Seriously polluted	Total
1987–1990	77.3	12.0	9.7	0.9	100
1991–1994	71.2	16.8	11.4	0.6	100
1995–1997	66.9	18.2	14.0	0.9	100
1998–2000	69.7	17.1	12.4	0.8	100
2001–2003	69.3	17.9	12.3	0.6	100
2004–200	71.4	18.2	9.9	0.5	100
2007–2009	68.9	20.7	10.0	0.4	100

Source: Environmental Protection Agency 2010, Water Quality 2007 - 2009

Table 12.2: Ireland: Municipal waste generated, recovered and landfilled			
Year	Waste generated (000 tonnes)	Waste recovered (% of waste generated)	Waste landfilled (% of waste generated)
2003	3,001.0	24.2	61.1
2004	3,034.6	30.3	59.9
2005	3,050.1	31.6	59.8
2006	3,384.6	33.1	58.5
2007	3,397.7	34.1	59.3
2008	3,224.3	36.1	60.1
2009	2,952.9	37.3	58.4
2010	2,846.1	42.0	45.0

Source: Environmental Protection Agency (2012), National Waste Report Series

Ireland has made significant improvements in increasing the amount of municipal waste recycled, which stood at 38 per cent in 2010. However there remains a significant challenge in meeting the 2013 target for diversion of household waste from landfill to recycling of 50 per cent (EPA, 2012).

The economic growth of recent decades has been accomplished mainly through drawing down natural resources without allowing stocks to regenerate, causing widespread degradation and loss to our eco-system. Careful stewardship of Ireland's natural resources is required to ensure the long term health and sustainability of our environment.

Climate Change

Climate change is one of the most significant and challenging issues currently facing humanity. Increased levels of greenhouse gases, such as CO_2, increase the amount of energy trapped in the atmosphere which leads to global effects such as increased temperatures, melting of snow and ice and rising global average sea-level. If these issues are not addressed with urgency, the projected effects of climate change present a very serious risk of dangerous and irreversible climate changes at national and global levels, with food production and ecosystems being particularly vulnerable.

Climate change and the implementation of climate policy to address it and its consequences has been a challenge for Ireland. Despite two National Climate Change Strategies (one in 2000 and one in 2007) there have been significant delays in implementing these policies. Some of these have still not been implemented. The mobilisation of vested interested has been a decisive factors in many of these delays and cases of non-implementation (Coughlin, O (2007). This is extremely disappointing because if these policies been implemented on time and as specified Ireland's climate policy commitments could have been met from domestic measures. Now, Ireland faces the prospect of not meeting its emissions targets, even if all measures are implemented immediately. Ireland is actually on course to overshoot its EU 2020 emissions targets as early as 2015 (EPA 2011).

Social Justice Ireland welcomes the *Roadmap for Climate Policy and Legislation* announced by the Department of Environment, Community and Local Government and the Minister's call for structured dialogue and consultation on policy and legislation on an open and inclusive basis, involving all stakeholders. It is crucial that all expert and evidence-based advice should be made available in an accessible manner to increase Irish people's understanding of, engagement with and participation in climate change policy and also to enhance political accountability and transparency on climate policy. However there are two areas of particular concern.

Social Justice Ireland is concerned that the Minister has stated that he does not intend to introduce sectoral targets[87]. The absence of sectoral targets and quantitative measures and outputs has already impeded climate change policy progress internationally (UNEP 2011: vii). Without these targets and a system whereby they are regularly reviewed, it will be extraordinarily difficult to monitor the progress of climate change policy. The absence of these targets will also make enforcing responsibility and accountability for implementation of climate policy across all government departments and stakeholders in all sectors extremely challenging.

As outlined in the roadmap, the government will not adopt a national policy position on climate legislation and the transition to a low carbon future until the end of 2013, while implementation of these policies will move out to 2014. This will give the government just six years to reach the targets set in the EU 2020 strategy (European Commission, 2010). Given that we are on course to overshoot

---

[87] http://www.environ.ie/en/Environment/Atmosphere/ClimateChange/ClimatePolicyReview 2011/News/MainBody,28331,en.htm Department of Environment, Community and Local Government, Press Release

emissions targets by 2015, there is a real danger that short-term planning in order to limit our liabilities in terms of overshooting some of these targets will subsume the need for long-term planning and policy goals towards a sustainable and low carbon future. The long-term goal of ensuring Ireland is a low carbon economy from 2020 onwards must be at the core of climate policy.

Emissions challenge

Ireland is already facing significant challenges in meeting its EU future emissions targets for greenhouse gases under the EU Climate and Energy package for 2020 and further anticipated longer term targets up to 2050. In 2009 Ireland's total greenhouse gas emissions declined by 7.9 per cent, a decrease across all sectors due to the effects of the economic downturn. However, effective action by all economic sectors is still required if the transition to a low emissions economy is to be achieved.

Ireland's emissions profile is dominated by emissions from the energy supply, transport and agriculture sectors, which together represent 71 per cent of our total national emissions (EPA 2011). Emissions from the industrial and commercial sector reduced by 20 per cent between 2008 and 2009, reflecting decreases in emissions from food process and cement production. Emissions from the energy industry reduced by 10.7 per cent in the same period, reflecting a reduced demand for electricity from end-users. The immediate challenge for Irish climate policy is to meet the EU 2020 targets for the domestic sector, the main being a reduction of at least 20 per cent on 2005 emission levels by 2020. The domestic sector comprises transport, agriculture and residential waste activities and is responsible for 72 per cent of Ireland's total emissions.

Transport and agriculture represent 70 per cent of Ireland's domestic sector emissions. These sectors are the most intractable in terms of carbon offsets and emissions mitigations with the transport sector recording a 156 per cent increase in emissions between 1990 and 2009. A national sustainable transport network will be a major part of moving towards a low carbon, resource efficient economy. Capital investment will be required in sustainable transport infrastructure projects in order to ensure the reduction of transport emissions. Agriculture, which accounted for 29 per cent of total emissions in 2009, faces major difficulties in limiting emissions and meeting future targets. In the agriculture sector progress towards changing farm practices has been limited and incentives to reduce on-farm greenhouse emissions have not been delivered on a wide scale (Curtin & Hanrahan 2012: 9). The agriculture and food sector must build on its scientific and technical knowledge base to meet the emissions challenge.

The European Network For Rural Development has highlighted a number of opportunities for Ireland to use the development of renewable energy to mitigate the effects of climate change by delivering additional reductions to Ireland's CHG emissions. The opportunity and capability exists to significantly mitigate climate change through growth in afforestation and renewable energy sources. Forestry can play a significant role in combating climate change but the development of the forestry sector and renewable energy lacks support in the Irish CAP Rural Development Programme (discussed further in chapter 13). It is important that Government departments work together to tackle climate change and that they also recognise that action on climate change is not just a challenge, but a great opportunity to create jobs and develop and genuine, indigenous, Irish low carbon economy.

Biodiversity

Nature and biodiversity are the basis for almost all ecosystem services. Biodiversity loss is the greatest challenge facing humanity (EPA 2011: vii). Biodiversity loss and ecosystem degradation directly affect climate change and undermine the way we use natural resources (EEAC 2011: 114). Pollution, over-exploitation of natural resources and the spread of non-native species are causing a decline in biodiversity in Ireland. The EPA has identified the four main drivers (EPA 2011: 11) of biodiversity loss in Ireland, all due to human activity. They are:

- habitat destruction and fragmentation; pollution; over exploitation of natural resources; and the spread of non-native species.

Our eco-system is worth €2.6 billion to Ireland annually (EPA 2011) yet our biodiversity capital is decreasing rapidly. Ireland missed the 2010 target to halt biodiversity loss and lacks fundamental information on such issues as the distribution of species and habitats which inform planning and policy in other countries. The fact that responsibility in this important area is now spread across two departments is a cause of some concern. The responsibility for biodiversity lies with the Department of Arts, Heritage and the Gaeltacht, while responsibility for all environmental issues lies with the Department of Environment, Community and Local Government. This requires close co-operation between the two departments to ensure that the policies they implement are complementary each will avoid negative consequences for other areas of environmental concern. Biodiversity underpins our eco-system, which in turn supports our natural capital and in particular the agriculture industry. It is critically important, therefore, that our biodiversity is preserved and maintained and that the effects of policies and developments on biodiversity are closely monitored in order to inform future environmental policies. The economic value of biodiversity, as well as its contribution to society's well-being, needs to more widely promoted and better understood. Climate change is not a problem which will simply go away of its own accord. Significant costs will have to be incurred in order to preserve and conserve our natural resources. The long-term benefits of these investments, however, for both the present and future generations, will far outweigh the initial cost.

Environmental taxation

One of the ways of tackling the challenges outlined above, whilst also broadening the tax base, is through environmental taxation. Eco-taxes put a price on the full costs of resource extraction and pollution and can help Ireland move towards a resource efficient, low carbon green economy. Carbon taxation was introduced in Ireland in Budget 2010 and was increased from €15 to €20 per tonne in Budget 2012. *Social Justice Ireland* welcomed the introduction of a carbon tax but is disappointed that the government has not used some of the money raised through it to target the low income families and rural dwellers who were most affected by this tax. When considering environmental taxation measures the government should ensure that they are structured to be equitable and effective and that they do not place a disproportionate burden on rural communities or lower socio-economic groups.

Key policy priorities on sustainability

- A common understanding of sustainable development must be communicated across all government departments, policy makers, stakeholders and civil society.
- All public policy decisions across Government departments must be underpinned by the principles of sustainability.
- The economic value of biodiversity must be accounted for in all environmental policy decisions.
- Shadow national accounts should be developed in order to move towards a more sustainable, resource efficient model of growth.
- A progressive and equitable environmental taxation system should be developed in a structured way that does not impose a disproportionate burden on certain groups.
- Investment should be made in sustainable infrastructure projects which will have substantial long-term dividends.

13. RURAL DEVELOPMENT

CORE POLICY OBJECTIVE:
RURAL DEVELOPMENT

To secure the existence of substantial numbers of viable communities in all parts of rural Ireland in which every person would have access to meaningful work, adequate income and the social services they require, and where infrastructures needed for sustainable development would be in place.

Rural Ireland continues to change dramatically. Approximately 40 per cent of the population live in rural areas. The need for an integrated transition from an agricultural to a rural development agenda to improve the quality of life of all rural dwellers has never been more pressing. Agriculture, forestry and fishing now account for only 82,500 people classified as employed in Ireland (CSO, 2011). At present those in farming comprise just one-quarter of the rural labour force and are a minority of the rural population.

Farm incomes
Rural income data from the SILC was reviewed in chapter 3. The SILC data reflects the fact that rural Ireland has high dependency levels, increasing out-migration and many small farmers living on very low incomes. The data from the most recent SILC study for 2010 (CSO 2011: 10) shows there is a very uneven national distribution of poverty. The risk of poverty in rural Ireland is 7 percentage points higher than in urban Ireland – 20.0per cent versus 13.1 per cent.

Key farm statistics:
* Family farm income rose from €12,190 in 2009 to €21,500 in 2011, an increase of 76 per cent. This can be attributed mainly to an increase in market value for gross output in 2011 (IFA, 2012).
* The number of farmers with work off the farm fell to 32 per cent in 2010 (Teagasc, 2010).
* Teagasc classified 36,000 Irish farms as being "economically vulnerable", meaning the farm business is not economically viable and neither the farmer nor the spouse works outside the farm in 2010.

- Only 10 per cent of cattle rearing farms were deemed economically viable by Teagasc in 2010.
- The preliminary results of the CSO Agricultural Census 2010 show that the number of farms in Ireland fell from 141,498 in 2000 to 139,800 in 2010, but that average farm size has increased by 4.1 per cent in the same period.
- In 2010 only 29 per cent of Irish farms were classified as full-time farms (Teagasc, 2010).
- Subsidies and direct farm payments accounted for 98 per cent of family farm income on average in 2010 (Teagasc, 2010).

According to Eurostat, real agricultural income per worker in 2011 increased by 30.1 per cent in Ireland. This was mainly due to the rise in the value of agricultural output and an increase in input costs in real terms.[88] As table 13.1 shows, these statistics mask the huge variation in farm income in Ireland as a whole. Only a minority of farmers are at present generating an adequate income from farm activity and even on these farms income lags considerably behind the national average. An important insight into the income of Irish farmers is provided by Teagasc in its National Farm Survey 2010 and the IFA's Farm Income Review 2011. The IFA Farm Income Review shows that overall national farm income (including direct payments) increased by 27 per cent between 2010 and 2011 in money terms. When inflation is taken into account this equates to an increase of 24 per cent in farm income in real terms. The IFA calculates the average farm income was €21,500 in 2011, 70 per cent below the average industrial wage. Table 13.1 below outlines the huge variations in farm income in Ireland in 2011, with 41 per cent of farms in Ireland producing an income of less than €6,500.

Table 13.1: Distribution of Family Farm Income in Ireland 2011

€	< 6,500	6,500 – 13,000	13,000 – 20,000	20,000 – 25,000	25,000 – 40,000	> 40,000
%	41	21	11	6	9	13
Number	40,395	20,695	11,044	5,572	8,457	13,332

Source: IFA Farm Income Review 2011

---

[88] http://ec.europa.eu/ireland/press_office/news_of_the_day/eurostat-agricultural-income-estimates_en.htm

The majority of farm families rely on income support and payments from the state to supplement their income. The latest CSO figures show that the value of subsidies to Irish farms was €1,841m in 2011 (CSO, 2012). Table 13.2 shows that by the end of 2011 there were 11,300 families receiving the Farm Assist payment, an increase of 3,598 since 2006. This increase can be attributed to a combination of falling product prices and the loss of off-farm employment. Off farm employment and income is extremely important to farming households and the fall in availability of off farm employment due to the recession will increase the dependence of farms on direct subsidies to avoid rural poverty and social exclusion.

Table 13.2: Farm Assist Expenditure (€m) 2006-2011

Year	Expenditure (€m)	Number Benefiting	Average Payment
2006	71	7,650	179
2007	79	7,400	205
2008	85	7,710	213
2009	96	8,845	209
2010	111	10,700 199	
2011	112	11,300	190

Source: IFA Farm Income Review 2011

Agriculture and direct employment from agricultural activities have been declining in Ireland. The Department of Agriculture, Food and the Marine has outlined its vision of the future of Irish Agriculture in *Food Harvest 2020* (Department of Agriculture, Food and the Marine, 2011). It envisages that by 2020 the Irish agri-food industry will have developed and grown in a sustainable manner by delivering high quality, natural-based produce. This requires the industry to adopt the "smart economy" approach by investing in skills, innovation and research. This signals a move away from traditional farming methods towards one of collaboration between the agricultural, food and fisheries industries. In tandem with implementation of this policy, significant investment is required in sustainable agriculture, rural poverty and social exclusion programmes to protect vulnerable farm household.

Rural development

Rural development is often confused with agricultural development. But many people living in rural Ireland are not engaged in agriculture and do not benefit from any increases which may occur in agriculture income. As agriculture declines a more comprehensive set of rural development policies is needed. Long-term strategies to address the failures of current and previous policies on critical issues such as infrastructure development, the national spatial imbalance, local access to public services, public transport and local involvement in core decision-making are urgently required. The 1999 White Paper on rural development provided a vision to guide rural development policy as we had advocated for over a decade previously. The current rural development policy, which has been developed within an EU framework and is dominated by the agri-model of rural development, lacks an inclusive, overarching vision. Ireland's rural development policy is outlined in the *CAP Rural Development Programme 2007-2013* under three main priorities (Department of Agriculture, Food and the Marine, 2011):

- improving the competitiveness of the agriculture sector;
- improving the environment and the countryside by support for land management;

and
- improving the quality of life in rural areas and encouraging diversification of economic activity.

The rural development programme is funded by the European Agricultural Fund for Rural Development and by member state contributions. The European Development Programme on which Irish rural development policy is based is divided into four different axes[89]:

- Axis 1: to improve the competitiveness of the agricultural and forestry sector including a range of measures that target human and physical capital in the agriculture, food and forestry sectors and quality production.
- Axis 2: to improve the environment and the countryside providing measures to protect and enhance natural resources, as well as preserving biodiversity, high nature value farming, forestry systems and cultural landscapes.
- Axis 3: to enhance the quality of life in rural areas and diversification of the rural economy offering support to help to develop local infrastructure and human capital in rural areas, to improve the conditions for growth and job creation in all sectors and the diversification of economic activities.
- Axis 4: based on the Leader experience, introduces possibilities for innovative governance through locally based, bottom-up approaches to rural development.

---

[89] For a more detailed breakdown see European Agricultural Fund for Rural Development: http://europa.eu/legislation_summaries/agriculture/general_framework/l60032_en.htm

In the Irish programme items under axis 3 and axis 4 are implemented together under LEADER. Table 13.3 outlines the expenditure on all four axes of the CAP Rural Development Programme in Ireland from 2007 – 2010.

Table 13.3: Financial Implementation of the Rural Development Programme and National

Axis and Total	Revised Funding Allocation in € Million (2007 – 2013) (EAFRD + Matching National +Health Check +EERP funds)	Actual Expenditure in € Million				Cumulative Expenditure -2007-2010 - € Million	Expenditure to date as % of RDP Allocation
		2007	2008	2009	January to June 2010		
Axis 1	483.5	63.2	65.7	74.2	27.6	230.6	47.7%
Axis 2	4,147.1	699.6	568.9	564.3	136.6	1,969.4	47.5%
Axis 3	370.9	0.0	0.0	10.0	6.4	16.4	4.4%
Axis 4	95.5	0.0	0.0	8.8	4.6	13.5	14.1%
Total Axes 1-4	**5,097**	**763**	**635**	**657**	**175**	**2,230**	**43.7%**
Technical	6.0	0.00	0.28	0.24	0.12	0.64	10.7%
Overall RDP	**5,103.1**	**762.8**	**634.8**	**657.5**	**175.3**	**2,230.5**	**43.7%**
% of Total Expenditure		34%	28%	29%	8%	100%	

Source: Indecon, Mid Term Evaluation of CAP Rural Development Plan

Up to late 2011 the Irish programme has used about 53% of the total public expenditure planned and emphasis has been given to agri-environmental payments which represented almost 52 per cent of total public expenditure of the programme up to June 2011. In Ireland activities and programmes aimed at developing a more sustainable rural economy, diversification of economic activity and an improved quality of life in rural areas are lagging being the policies being implemented in axis 1 and axis 2. Measures under axis 3 and 4 only commenced in mid-2009 and only 18.5 per cent of this budget had been spent by June 2010. This poses a significant challenge for government in trying to ensure that the Leader Local Action Groups have the infrastructure and capacity required to accelerate the allocation of funding to projects and actions in order to meet the programme targets.

The primary goals of axes 3 and 4 are to increase the diversification of economic activity in rural areas, enhance the opportunities for alternative business creation in rural areas and to improve the quality of life for rural dwellers. Actions contained in axis 3 and axes 4 are designed to:

- increase economic activity and employment rates in the wider rural economy through encouraging diversification into non-agricultural activities;
- support the creation and development of micro-enterprises in the broader rural economy;
- encourage rural tourism which is built on the sustainable development of Ireland's natural resources, cultural and natural heritage;
- improve access to basic services by rural dwellers e.g. inadequate recreational facilities;
- regenerate villages and their surrounding areas by improving their economic prospects and the quality of life; and
- maintain, restore and upgrade the natural and built heritage.

(Department of Agriculture, Food and the Marine, 2011)

These actions are in line with the AGRI Vision 2015 report (Department of Agriculture, Food and the Marine, 2004), which stated that the primary purpose of rural policy development is to underpin the economic and social well-being of rural communities. This report highlighted the fact that many rural dwellers are not linked to agriculture and that in order to improve the standard of living and quality of life in rural communities opportunities must be created so that the rural economy can develop agriculture in conjunction with much needed alternative enterprises.

It is of concern that the mid-term evaluation of the Rural Development Plan (Indecon, 2010) highlights the need for careful monitoring of expenditure in axes 3 and 4 and the possibility that the expenditure targets will not be met because of the delay in implementing actions under these axes. It is also of concern that the Department of Agriculture, Food and the Marine notes that the on-going reduction in services and enterprise opportunities due to the disproportionate effect of transport and fuel costs represents a threat to the quality of life in rural areas. The National Rural Network should be given adequate funding to ensure that it can continue to be a valuable source of information and in particular can highlight the resources and opportunities available to local rural communities under axes 3 and 4, and to play a role in ensuring this funding is allocated effectively.

With the on-going challenges facing traditional rural sectors, including agriculture, the future success of the rural economy is inextricably linked to the capacity of rural entrepreneurs to innovate and to develop new business opportunities that create jobs and income. The key needs of rural entrepreneurs have been highlighted as (EU Rural Winter Review, 2011):

- better, more locally-led access to finance;
- a shift in the focus of funders from being risk averse and administratively burdensome to effective risk management and outcome orientation;
- harnessing local knowledge at all stages of policy formulation, delivery and evaluation;
- tailoring the speed of funding approval and payment to the speed of business development;
- ensuring the broader community is understanding and supportive of entrepreneurial activity, including the risk of failure;
- developing better communication between national, regional and local participants to ensure the needs of entrepreneurs can be met;
- acknowledging that rising costs and government revenue raising measures can hit rural businesses disproportionately compared to their urban counterparts e.g. fuel is often a bigger cost for rural businesses and entrepreneurs who need to transport produce or goods greater distances.

To support the development of rural enterprise and the creation of employment in rural areas priority must be given to developing an integrated public transport system and a communications and technological infrastructure that will allow them to grow.

Rural transport

The rural transport network is vital for rural communities as a reliable and sustainable transport service. We will maintain and extend the Rural Transport Programme with other local transport services as much as possible (Government of Ireland 2011: 63).

The lack of an accessible, reliable and integrated rural transport system is one of the key challenges facing people living in rural areas. Rural dwellers at present shoulder a disproportionate share of the burden of insufficient public transport. A recent report (EPA 2011: 10) found that 45 per cent of the rural district electoral divisions in Ireland have a minimal level of scheduled public transport services with varying frequency and timing. Among the main identified issues contributing to rural deprivation and depopulation are (McDonagh, Varley & Shortall 2009: 16):

- access to secure and meaningful employment;
- availability of public transport in order to access employment and public services;
- access to childcare; and
- access to transport.

Small rural firms and rural entrepreneurs need to be supported in order to develop their businesses and to overcome their spatial disadvantage and to benefit from the growth of the 'knowledge economy'. Access to sustainable, integrated public transport serving rural Ireland and to reliable high speed broadband must be given priority in order to support rural businesses and the development of the rural economy through diversification and innovation. The current strategy of relying on 'global demand' and FDI led investment has resulted in a widening of the development gap between urban and rural areas. One of the major problems faced by the government in trying to develop and promote sustainable rural communities is the restricted opportunities in secondary labour markets in rural areas. The reliance of rural dwellers on private cars to avail of public services, employment opportunities, healthcare and recreational activities is a key challenge for policy makers. Transport policy must be embedded within access to services, equity and social inclusion. The Rural Transport Programme (formerly the Rural Transport Initiative) has certainly improved access in some areas. However, the lack of a mainstream public transport system means that many rural areas are still not adequately served. People with disabilities, women, older people, low income households and young people are rural groups still at a significant disadvantage in terms of access to public transport. Policy makers must ensure that local government and the local community are actively involved in developing, implementing and evaluating rural transport policies. In 2000 there was a call for a national rural transport policy and the prioritisation of government funding in this area (Farrell, Grant Sparks, 2000). Twelve years later this policy has yet to be delivered. By 2021 it is estimated that 450,000 people could have unmet transport needs, of whom some 240,000 will be from the groups of vulnerable rural dwellers indicated above.

The importance of the rural transport network was highlighted in the *Programme for National Recovery*, yet in Budget 2012 the funding for this initiative was reduced by €0.9m and funding for the Local Community Development programme introduced to tackle poverty and social exclusion was reduced by €8m. It is important that government does not continue to rely on community and voluntary groups as the so called 'provider of last resort' of transport services to vulnerable rural dwellers.

The Department of Transport published its *Value for Money Review of the Rural Transport Programme* (Department of Transport, Tourism and Sport, 2012) in early 2012. Throughout this report reference is made to the lack of data and the evidence needed to evaluate the programme. The government must address this data gap immediately by putting in place structures which enable the providers of the RTP to collect this data. The high administrative costs associated with the RTP are also highlighted by the report, as they were in the earlier Fitzpatrick Report in 2006. Fitzpatrick noted that running the Rural Transport Initiative (now the RTP) had placed a considerable burden of management, administration and governance on RTI groups with little prior experience of such matters. Any expansion to the programme, he cautioned, would lead to an increase to the administrative needs of the RTP groups and the administrative costs to Pobal. This is directly linked to devolving the service to local communities and the lack of a clearly articulated framework for rural transport policy within public transport policy (Fitzpatrick 2006: IV:13:63). The recently published *Value for Money Review of the RTP* does not adequately address the issue of sustainable development and sustainable transport, which should be a key component of any future rural development policy. The main outcome of this review is to highlight the degree of inertia in progressing rural transport policy since the last review in 2006.

A mainstream rural public transport service is required to meet the needs of both existing and potential users. Investment in a national sustainable rural transport network is required to support rural development and to ensure access to employment, and services and to ensure that rural economies are supported in terms of economic diversification. Improved rural public transport and improved accessibility to services also provide Ireland with an opportunity to achieve a modal shift and deliver a significant reduction in CHG emissions (Browne 2011: 12). This is all the more pressing in terms of our EU 2020 emissions target and CHG emissions from private vehicles. By investing in a sustainable national public transport system covering all rural areas government could significantly reduce CHG emission in the longer term.

Future of rural Ireland

The social inclusion aspect of an integrated rural public transport system can no longer be ignored. The links between better participation, better health, access to public services, access to employment opportunities and a public integrated rural transport service have been well documented (Fitzpatrick, 2006). This knowledge, however, has yet to be incorporated fully into rural development policy. Rural Ireland and rural communities are coming under unprecedented pressures and many are fighting for survival. Measures introduced in Budget 2012 are likely to have a negative impact on the weakest people in rural Ireland as inflation rises, unemployment persists and the carbon levy is increased.

The reduction in funding for the Rural Transport Programme will have a negative impact on rural communities for whom adequate public transport infrastructure, services and accessibility of transport is vital to support employment, to develop local enterprise and to provide access to services. Cuts to funding for REPs and changes to the terms of the Disadvantaged Areas and Farm Assist programmes will put further pressure on family farm income, particularly the 41 per cent of farms generating an income of less than €6,500 per year. The continued high rate of general unemployment suggests that people seeking off farm work in order to supplement their farm income will find it increasingly difficult to secure such work.

Rural family incomes are being hit by the increased carbon levy, the doubling of the charge for school transport at primary level, the €50 reduction in the Back to School Clothing and Footwear allowance and the 3 per cent reduction in the maintenance grant for higher education. Small rural schools are under threat with 100 posts due to be lost in 2012 due to the increase in the pupil threshold for teacher allocations in these schools. A value for money review of smaller schools is currently being undertaken by the Department of Education and concerns have already been raised about the significant socio-economic impact of the possible closure of these schools on rural communities. Combined with the planned closure of over 17 rural Garda stations in 2012, the quality of life for rural dwellers and the sustainability of our rural communities are under significant threat. *Social Justice Ireland* believes that we are now reaching a crucial juncture. Important decisions need to be made as a matter of urgency to ensure the very survival of our rural communities.

Key policy priorities on rural development

- Adopt integrated rural development policies in which access to public services and rural transport are priorities.
- Recognise that rural Ireland encompasses far more than just agriculture; develop policies to promote the diversification of the rural economy and support local enterprise.

- Prioritise the roll out of high speed broadband in rural areas.
- Invest in the development of renewable energies to ensure the sustainability of the rural environment.
- Ensure that policies do not have a disproportionate impact on rural dwellers (e.g. carbon levy).
- Ensure all policies are based on equity and social justice and take account of rural disadvantage.

14. THE DEVELOPING WORLD

CORE POLICY OBJECTIVE: THE DEVELOPING WORLD

To ensure that Ireland plays an active and effective part in promoting genuine development in the developing world and to ensure that all Ireland's policies are consistent with such development.

Globally, the scale and extent of underdevelopment and inequality remains large, as indicated by The United Nations *2011 Human Development Report*.

Table14.1:United Nations development indicators by region and worldwide			
Region	GDP per capita (US$ PPP)★	Life Expectancy at Birth (yrs)	Adult Literacy %★★
Least Developed Countries	1,327	59.1	59.2
Arab States	8,554	70.5	72.9
East Asia + Pacific	6,466	72.4	93.5
Europe + Central Asia	12,004	71.3	98.0
L. America + Caribbean	10,119	74.4	91.0
South Asia	3,435	65.9	62.8
Sub-Saharan Africa	1,966	54.4	61.6
Very High HDI^	33,352	80.0	n/a
Worldwide total	**10,082**	**69.8**	**80.9**

Source: UNDP (2011: 130, 161)

Notes: ★ Data adjusted for differences in purchasing power.

★★ Adult defined as those aged 15yrs and above

^47 Countries including the OECD with very high human development indicators

Tables 14.1 (above) and 14.2 (below) show the sustained differences in the experiences of various regions in the world. There are sizeable differences in income levels (GDP per person) between the most developed countries of the world, those in the OECD, and the rest (i.e. the vast majority) of the world. These differences go beyond just income and are reflected in each of the indicators reported in both tables. Today, life expectancies are 25 years higher in the richest countries than in Sub-Saharan Africa. Similarly, the UN reports that more than one in three Southern Asians and Sub-Saharan Africans are unable to read.

These phenomena are also reflected in high levels of absolute poverty, with over 920m people worldwide living below the international poverty line of $1.25 a day, and in the disparate mortality rates shown in table 14.2. The *2011 Human Development Report* shows that almost 13 per cent of all children born in Sub-Saharan Africa died before their fifth birthday. The comparable figure for countries with a very high development index was 6 per cent. There has been some progress on this front as the deaths of children under five declined from 12.4 million in 1990 to 8.1 million in 2009. Despite many successful health aid programmes, however, maternal mortality rates are still very high in developing countries. Table 14.2 shows that there are 537 deaths per 100,000 live births in Least Developed Countries as against 16 in OECD countries.

Table 14.2:Maternal and Infant Mortality Rates		
Region	Maternal Mortality Ratio#	Under-5yrs mortality rate★
Least Developed Countries	537	120
Arab States	192	49
East Asia + Pacific	79	26
Europe + Central Asia	29	19
L. America + Caribbean	80	22
South Asia	252	69
Sub-Saharan Africa	619	129
Very High HDI	16	6
Worldwide total	**176**	**58**

Source: UNDP 2011:142, 161

Notes: # ratio of the number of maternal deaths to the number of live births expressed per 100,000 live births

^47 Countries including the OECD with very high human development indicators

UN millennium development goals

In response to these problems the UN Millennium Declaration was adopted in 2000 at the largest-ever gathering of heads of state. It committed both rich and poor countries to doing all they can to eradicate poverty, promote human dignity and equality and achieve peace, democracy and environmental sustainability. World leaders promised to work together to meet concrete targets for advancing development and reducing poverty by 2015 or earlier. Emanating from the Millennium Declaration, a set of Millennium Development Goals was agreed. These bind countries to do more in the attack on inadequate incomes, widespread hunger, gender inequality, environmental deterioration and lack of education, healthcare and clean water. They also include actions to reduce debt and increase aid, trade and technology transfers to poor countries. These goals and their related targets are:

Goal 1: Eradicate extreme poverty and hunger
Target 1: Between 1990 and 2015, halve the proportion of people whose income is less than $1 a day.
Target 2: Between 1990 and 2015, halve the proportion of people who suffer from hunger.

Goal 2: Achieve universal primary education
Target 3: Ensure that by 2015 children everywhere, boys and girls alike, will be able to complete a full course of primary schooling.

Goal 3: Promote gender equality and empower women
Target 4: Eliminate gender disparity in primary and secondary education, preferably by 2005 and in all levels of education no later than 2015.

Goal 4: Reduce child mortality
Target 5: Between 1990 and 2015 reduce by two-thirds, the under-five mortality rate.

Goal 5: Improve maternal health
Target 6: Between 1990 and 2015 reduce by three-quarters the maternal mortality ratio.

Goal 6: Combat HIV/AIDS, malaria and other diseases
Target 7: Have halted and begun to reverse the spread of HIV/AIDS by 2015.
Target 8: Have halted and begun to reverse the incidence of malaria and other major diseases by 2015.

Goal 7: Ensure environmental sustainability

Target 9: Integrate the principles of sustainable development into country policies and programmes and reverse the loss of environmental resources.

Target 10: Halve the proportion of people without sustainable access to safe drinking water by 2015.

Target 11: Have achieved a significant improvement in the lives of at least 100 million slum dwellers by 2020.

Goal 8: Develop a global partnership for development

Target 12: Develop further an open, rule based, predictable, nondiscriminatory trading and financial system (includes a commitment to good governance, development, and poverty reduction – both nationally and internationally).

Target 13: Address the special needs of the least developed countries (includes tariff and quota free access for exports, enhanced programme of debt relief for and cancellation of official bilateral debt and provide more generous official development assistance for countries committed to poverty reduction).

Target 14: Address the special needs of landlocked countries and small island developing states (through the Programme of Action for the Sustainable Development of Small Island Developing States and 22nd General Assembly provisions).

Target 15: Deal comprehensively with the debt problems of developing countries through national and international measures in order to make debt sustainable in the long term.

Target 16: In cooperation with developing countries, develop and implement strategies for decent and productive work for youth.

Target 17: In cooperation with pharmaceutical companies, provide access to affordable essential drugs in developing countries.

Target 18: In cooperation with the private sector, make available the benefits of new technologies, especially information and communications technologies.
(UNDP, 2003: 1-3)

In September 2010 the world recommitted itself to accelerate progress towards these goals. While we are 10 years into the MDG process, progress on these goals and targets has been mixed with some regions doing better than others. In particular, the UN suggests that East Asia and the Pacific are progressing satisfactorily but that overall human development is proceeding too slowly. Writing in the *2011 MDG Progress Report* the UN Secretary General Ban Ki-Moon, while acknowledging the progress made, said: "we still have a long way to go in empowering women and girls, promoting sustainable development, and protecting the most vulnerable from the devastating effects of multiple crises, be they conflicts, natural disasters or volatility in prices for food and energy. Progress tends to bypass those who are lowest on the economic ladder or are otherwise disadvantaged because of their sex, age, disability or ethnicity. Disparities between urban and rural areas are also pronounced and daunting. Achieving the goals will require equitable and inclusive economic growth – growth that reaches everyone and that will enable all people, especially the poor and marginalized, to benefit from economic opportunities. We must also take more determined steps to protect the ecosystems that support economic growth and sustain life on earth." (UNDP 2011:3) *Social Justice Ireland* believes that the international community needs to play a more active role in assisting less developed countries achieve these goals. The provision of additional financial support will be central to this, while any cutbacks in this support (see below) are likely to undermine progress.

Poverty and its associated implications remain the root causes of regional conflicts and civil wars in many of these poor countries. States and societies that are poor are prone to conflict. It is very difficult for governments to govern effectively when their people cannot afford to pay taxes and industry and trade are almost non-existent. Poverty is also a major cause of environmental degradation. Large-scale food shortages, migration and conflicts lead to environmental pressures.

Clearly poverty in the southern world threatens the very survival of all peoples. It is the major injustice in a world that is not, as a unit, poor. Now, more than ever, the Irish government must exercise its voice within the European Union and in world institutions to ensure that the elimination of poverty becomes the focus of all policy development.

Under the auspices of the OECD Development Co-operation Directorate the fourth High Level Forum on Aid Effectiveness met in Busan, Korea in November 2011. The declaration from the Forum established an agreed framework for development co-operation that embraces the traditional donors, governments, civil society organisations and private funders. Building on previous work, signatories agreed to shared principles to achieve common goals. Because of the broad spectrum of its participants, the Forum provided some hope of progress. However, the outcome is highly dependent on reaching agreement on a set of indicators and targets to monitor progress which has been deferred to June 2012.

Trade and debt

The data in tables 14.1 and 14.2 above underscore the totally unacceptable division that currently exists between rich and poor regions of the world. The persistence of this phenomenon is largely attributable to unfair trade practices and to the backlog of un-payable debt owed by the countries of the South to other governments, to the World Bank, the International Monetary Fund (IMF) and to commercial banks.

The effect of trade barriers cannot be overstated. By limiting or eliminating access to potential markets the Western world is denying poor countries substantial income. A decade ago at the 2002 UN Conference on Financing and Development the President of the World Trade Organisation (WTO), Michael Moore, stated that the complete abolition of trade barriers could "boost global income by $2.8 trillion and lift 320 million people out of poverty by 2015". Research by Oxfam (2002) further shows that goods from poor countries are taxed at four times the rate of goods from rich countries and that 120 million people could be lifted out of poverty if Africa, Latin America and Asia increased their share of world markets by just 1 per cent. It is clear that all countries would gain from trade reform. Such reform is now long overdue.

The high levels of debt experienced by Third World countries have disastrous consequences for the populations of indebted countries. Governments that are obliged to dedicate large proportions of their country's national income to debt repayment cannot afford to pay for health and educational programmes for their people. In 1997, Third World debt totalled over $2.2 trillion. In the same year nearly $250 billion was repaid in interest and loan principal. Africa alone spends four times more on interest on its loans than on healthcare. For every €1 given in aid by rich countries, poor countries pay back nearly €4 in debt repayments. It is not possible for these countries to develop the kind of healthy economies that would facilitate debt repayment when millions of their people are being denied basic healthcare and education and are either unemployed or earn wages so low that they can barely survive.

A process of debt cancellation has been argued for over a number of years and should be further developed beyond the basic schemes introduced in recent years. *Social Justice Ireland* welcomes moves in this direction and, in particular, we welcome the on-going commitment of the Irish government to support such a move. This was a major policy shift, following entrenched opposition by the Department of Finance. It is now important that Ireland campaign on the international stage for this process to be implemented. Given Ireland's current economic circumstances, the Irish population now has a greater appreciation of the implications of these debts and the merit in having them reduced.

Social Justice Ireland believes that Ireland's representatives at the World Bank and the IMF should be more critical of the policies adopted by these bodies. The Department of Finance's annual reports on Ireland's involvement in these organisations reveal an alarming degree of unconditional support. According to these reports, Ireland has unconditionally supported the World Bank's positions in all of the following areas: poverty reduction, gender issues, private-sector development, governance issues and corruption, military spending, post-conflict initiatives and environmentally sustainable projects. This level of support does not match Irish public opinion. NGOs, such as the Debt and Development Coalition, which have done much work on these issues, are very critical of the World Bank policies on issues such as poverty reduction, gender and the environment. We believe that this criticism of government is well founded.

Ireland's commitment to ODA

The international challenge to significantly increase levels of Overseas Development Assistance (ODA) was set out by the former UN Secretary General Kofi Annan shortly after the adoption of the MDGs. He stated that:

> *We will have time to reach the Millennium Development Goals – worldwide and in most, or even all, individual countries – but only if we break with business as usual. We cannot win overnight. Success will require sustained action across the entire decade between now and the deadline. It takes time to train the teachers, nurses and engineers; to build the roads, schools and hospitals; to grow the small and large businesses able to create the jobs and income needed. So we must start now. And we must more than double global development assistance over the next few years. Nothing less will help to achieve the Goals.*

These comments lay down a clear challenge to the international community. *Social Justice Ireland* believes that Ireland can lead the way in responding to that challenge, even against the background of our current economic difficulties.

As table 14.3 shows, over time Ireland has achieved sizeable increases in our ODA allocation. In 2006 a total of €814m (0.53 per cent of GNP) was allocated to ODA – reaching the interim target set by the Government. Budget 2008 further increased the ODA budget to €920.7m (0.6 per cent of GNP). However, since then the

ODA budget has been a focus of government cuts and has fallen by €285m – more than 31 per cent. In 2009 and 2010 these cuts have been focused on the poorest countries and people in the world and we regret this policy choice. Budget 2011 adopted a better approach and focused that Budget's cut, of €35m, on Ireland ODA contributions to international institutions such as the World Bank and the IMF.

Table 14.3: Ireland's net overseas development assistance, 1993-2012		
Year	€m's	% of GNP
1993	69.4	0.18
1994	95.5	0.23
1995	122	0.26
1996	142.3	0.27
1997	157.6	0.26
1998	177.3	0.26
1999	230.3	0.30
2000	254.9	0.28
2001	319.9	0.33
2002	422.1	0.40
2003	445.7	0.38
2004	488.9	0.39
2005	578.5	0.42
2006	814.0	0.53
2007	870.9	0.53
2008	920.7	0.60
2009	696	0.55
2010	671	0.53
2011	636	0.50
2012	639	0.50

Source: CSO (2010:45), Irish Aid (2010:67-69) and various Budget Documents.

Rebuilding our commitment to ODA and honouring the UN target should be important policy paths for Ireland to pursue in the years to come. Not only would they be major successes for government, and an important element in the delivery of promises made in the national agreement, but they would also be of significance internationally. Ireland's success would not only provide additional assistance to needy countries but would also provide leadership to those other European countries who do not meet the target. To date the Irish Aid programme has received deserved praise from the OECD's Development Assistance Committee, which Ireland's aid budget performance in 2007 and as being in international terms at the 'cutting edge' (OECD, 2009). Despite the economic challenges, Ireland currently faces we believe that our commitments in respect of ODA should be honoured. We welcome the commitment of the Government to the 0.7 per cent of GNP target for Overseas Development Aid to be achieved by 2015.

HIV/AIDS

In March 2011 the *UN AIDS Report* showed there were 33.3 million people living with HIV. This was a 27 per cent increase since 1999. However, there was a decrease in new HIV infections in 2010, down about 21 per cent from its peak in 1997. Worldwide, nearly 23 per cent of all people living with HIV are under 24 years and people aged 15-24 years account for 35 per cent of all people becoming newly infected. The poorer African countries are the most severely affected, accounting for 68 per cent of all people living with HIV. They also have 72 per cent of AIDS deaths.

In launching the *UN Aids Report*, UN Secretary General Ban Ki-Moon noted "Every day 7,000 people are newly infected, including 1,000 children. Weak national infrastructures, financing shortfalls and discrimination against vulnerable populations are among the factors that continue to impede access to HIV prevention, treatment, care and support services". The current uncertain economic climate is very challenging for those combating the HIV/AIDS epidemic. The UN notes that in 2009 the funding was lower than in 2008. Despite our difficulties *Social Justice Ireland* urges Government to meet its commitments in this area.

Key policy priorities on the developing world
*   Ensure that Ireland delivers on its promise to meet the United Nations target of contributing 0.7 per cent of GNP to Overseas Development Assistance by the EU deadline of 2015.
*   Take a far more proactive stance at government level on ensuring that Irish and EU policies towards countries in the South are just.
*   Continue to support the international campaign for the liberation of the poorest nations from the burden of the backlog of un-payable debt and take steps to ensure that further progress is made on this issue.
*   Continue to support the implementation of the Millennium Development Goals.

- Engage pro-actively and positively in the Rio+20 process (see chapter 12 on sustainability).
- Work for changes in the existing international trading regimes to encourage fairer and sustainable forms of trade. In particular, resource the development of Ireland's policies in the WTO to ensure that this goal is pursued.
- Ensure that the government takes up a leadership position within the European and international arenas to encourage other states to fund programmes and research aimed at resolving the AIDS/HIV crisis.

15. VALUES

"Few can doubt that we have been in a period of economic transition. The financial collapse has shown that many aspects of the 'new economy', so widely praised just a few years ago, are unstable and unsustainable. For years we were told that we had entered a brand new world of unlimited financial possibilities, brought about by sophisticated techniques and technologies, starting with the internet and the information technology revolution, spread through the world by "globalisation" and managed by 'financial engineers' who, armed with the tools of financial derivatives, could eliminate risk and uncertainty. Now we can see that the new financial structure was a house of cards built on sand, where speculation replaced enterprise and the self-interest of many financial speculators came at the expense of the common good.

While there were many factors that contributed to the financial meltdown of 2008, they start with the exclusion of ethics from economic and business decision making. The designers of the new financial order had complete faith that the 'invisible hand' of market competition would ensure that the self-interested decisions of market participants would promote the common good." (Clark and Alford, 2010).

When the initial shock of the meltdown had been absorbed many questions remained. Why had we failed to see the crash coming? Where did the wealth go? Who benefitted from the meltdown? It is obvious who is bearing the cost of the crash – the unemployed, emigrants who were forced to leave Ireland, poor, sick and vulnerable people who have had their income and social services cut. There is, as a result, much fear, anxiety and anger in our communities. Today, more and more people in society are questioning how the policies and decisions of the past decade could have failed us so badly. The critical issue now is how to prevent a recurrence of this type of economic crash. While some people suggest good regulation as the solution, others believe more radical approaches are necessary.

These reflections and questions bring to the fore the issue of values. Our fears are easier to admit than our values. Do we as a people accept a two-tier society at the same time we deride it in principle? The earlier chapters of this review document many aspects of this divided society. It is obvious that we are becoming an ever more unequal society. Scare resources are being taken from poorer people to offset the debts of bankers and speculators. This shift of resources is made possible by the support of our national value system. This dualism in our values allows us to continue with the status quo. It allows us to implicitly find acceptable the exclusion of almost one sixth of the population from the mainstream of our society while substantial resources and opportunities are channelled towards other groups in society. This dualism operates at the levels of the individual, communities and sectors.

To change this reality requires a fundamental change of values. We need a rational discussion about the kind of society in which in wish to live. To be realistic, this discussion should challenge our values, support us in articulating our goals and help us formulate the way forward. *Social Justice Ireland* wishes to contribute to this dialogue. We approach the task from the concerns and values of the Christian ethos.

Christian values

Christianity subscribes to the values of both human dignity and the centrality of the community. The person is seen as growing and developing in a context that includes other people and the environment. Justice is understood in terms of relationships. The Christian scriptures describe justice as a harmony that comes from fidelity to right relationships with God, people and the environment. A just society is one that is structured in a way which promotes these right relationships so that human rights are respected, human dignity is protected, human development is facilitated and the environment is respected and protected (Healy and Reynolds, 2003:188).

As our societies have grown in sophistication, the need for appropriate structures has become more urgent. The aspiration that everyone should enjoy "the good life" – and the goodwill to make it available to all – are essential ingredients in a just society. But this good life will not happen without the deliberate establishment of structures to facilitate its development. In the past charity, in the sense of alms-giving by some individuals, organisations and Churches on an arbitrary and ad hoc basis, was seen as sufficient to ensure that everyone could cross the threshold of human dignity. Calling on the work of social historians, it could be argued that charity in this sense was never an appropriate method for dealing with poverty. Certainly it is not a suitable methodology for dealing with the problems of today. As recent world disasters have clearly shown, charity and the heroic efforts of voluntary agencies cannot solve these problems on a long-term basis. Appropriate structures are necessary to ensure that every person has access to the resources needed to live life with dignity.

Few people would disagree that the resources of the planet are not just for the use of the present generation but also for the generations still to come. In Old Testament times these resources were closely tied to land and water. A complex system of laws about the Sabbatical and Jubilee years (Lev 25: 1-22, Deut 15: 1-18) was devised to ensure, on the one hand, that no person could be disinherited, and, on the other, that land and debts could not be accumulated. This system also ensured that the land was protected and allowed to renew itself.

These reflections raise questions about ownership. Obviously there was an acceptance of private property, but it was not an exclusive ownership. It carried social responsibilities. We find similar thinking among the leaders of the early Christian community. St John Chrysostom, speaking to those who could manipulate the law so as to accumulate wealth to the detriment of others, taught that "*the rich are in the possession of the goods of the poor even if they have acquired them honestly or inherited them legally*" (Homily on Lazarus). These early leaders also established that a person in extreme necessity has the right to take from the riches of others what he or she needs, since private property has a social quality deriving from the law of the communal purpose of earthly goods (*Gaudium et Spes* 69-71).

In more recent times, Pope Paul VI said "*private property does not constitute for anyone an absolute and unconditional right. No one is justified in keeping for his/her exclusive use what is not needed when others lack necessities....The right to property must never be exercised to the detriment of the common good*" (*Populorum Progressio* No. 23). Pope John Paul II has developed the understanding of ownership, especially in regard to the ownership of the means of production.

One of the major contributors to the generation of wealth is technology. The technology we have today is the product of the work of many people through many generations. Through the laws of patenting and exploration, a very small group of people has claimed legal rights to a large portion of the world's wealth. Pope John Paul II questions the morality of these structures. He says "*if it is true that capital as the whole of the means of production is at the same time the product of the work of generations, it is equally true that capital is being unceasingly created through the work done with the help of all these means of production*". Therefore, no one can claim exclusive rights over the means of production. Rather, that right "*is subordinated to the right to common use, to the fact that goods are meant for everyone*". (*Laborem Exercens* No. 14). Since everyone has a right to a proportion of the goods of the country, society is faced with two responsibilities regarding economic resources. Firstly, each person should have sufficient to access the good life. Secondly, because the earth's resources are finite, and because "more" is not necessarily "better", it is time that society faced the question of putting a limit on the wealth that any person or corporation can accumulate. Espousing the value of environmental sustainability requires a commitment to establish systems that ensure the protection of our planet.

Interdependence, mutuality, solidarity and connectedness are words that are used loosely today to express a consciousness which resonates with Christian values. All of creation is seen as a unit that is dynamic – each part is related to every other part, depends on it in some way and can also affect it. When we focus on the human family, this means that each person depends on others initially for life itself and subsequently for the resources and relationships needed to grow and develop. To ensure that the connectedness of the web of life is maintained, each person, depending on age and ability, is expected to reach out to support others in ways that are appropriate for their growth and in harmony with the rest of creation. This thinking respects the integrity of the person, while recognising that the person can achieve his or her potential only in right relationships with others and the environment.

As a democratic society we elect our leaders regularly. This gives an opportunity to scrutinise the vision politicians have for our society. Because this vision must be based on values, it is worth evaluating the values being articulated and check that the plans proposed will deliver what they are proposed to in terms of advancing these values.

Many people in Irish society would subscribe to the values articulated here. However, appropriate structures and infrastructures are essential for such values to become tangible. These are the values that *Social Justice Ireland* wishes to promote. We wish to work with others to develop and support appropriate systems, structures and infrastructures which will give practical expression to these values in Irish society.

16. REFERENCES

Advisory Group on Unfinished Housing Developments (2011), *Resolving Irelands Unfinished Housing Developments Report of Advisory Group on Unfinished Housing Developments,*
http://www.environ.ie/en/Publications/DevelopmentandHousing/
Housing/FileDownLoad,26678,en.pdf Accessed February 2012

All Ireland Traveller Health Study Team, (2010), *All Ireland Traveller Health Study: Our Geels Summary Of Findings,* School of Public Health, Physiotherapy and Population Science, University College Dublin, Dublin.

Allied Irish Banks (2012), *Housing Market Bulletin – February 2012* AIB Global Treasury Economic Research.

Allied Irish Banks (2011), *Macroeconomic Forecasts*, Dublin, AIB Bank.

An Chomhairle Leabharlanna (2010), *Public Library Authority Statistics Actuals,*
http://www.librarycouncil.ie/publications_archive/documents/2010Actuals.pdf
Accessed February 2012

Bank for International Settlements (2010), *Triennial Central Bank Survey of Foreign Exchange and Derivatives Market Activity*, Basel, BIS

Barrett, A. and C. Wall (2006), *The Distributional Impact of Ireland's Indirect Tax System,* Dublin, Combat Poverty Agency.

Begg, D. (2003), "The Just Society - Can we afford it?" in Reynolds B. and S. Healy (eds.) *Ireland and the Future of Europe: leading the way towards inclusion?*, Dublin, CORI.

Bennett M., D. Fadden,. D. Harney, P. O'Malley, C. Regan and. L. Sloyan (2003) *Population Ageing in Ireland and its Impact on Pension and Healthcare Costs.* Report of Society of Actuaries Working Party on Population Studies. Society of Actuaries in Ireland.

Bergin A., Fitz Gerald J. and Kearney I. (2002), *The Macro-economic Effects of Using Taxes or Emissions Trading Permits to Reduce Greenhouse Gas Emissions,* paper presented to ESRI conference entitled "The sky's the limit: efficient and fair policies on global warming", December, Dublin.

Bristow, J. (2004). *Taxation in Ireland: an economist's perspective*, Dublin, Institute of Public Administration.

Browne, D, Caulfield, B and O'Mahony, M (2011), *Barriers to Sustainable Transport in Ireland* in Climate Change Research Programme (CCRP) 2007-2013 Report Series No. 7; Dublin; EPA available at http://www.epa.ie/downloads/pubs/research/climate/CCRP%20Report%20Series%20No.%207%20%20Barriers%20to%20Sustainable%20Transport%20in%20Ireland.pdf Accessed March 2012

Browne, M. (2007), *The Right Living Space, Housing and Accommodation Needs of People with Disabilities,* A Citizens Information Board/Disability Federation of Ireland Social Policy Report.

Brueggeman, W. (2009), *From Anxiety and Greed to Milk and Honey,* available at http://sojo.net/magazine/2009/02/anxiety-and-greed-milk-and-honey Accessed March 2012.

Cafferkey, G. and B. Caulfield (2011), Examining the barriers to sustainable inter-city transport in Ireland http://www.itrn.ie/uploads/sesD2_ID123.pdf Accessed March 2012

Carers Association (2010), *Pre-Budget Submission,* Tullamore, Carers Association.

Caritas Europa (2011), *Shadow Report on Europe 2020 Strategy,* Brussels, Caritas Europa.

Carneiro, P and J. Heckman (2003), *NBER Working Paper Series: Human Capital Policy* Cambridge MA; National Bureau of Economic Research.

Carrie, A. (2005), "Lack of long-run data prevents us tracking Ireland's social health" in *Feasta Review No2 Growth: the Celtic Cancer* Dublin, Feasta.

Central Bank (2012), *Residential Mortgage Arrears, Restructures and Repossessions Statistics - Trend Data,* http://www.centralbank.ie/press-area/press-releases/Documents/Residential%20Mortgage%20Arrears%20and%20Repossession%20Statistics%20-%20Trend%20to%20December%202011.pdf Accessed February 2012

Central Statistics Office (2012), *Live Register – February 2012,* Dublin, Stationery Office.

Central Statistics Office (2012), *Census of Agriculture 2010 Preliminary Results* Dublin, Stationery Office.

Central Statistics Office (2012), Statistical Data Bank, National Income and Expenditure annual results, various years, selected from table N1022:T22. *Details on Taxation by Statistical Indicator and Year,* available at www.cso.ie Accessed February 2012

Central Statistics Office (2012), *Output, Input and Income in Agriculture 2011- Preliminary estimate* Dublin, Stationery Office.

Central Statistics Office (2012), *Quarterly National Household Survey Quarter 4 2011* Dublin, Stationery Office.

Central Statistics Office (2012) *Quarterly National Household Survey Quarter 2 2011, Response of Households to the Economic Downturn – Pilot module* Dublin, Stationery Office.

Central Statistics Office (2011), *Household Budget Survey,* Dublin, Stationery Office.

Central Statistics Office (2011) *Information Society and Telecommunications in Households 2009-2011,* http://www.cso.ie/en/media/csoie/releasespublications /documents/informationtech/2011/isth2009-2011.pdf Accessed February 2012

Central Statistics Office (2011), *Census of Population 2011 Preliminary Results,* http://www.cso.ie/en/media/csoie/census/documents/Prelim%20complete.pdf Accessed February 2012

Central Statistics Office (2011), *Measuring Ireland's Progress 2010,* Dublin, Stationery Office.

Central Statistics Office (2011), *Population and Migration Estimates April 2011* Dublin, Stationery Office.

Central Statistics Office (2011). *National Income and Expenditure Accounts 2010,* Dublin, Stationery Office.

Central Statistics Office (2011), *Quarterly National Household Survey Quarter 3 2011* Dublin, Stationery Office.

Central Statistics Office (2011), *Quarterly National Household Survey Voter Participation Quarter 2 2011* Dublin, Stationery Office.

Central Statistics Office (2011), *Statistical Yearbook of Ireland 2011*, Dublin, Stationery Office.

Central Statistics Office (2011), *Quarterly National Household Survey Quarter 2 2011 Educational Thematic Report 2011* Dublin, Stationery Office.

Central Statistics Office (2011) *Survey on Income and Living Conditions 2010 – Preliminary Results,* Dublin, Stationery Office.

Central Statistics Office (2011) *Quarterly National Household Survey Quarter 3 2010, Health Status and Health Service Utilisation* Dublin, Stationery Office.

Central Statistics Office (2011), *Quarterly National Accounts*, Dublin, Stationery Office

Central Statistics Office (2010), *Quarterly National Household Survey Equality Quarter 4 2010* Dublin, Stationery Office.

Central Statistics Office (2010), *Survey on Income and Living Conditions 2009 Results,* Dublin, Stationery Office.

Central Statistics Office (2010), *National Disability Survey 2006 – Volume two.* Dublin, Stationery Office.

Central Statistics Office (2010), *Quarterly National Household Survey: Special Module on Carers Quarter 3 2009*, Dublin, Stationery Office.

Central Statistics Office (2009), *Quarterly National Household Survey Quarter 3 2009,* Dublin, Stationery Office.

Central Statistics Office (2009), *Survey on Income and Living Conditions 2008 Results,* Dublin, Stationery Office.

Central Statistics Office (2009), *Measuring Ireland's Progress 2008,* Dublin, Stationery Office.

Central Statistics Office (2008), *Population and Labour Force Projections 2011-2041,* Dublin, Stationery Office.

Central Statistics Office (2008), *National Disability Survey 2006 – First Results.* Dublin, Stationery Office.

Central Statistics Office (2007), *Census 2006: Various Volumes,* Dublin, Stationery Office.

Central Statistics Office (2007), *Census 2006: Principal Demographic Results,* Dublin, Stationery Office.

Central Statistics Office (2007), *Census 2006: Volume 11 Disability, Carers and Voluntary Activities,* Dublin, Stationery Office.

Central Statistics Office (2007), *Household Budget Survey,* Dublin, Stationery Office.

Central Statistics Office (2007), *Quarterly National Household Survey Quarter 4 2006* Dublin, Stationery Office.

Central Statistics Office (2006), *Industrial Earnings and Hours Worked,* Dublin, Stationery Office.

Central Statistics Office (2004), *Industrial Earnings and Hours Worked,* Dublin, Stationery Office.

Central Statistics Office (2004), *Quarterly National Household Survey: Special Module on Disability Quarter 1 2004,* Dublin, Stationery Office.

Central Statistics Office (2003), *Census 2002: Various Volumes,* Dublin, Stationery Office.

Central Statistics Office (various), *Quarterly National Accounts,* Dublin, Stationery Office

Central Statistics Office (various), *Earnings and Labour Costs,* Dublin, Stationery Office.

Central Statistics Office (various), *Survey on Income and Living Conditions Results,* Dublin, Stationery Office.

Chambers of Commerce of Ireland (2004), *Local Authority Funding – Government in Denial,* Dublin

Clark C.M.A. and H. Alford (2010), *Rich and Poor: Rebalancing the economy*, London CTS.

Clark C.M.A. (2002), *The Basic Income Guarantee: ensuring progress and prosperity in the 21st century*, Dublin, Liffey Press and CORI Justice Commission.

Coates, D., Kane, F. & Treadwell Shine, K. (2008) *Traveller Accommodation in Ireland Review of Policy and Practice (Housing Policy Discussion series 3)*, Centre for Housing Research, Dublin.

Collins, M.L. and A. Larragy (2011), 'A Site Value Tax for Ireland: approach, design and implementation' *Trinity Economics Papers Working Paper 1911*. Dublin, Trinity College Dublin.

Collins M.L. (2011). "Taxation". In O'Hagan, J. and C. Newman (eds.), *The Economy of Ireland* (11th edition). Dublin, Gill and Macmillan.

Collins, M.L. (2011), *Establishing a Benchmark for Ireland's Social Welfare Payments.* Paper for Social Justice Ireland. Dublin, Social Justice Ireland.

Collins, M.L. and M. Walsh (2010), *Ireland's Tax Expenditure System: International Comparisons and a Reform Agenda – Studies in Public Policy No. 24*, Dublin, Policy Institute, Trinity College Dublin.

Collins, M.L. (2006), *"Poverty: Measurement, Trends and Future Directions"*, in Healy, S., B. Reynolds and M.L. Collins, Social Policy in Ireland: Principles, Practice and Problems, Dublin, Liffey Press.

Collins M.L. and S. Healy (2006), "Work, Employment and Unemployment", in Collins, M.L., S. Healy and B. Reynolds (eds.), *Social Policy in Ireland, Principles, Practice and Problems (2nd edition)*. Dublin, Liffey Press.

Collins, M.L. and C. Kavanagh (2006), *"The Changing Patterns of Income Distribution and Inequality in Ireland, 1973-2004"*, in Healy, S., B. Reynolds and M.L. Collins, Social Policy in Ireland: Principles, Practice and Problems, Dublin, Liffey Press.

Collins, M.L. (2004), "Taxation in Ireland: an overview" in B. Reynolds, and S. Healy (eds.) *A Fairer Tax System for a Fairer Ireland,* Dublin, CORI Justice Commission.

Collins, M.L. and C. Kavanagh (1998), *"For Richer, For Poorer: The Changing Distribution of Household Income in Ireland, 1973-94",* in Healy, S. and B. Reynolds, Social Policy in Ireland: Principles, Practice and Problems, Dublin, Oak Tree Press.

Collins, M.L., B. Mac Mahon, G. Weld and R. Thornton (2012), *A Minimum Income Standard for Ireland – a consensual budget standards study examining household types across the lifecycle – Studies in Public Policy No. 27,* Dublin, Policy Institute, Trinity College Dublin.

Comhar (2008), *A Study in Carbon Allocation: Cap and Share,* Dublin, Comhar Sustainable Development Council.

Comhar (2002), *Principles for Sustainable Development,* Dublin; Stationery Office.

Comhar and Irish Rural Link (2009), *Towards a Sustainable Rural Transport Policy* http://www.comharsdc.ie/_files/Final%20Rural%20Transport%20Report_Website%20Version.pdf Accessed February 2012

Commission for Communications Regulation, (2011), *Provision of Universal Service by eircom, Performance Data – Q3 2011 (1 July 2011 to 30 September 2011),* http://www.comreg.ie/_fileupload/publications/ComReg11104.pdf Accessed February 2012

Commission on Taxation (2009), *Commission on Taxation Report 2009.* Dublin, Stationery Office.

Commission on Taxation (1982), *Commission on Taxation First Report.* Dublin, Stationery Office.

Considine, M & F. Dukelow (2009), *Irish Social Policy a Critical Introduction,* Gill and Macmillan, Dublin.

Costanza, R., Hart, M., Posner S. and Talberth, J. (2009), *Beyond GDP: The Need for New Measures of Progress,* Boston University, The Pardee Papers.

Coughlan, O (2007), *Irish Climate Change Policy from Kyoto to the Carbon Tax: a Two-level Game Analysis of the Interplay of Knowledge and Power,* available at http://www.climatechange.ie/pdf/carbon_tax_2007.pdf, Accessed February 2012

Council for Justice and Peace of the Irish Episcopal Conference (2012), *Caring for Health in Ireland*, Veritas, Dublin.

Council of Europe (2011), *Charter on Shared Social Responsibilities* Strasbourg, Council of Europe.

Curtin, J. and G. Hanrahan (2012), *Why Legislate? Designing a Climate Law for Ireland*, Dublin, The Institute of International and European Affairs.

Daft (2012) The Daft.ie Rental Report, *An analysis of recent trends in the Irish rental market, 2011 in review* www.daft.ie/report/Daft-Rental-Report-Q4-2011.pdf Accessed March 2012

Dalal-Clayton, B. & S. Bass (2002), *Sustainable development strategies: a resource book,* OECD: Paris.

Daly, H.E and J.B. Cobb (1987), *For the Common Good: Redirecting the Economy toward Community, the Environment and a Sustainable Future,* Boston: Beacon Press

Department of Agriculture, Food and the Marine (2011), *Food Harvest 2020* http://www.agriculture.gov.ie/media/migration/agri-foodindustry/foodharvest2020/2020FoodHarvestEng240810.pdf Accessed February 2012

Department of Agriculture, Food and the Marine (2007), *Ireland CAP Rural Development Programme 2007-2013* Dublin, Department of Agriculture, Food and the Marine.

Department of Agriculture, Food and the Marine (2004), *Agri-Vision 2015* http://www.agri-vision2015.ie/AgriVision2015_PublishedReport.pdf Accessed February 2012

Department of An Taoiseach (2011), *Ireland's National Reform Programme* Dublin, Stationery Office.

Department of An Taoiseach (2006) *Towards 2016 - Ten-Year Framework Social Partnership Agreement 2006-2015*, Dublin, Stationery Office.

Department of An Taoiseach (2002), *Basic Income, A Green Paper*, Dublin, Stationery Office.

Department of An Taoiseach (2001), *Final Report of the Social Welfare Benchmarking and Indexation Group*, Dublin, Stationery Office.

Department of Communications, Energy and Natural Resources, (2011), *Government convenes CEO Taskforce on High Speed Broadband Rollout* (press releases) http://www.dcenr.gov.ie/Press+Releases/2011/Faster+Broadband+to+More+Places+Quicker.htm Accessed February 2012

Department of Education and Skills (2012), *Report to the Minister for Education and Skills on the impact in terms of posts in Budget measures in relation to The Withdrawal form DEIS Band 1 and Band 2 Urban Primary Schools of Posts from Disadvantage Schemes pre-dating DEIS* available at http://www.education.ie/servlet/blobservlet/ deis_legacy_posts_report_2012.pdf Accessed March 2012

Department of Education and Skills (2012), *Minister Quinn announces details of 275 major school building projects* (press release) available at http://www.education.ie/ home/home.jsp?maincat=10861&pcategory=10861&ecategory=10876&section page=12251&language=EN&link=link001&page=1&doc=56781 Accessed March 2012

Department of Education and Skills (2011), *2011-2031, Twenty Years of Radical Reform* Speech by Minister for Education and Skills Ruairi Quinn, TD at the MacGill Summer School, Glenties, Co. Donegal available at http://www.education.ie/robots/view.jsp?pcategory=10861&language= EN&ecategory=10876&link=link001&doc=55526 Accessed March 2012

Department of Education and Skills (2011), *An Evaluation of Planning Processes in DEIS Post-Primary Schools* Dublin, Stationery Office.

Department of Education and Skills (2011), *An Evaluation of Planning Processes in DEIS Primary Schools* Dublin, Stationery Office.

Department of Education and Skills (2011), *Comprehensive Review of Current Expenditure* available at http://per.gov.ie/wp-content/uploads/Department-of-Education-Skills.pdf last Accessed 3 March 2012

Department of Education and Skills (2011), *Information Note regarding main features of 2012 Estimates for Education and Skills Vote* available at http://www.education.ie/admin/servlet/blobservlet/pr_list_final_051211a.pdf?l anguage=EN&igstat=true Accessed March 2012

Department of Education and Skills (2011), *Literacy and Numeracy for Learning and Life* Dublin, Stationery Office.

Department of Education and Skills (2011), *National Strategy for Higher Education to 2030* Dublin, Stationery Office.

Department of Education and Skills (2009), *Policy Options for New Student Contributions in Higher Education: Report to Minister for Education and Science* Dublin.

Department of Environment, Community and Local Government (2012) Minister for Housing and Planning, Ms. Jan O'Sullivan T.D announces first Transaction under the Mortgage to Rent scheme, http://www.environ.ie/en/Development Housing/Housing/News/MainBody,29400,en.htm Accessed February 2012

Department of Environment, Community and Local Government (2011), *Interim Report of the Local Government/Local Development Alignment Steering Group* available at http://www.environ.ie/en/Community/AlignmentofLocalGovtLocalDev/Publi cationsDocuments/FileDownLoad,28839,en.pdf Accessed March 2012

Department of Environment, Community and Local Government (2011), *A Draft Framework for Sustainable Development for Ireland,* available at http://www.environ.ie /en/Publications/Environment/Miscellaneous/FileDownLoad,29081,en.pdf Accessed February 2012

Department of Environment, Community and Local Government (2011), *A Roadmap for Climate Policy and Legislation* available at http://www.environ.ie/en/Environment/Atmosphere/News/MainBody,29241, en.htm Accessed March 2012

Department of the Environment, Community and Local Government (2011*), Press release announcing climate policy review,* available at http://www.environ.ie/en/Environment/Atmosphere/ClimateChange/Climate

PolicyReview2011/News/MainBody,28331,en.htm Accessed March 2012

Department of Environment, Community and Local Government (2011), *Review of National Climate Policy* available at http://www.environ.ie/en/Environment/Atmosphere/ClimateChange/Climate PolicyReview2011/PublicationsDocuments/FileDownLoad,28328,en.pdf Accessed February 2012

Department of Environment, Community and Local Government, (2011a), *2011 National Housing Development Survey Summary Report,* *http://www.environ.ie/en/Publications/DevelopmentandHousing/Housing/HousingSur vey2011/FileDownLoad,28126,en.doc* Accessed February 2012

Department of Environment, Community and Local Government, (16 June 2011b) *Housing Policy Statement* http://www.environ.ie/en/Publications/DevelopmentandHousing/Housing/Fil eDownLoad,26867,en.pdf Accessed February 2012

Department of Environment, Community and Local Government, (2011c), *National Housing Strategy for People with a Disability 2011-2016* http://www.environ.ie/en/DevelopmentHousing/Housing/PublicationsDocum ents/FileDownLoad,28016,en.pdf Accessed February 2012

Department of Environment, Community and Local Government, (2011d), *Hogan and NAMA Agree 2,000 New Housing Units for those on Social Housing Lists,* http://www.environ.ie/en/DevelopmentHousing/Housing/News/MainBody,2 9071,en.htm Accessed February 2012

Department of Environment Heritage and Local Government, (2009) *Annual Housing Statistics Bulletin 2008* http://www.environ.ie/en/Publications/StatisticsandRegularPublications/Housi ngStatistics/FileDownLoad,20957,en.pdf Accessed February 2012
Department of Environment, Heritage and Local Government (2008), *Statement of Strategy* Dublin, Stationery Office.

Department of the Environment Heritage and Local Government, (2008), *The Way Home: A Strategy to Address Adult Homelessness in Ireland 2008 - 2013* http://www.homelessagency.ie/getdoc/2b0b1ff1-7527-466a-b973-2fe320346d8e/The-Way-Home—-A-Strategy-to-Address-Adult-Homeles.aspx Accessed February 2012

Department of the Environment, Heritage and Local Government (various), *Housing Statistics Bulletin,* Dublin, Stationery Office.

Department of Finance (2012), *Monthly Economic Bulletin- February 2012,.* Department of Finance

Department of Finance (2012), *Finance Bill,* Dublin, Stationery Office.

Department of Finance (2011*), Budget 2012,* Dublin, Stationery Office.

Department of Finance (2011), *Medium Term Fiscal Statement* Dublin, Stationery Office.

Department of Finance (2007), *Budget 2008 – Income Tax Ready Reckoner,* Dublin, Stationery Office.

Department of Finance (2006), *Budget 2006 – Review of Tax Schemes Volumes I, II and III.* Dublin, Stationery Office.

Department of Finance (various*), Budget Documentation – various years,* Dublin, Stationery Office.

Department of Health (2011), *Primary Care – A New Direction* Dublin, Stationery Office.

Department of Health, (2011) *Key Trends 2011* Dublin, Stationery Office.

Department of Health (2010), *Medical Cards/GP Visit Cards October 2010: Fact Sheet.* Dublin available at http://www.dohc.ie/fact_sheets/medicalcards_factsheet102010.pdf?direct=1 Accessed March 2012.

Department of Health (2008), *A Fair Deal – The Nursing Home Care Support Scheme,* Dublin; Stationery Office.

Department of Health (2006), *A Vision for Change – Report of the Expert Group on Mental Health Policy,* Dublin; Stationery Office

Department of Health and Children (2002) *Annual Report of the Chief Medical Officer 2002* Department of Health and Children, Dublin, Stationery Office.

Department of Health and Children (2001), *Quality and Fairness: A Health System for You,* Dublin, Stationery Office.

Department of Health and Children (2000), *National Children's Strategy, Our Children their Lives* Dublin; Stationery Office.

Department of Justice, Equality and Defence (2011), *Immigration in Ireland 2011 – a year end snapshot* available at http://www.inis.gov.ie/en/INIS/Pages/Immigration%20in%20Ireland%202011%20%E2%80%93%20a%20year-end%20snapshot%20%E2%80%93%20major%20changes%20and%20more%20to%20follow Accessed March 2012

Department of Public Expenditure and Reform (2011) *Comprehensive Expenditure Review 2012-2014,* Government Publications December 2011 available at http://www.budget.gov.ie/Budgets/2012/Documents/CER%20-%20Estimates%20Final.pdf Accessed March 2012

Department of Social Protection (2011) *Comprehensive Review of Expenditure,* http://www.welfare.ie/EN/Policy/CorporatePublications/Finance/exp_rev/Documents/Comprehensive_Review_of_Expenditure_2011.pdf Accessed February 2012

Department of Social, Community and Family Affairs (2000), *Supporting Voluntary Activity*, Dublin, Stationery Office.

Department of Social, Community and Family Affairs (1999), *Report of the Working Group Examining the Treatment of Married, Cohabiting and One-Parent Families under the Tax and Social Welfare Codes,* Dublin, Stationery Office

Department of Transport, Tourism and Sport (2012), *Value for Money and Policy Review of the Rural Transport Programme* http://www.dttas.ie/uploads/documents/feature/20110630%20VFM%20FINAL%20REPORT.pdf Accessed February 2012

Department of Transport (2009), *A Sustainable Transport Future A New Transport Policy for Ireland 2009 - 2020* http://smartertravel.ie/sites/default/files/uploads/pdfs/NS1264_Smarter_Travel_english_PN_WEB.pdf Accessed February 2012 Accessed March 2012

Disability Federation of Ireland (2007), *Pre-Budget Submission for Budget 2008*, Dublin, DFI.

Douthwaite, R. (2004), "Tradable Quotas: the fairer alternative to eco-taxation" in B. Reynolds, and S. Healy (eds.) *A Fairer Tax System for a Fairer Ireland*, Dublin, CORI Justice Commission.

Drudy, P.J. and M.L. Collins (2011), Ireland: From Boom to Austerity. *Cambridge Journal of Regions, Economy and Society* - September.

Drudy, P.J. (2006), "Housing in Ireland: Philosophies, Problems and Policies", in Healy, S., B. Reynolds and M.L. Collins, *Social Policy in Ireland: Principles, Practice and Problems*, Dublin, Liffey Press.

Drudy, P.J. and M. Punch (2005), *Out of Reach: Inequalities in the Irish Housing System*, Dublin, Tasc at New Island.

Dunne, T. (2004), "Land Values as a Source of Local Government Finance" in B. Reynolds, and S. Healy (eds.) *A Fairer Tax System for a Fairer Ireland*, Dublin, CORI Justice Commission.

Economic and Social Research Institute (2011), *Quarterly Economic Commentary - November 2011*, ESRI: Dublin.

Economic and Social Research Institute (2003), *National Development Plan Mid-Term Review*, Dublin, ESRI.

http://www.eeac.eu/images/doucments/eeac-statement-backgr2011_rio_final_144dpi.pdf Accessed February 2012

Employers' Diversity Network (2009), *Issues and Challenges in the Recruitment and Selection of Immigrant Workers in Ireland* Dublin, Stationery Office.

EPA (2012), *A Focus on Urban Waste Water Discharges in Ireland* EPA; Dublin.

EPA (2012), *A Year in Review – Highlights from 2011* available at
http://epa.ie/downloads/pubs/other/corporate/Statement%202011.pdf
Accessed March 2012

EPA (2012), *National Waste Report 2010* available at
http://epa.ie/downloads/pubs/waste/stats/National%20Waste%20Report_web.
pdf Accessed March 2012

EPA (2011), *Biochange: Biodiversity and Environmental Change: An Integrated Study
Encompassing a Range of Scales, Taxa and Habitats*; Wexford, EPA.

EPA (2011), *Ireland's Greenhouse Gas Emissions in 2010* available at
http://www.epa.ie/downloads/pubs/air/airemissions/GHG_1990-
2010_Provisional_2012.pdf Accessed March 2012

EPA (2011), *Ireland's Greenhouse Gas Emissions Projections 2010-2020,* available at
http://epa.ie/downloads/pubs/air/airemissions/EPA%20GHG%20Emission%20
Projections_FINAL.pdf, Accessed February 2012

EPA (2010), *Environmental Protection Agency Biodiversity Action Plan,* available at
http://epa.ie/downloads/pubs/biodiversity/EPA%20Bio%20AP_final.pdf
Accessed February 2012

EPA (2010), *Water Quality in Ireland 2007-2009*; Dublin, EPA.

Economic and Social Research Institute (2012), *Quarterly Economic Commentary
Winter 2011/Spring 2012,* Dublin, ESRI.

Eurofound (2011), *Shifts in the job structure in Europe during the Great Recession*
Luxembourg: Publications Office of the European Union.
European Council (2012), *Treaty on Stability, Coordination and Governance in the
Economic and Monetary Union,* Brussels: European Union.

Eurostat (2011), *Taxation trends in the European Union,* Luxembourg, Eurostat.

Eurostat (2010), *Taxation Trends in the European Union,* Luxembourg, Eurostat.

Eurostat (2008), *Taxation Trends in the European Union,* Luxembourg, Eurostat.

Eurostat (2004), *Taxation trends in the European Union,* Luxembourg, Eurostat.

European Commission, (2011), *Commission Staff Working Paper Accompanying the White Paper - Roadmap to a Single European Transport Area – Towards a competitive and resource efficient transport system* http://eurlex.europa.eu/LexUriServ/LexUriServ.do?uri=SEC:2011:0391:FIN: EN:PDF Accessed February 2012

European Commission (2011), *The Social Dimension of the Europe 2020 Strategy A report of the Social Protection Committee,* Luxembourg: Publications Office of the European Union.

European Commission (2011), A *resource-efficient Europe – Flagship initiative under the Europe 2020 Strategy,* available at http://ec.europa.eu/resource-efficient-europe/pdf/resource_efficient_europe_en.pdf, Accessed February 2012

European Commission (2011), *Early Childhood Education and Care: Providing all our children with the best start for the world of tomorrow,* Brussels available at http://ec.europa.eu/education/school-education/doc/childhoodcom_en.pdf Accessed March 2012

European Commission (2011), *Our life insurance, our natural capital: an EU biodiversity strategy to 2020,* available at http://ec.europa.eu/environment/nature/biodiversity/comm2006/pdf/2020/1_ EN_ACT_part1_v7%5B1%5D.pdf, Accessed February 2012

European Commission (2011), *Strategic framework for European cooperation in education and training (ET 2020)* Brussels, European Commission.

European Commission (2011), *Proposal for a Council Directive on a common system of financial transaction tax and amending Directive 2008/7/EC* Brussels, European Commission available at http://ec.europa.eu/taxation_customs/resources/documents/taxation/other_tax es/financial_sector/com%282011%29594_en.pdf Accessed March 2012.

European Commission (2010), *Digital Scorecard,* http://ec.europa.eu/information_society/digital-agenda/scoreboard/countries/ie/index_en.htm Accessed March 2012

European Commission (2010), *Eurobarometer 74 Autumn 2010 Report* Brussels, European Commission.

European Commission (2010), *Europe 2020: A strategy for smart, sustainable and inclusive growth;* Brussels, European Commission available at http://eur-lex.europa.eu/LexUriServ/LexUriServ.do?uri=COM:2010:2020:FIN:EN:PDF Accessed March 2012

European Commission (staff working document), (2008) *Digital Literacy Report: a review for the i2010 eInclusion Initiative Digital Literacy: High-Level Expert Group Recommendations,* http://ec.europa.eu/information_society/eeurope/i2010/docs/digital_literacy/digital_literacy_review.pdf Accessed February 2012

European Commission against Racism and Intolerance (2007), *Third Report on Ireland* Strasbourg.

European Migration Network (2012), *Useful Statistics* available at http://www.emn.ie/index.jsp?p=100&n=128&a=0 Accessed March 2012

European Network for Rural Development (2011), *Climate Change and Renewable Energy measures in EU RDPs 2007-2013 Member state profile – Ireland* http://enrd.ec.europa.eu/app_templates/filedownload.cfm?id=FAE991FE-AB14-65CF-0E42-934C9205DAAB Accessed February 2012

European Network for Rural Development (2011), *EU Rural Review Winter 2011* Belgium http://enrd.ec.europa.eu/app_templates/filedownload.cfm?id=1E1424B0-CF45-6AB3-5A47-F709F850C016 Accessed February 2012

European Network for Rural Development (2010), *Climate Change and Renewable Energy measures in EU RDPs 2007-2013 Ireland* http://enrd.ec.europa.eu/app_templates/filedownload.cfm?id=FAE991FE-AB14-65CF-0E42-934C9205DAAB, Accessed February 2012

European Parliament & Council of Europe (2006), *Key Competences for Lifelong Learning,* Brussels

Expert Group on Future Skills Needs (2007), *Tomorrow's skills – Towards a National Skills Strategy,* Dublin; Stationery Office

Farrell, C., McAvoy, H. Wilde, J. & Combat Poverty Agency, (2008), *Tackling Health Inequalities an All-Ireland Approach to Social Determinants,* Dublin, Combat Poverty Agency/Institute of Public Health.

Feasta and New Economics Foundation (NEF) (2006), *The Great Emissions Rights Give-Away*. Feasta and NEF.

Fitzpatrick & Associates for Department of Transport (2006), *Progressing Rural Public Transport in Ireland* https://www.pobal.ie/Funding%20Programmes/RTP/Beneficiaries/Publication s/2006%20report%20Progressing%20Rural%20Public%20Transport.pdf Accessed February 2012

Forfás & National Competitiveness Council (2011), *Ireland's Competitiveness Challenge 2011* Dublin, Stationery Office.

Forfás (2011), *Ireland's Advanced Broadband Performance and Policy Priorities,* http://www.forfas.ie/publication/search.jsp?ft=/publications/2011/Title,8528,e n.php Accessed March 2012

Forfás (2009), *Sharing our future: Ireland 2025,* Dublin; Stationery Office

Goldberg, F.T., L.L. Batchelder and P.R. Orszag (2006), *Reforming Tax Incentives into Uniform Refundable Tax Credits,* Washington, Brookings.

Government of Ireland (2011), *Towards Recovery: Programme for a National Government 2011-2016* Dublin, Stationery Office.

Government of Ireland (2010), *National Pensions Strategy.* Dublin, Stationery Office.

Government of Ireland (2007), *National Climate Change Strategy.* Dublin, Stationery Office.

Government of Ireland (2007), *National Action Place for Social Inclusion 2007-2016,* Dublin, Stationery Office.

Harrington, J., Perry, I., Lutomski, J., Morgan, K., McGee, H., Shelley, E., Watson, D. and Barry, M. (2008), *SLÁN 2007: Survey of Lifestyle, Attitudes and Nutrition in Ireland. Dietary Habits of the Irish Population,* Department of Health and Children Dublin, Stationery Office.

Healy, S. and M.L. Collins, M.L. (2006), "Work, Employment and Unemployment", in Healy, S., B. Reynolds and M.L. Collins, *Social Policy in Ireland: Principles, Practice and Problems*, Dublin, Liffey Press.

Healy, S. and B. Reynolds (2003), *"Christian Critique of Economic Policy and Practice"* in J.P. Mackey and E. McDonagh (eds.) *Religion and Politics in Ireland at the turn of the millennium*, Dublin, Columba Press.

Healy, S. and B. Reynolds (2003), *"Ireland and the Future of Europe – a social perspective"* in Reynolds, B. and S. Healy (eds.) *Ireland and the Future of Europe: leading the way towards inclusion?* Dublin, CORI.

Higher Education Authority (2012), *Springboard 2011 First Stage Evaluation* Dublin; HEA.

Higher Education Authority (2012), *Towards a Future Higher Education Landscape* Dublin; HEA.

Higher Education Authority (2011), *10/11 Higher Education Key Facts and Figures* Dublin; HEA.

Higher Education Authority (2011), *Report on the Social and Living Conditions of Higher Education Students in Ireland 2009/2010* Dublin, HEA.

Higher Education Authority (2010), *Review of Student Charge: August 2010* Dublin; HEA

Higher Education Authority (2010), *A Study of Progression in Irish Higher Education* Dublin; HEA.

Higher Education Authority (2010), *National Plan for Equity of Access to Higher Education 2008-2013 Mid-Term Review* Dublin, HEA.

Higher Education Authority (2010), *What do graduates do? The Class of 2008* Dublin, HEA.

H.M. Treasury (2004). *Financial Statement and Budget Report, 2004*. London, H.M. Treasury.

Hoegen, M. (2009), *Statistics and the quality of life. Measuring progress – a world beyond GDP,* Bonn, InWent.

Housing Agency (2011), *Housing Needs Assessment 2011* www.housing.ie
Accessed February 2012

Homeless Agency (2008) *Counted In, 2008 A report on the extent of homelessness in Dublin, http://www.homelessagency.ie/Research-and-Policy/Publications/Assessments-of-Homelessness/Counted-In,-2008.aspx* Accessed February 2012

Houses of the Oireachtas (2005). *Report on Voluntary Work to the Joint Oireachtas Committee on Arts, Sport, Tourism, Community, Rural and Gaeltacht Affairs.* Dublin, Houses of the Oireachtas.

Hyland, A. (2011), *Entry to Higher Education in Ireland in the 21ˢᵗ Century* (Discussion Paper for the NCCA/HEA Seminar 2011) Dublin, HEA.

IMD (2007), *IMD World Competitiveness Yearbook*, Lausanne, Switzerland.

Immigrant Council of Ireland (2011), *Taking Racism Seriously: Migrants experiences of violence, harassment and anti-social behaviour in the Dublin Area* Dublin, Immigrant Council of Ireland.

Indecon (2012), *Mid-Term Evaluation of the rural Development Programme Ireland (2007-2013)* http://ec.europa.eu/agriculture/rurdev/countries/irl/mte-rep-irl_en.pdf Accessed February 2012

Indecon International Economic Consultants (2010) *Assessment of Economic Impact of Sports in Ireland,* http://www.irishsportscouncil.ie/News_Events/Latest_News/2010_Archive/Indeconreport.pdf Accessed March 2012

Indecon (2005), *Indecon Review of Local Government Funding – Report commissioned by the Minister for Environment, Heritage and Local Government.* Dublin, Stationery Office.

Institute of Public Health, (2011), *Facing the Challenge. The Impact of Recession and Unemployment on Men's Health in Ireland* Dublin, Institute of Public Health in Ireland.

Institute of Public Health (2007), *"Fuel Poverty and Health"*, Dublin, IPH.

International Monetary Fund (2008), *World Economic Outlook*, Washington DC, IMF.

International Monetary Fund (2004), *World Economic Outlook*, Washington DC, IMF.

Inter-Departmental Mortgage Arrears Working Group, (2011) http://www.finance.gov.ie/documents/publications/reports/2011/mortgagearr2 .pdf Accessed February 2012

Irish Aid, *Annual Report 2010*, Dublin, Stationery Office.

Irish Farmers Association (2012), *Farm Income Review 2011* http://www.ifa.ie/LinkClick.aspx?fileticket=fduGptijnhw%3D&tabid=586 Accessed February 2012

Joint Oireachtas Committee on Arts, Sport, Tourism, Community, Rural and Gaeltacht Affairs (2005), *Volunteers and Volunteering in Ireland*, Dublin, available at http://www.volunteeringireland.ie/docs/volunteering_in_ireland_january_2005 .pdf Accessed March 2012

Kitchin, R. Gleeson, J. Keaveney, K. & O' Callaghan, C. (2010), A Haunted Landscape: Housing and Ghost Estates in Post Celtic Tiger Ireland *Working Paper Series no. 59, National Institute for Regional and Spatial Analysis,* NUI Maynooth.

International Monetary Fund (2004), *World Economic Outlook*, Washington DC, IMF

Leahy, E., S. Lyons, & R. Tol (2011), The Distributional Effects of Value Added Tax in Ireland. *The Economic and Social Review, Vol. 42, No. 2, Summer 2011, pp. 213-235*

Legal Aid Board (2010) Annual Report, http://www.legalaidboard.ie/lab/publishing.nsf/650f3eec0dfb990fca256921000 69854/0a605c18c2547a2b8025791b003e76c8/$FILE/LAB%20Annual%20Rep ort%202010%20Final%20-%20English.pdf Accessed March 2012

Lucas, K. Grosvenor, T. & Simpson, R. (2001), *Transport, the Environment and social exclusion,* Joseph Rowntree Foundation, York.

Lunn, P. and R. Layte (2009), *The Irish Sports Monitor Third Annual Report,* http://www.irishsportscouncil.ie/Research/The_Irish_Sports_Monitor/The_Iri sh_Sports_Monitor_2009/ISM_2009.pdf Accessed March 2012

Mallon, S. and S. Healy (2012), *Ireland and the Europe 2020 Strategy – Unemployment, Education and Poverty*. Dublin, Social Justice Ireland.

McCoy, S, Byrne, D, O'Connell, P, Kelly, E & C. Doherty (2010), *Hidden Disadvantage? A Study on the Low Participation in Higher Education by the Non-Manual Group* Dublin, HEA.

McCashin A (2000), *The Private Rented Sector in the 21ˢᵗ Century – Policy Choices.* Dublin, Threshold and St Pancras Housing Association

Mc Daid, S. & K. Cullen (2008), *ICT accessibility and social inclusion of people with disabilities and older people in Ireland: The economic and business dimensions,* http://www.cfit.ie/news-and-commentary-archive/22-wrc-research Accessed February 2012

McDonagh, J, Varley, T and Shortall, S (eds) (2009), *A living countryside?: the politics of sustainable development in rural Ireland;* Ashgate, England.

McGing, C (2012), *'Why do we need more women in politics and how do we get there'* presentation at "How to elect more women?" conference, Dublin Castle, 21 January 2012.

McGinnity, F. and H. Russell (2008), *Gender Inequalities in Time,* Dublin, ESRI.

McGrath, B., Rogers, M. & Gilligan, R. (2010), *Young People and Public libraries in Ireland: Issues and Opportunities,* Department of Health and Children, Dublin.

Morrone, Adolfo (2009), "The OECD Global Project on Measuring Progress and the challenge of assessing and measuring trust" in Reynolds, B. and Healy S. (eds.), *Beyond GDP: what is progress and how should it be measured,* Dublin.

National Anti-Poverty Strategy Review (2002), *Building an Inclusive Society* Dublin, Stationery Office.

National Anti-Poverty Strategy (1997), *Sharing in Progress,* Dublin, Stationery Office

National Disability Authority (2006), *Indecon Report in the Cost of a Disability,* Dublin, NDA.

National Economic and Social Council (2009), *Ireland's Five Part Crisis,* Dublin, NESC.

National Economic and Social Council (2006), *NESC Strategy 2006: People, Productivity and Purpose*, Dublin, NESC

National Economic and Social Council (2005), *The Welfare State*, Dublin, NESC.

National Economic and Social Council (2003), *An Investment in Quality: Services, Inclusion and Enterprise*, Dublin, NESC.

National Economic and Social Forum (2006), *Improving the Delivery of Quality public Services,* Dublin, NESF

National Office for Suicide Prevention (2010), *Annual Report 2010* Dublin.

National Traveller Accommodation Consultative Committee, (2010) *Annual Report 2010*
http://www.environ.ie/en/Publications/DevelopmentandHousing/Housing/Fil eDownLoad,28665,en.pdf Accessed February 2012

Niestroy, I (2005), *Sustaining Sustainability,* Brussels, EEAC.

Nolan, B. (2006), "*The EU's Social Inclusion Indicators and Their Implications for Ireland*", in Healy, S., B. Reynolds and M.L. Collins, Social Policy in Ireland: Principles, Practice and Problems, Dublin, Liffey Press.

OECD (2012), *Labour Force* 2012 Paris, OECD.

OECD (2012), OECD *Factbook 2011-2012: Economic, Environmental and Social Statistics* Paris, OECD Publishing.

OECD (2012), *Equity and Quality in Education: Supporting Disadvantaged Students and Schools Spotlight on Ireland* Paris, OECD.

OECD (2011) *How's Life? Measuring well –being* Paris, OECD Publishing.

OECD (2011), *Education at a Glance 2011: OECD Indicators* Paris, OECD Publishing.

OECD (2011), *Employment Outlook 2011* Paris, OECD Publishing.

OECD (2011) *Busan Partnership for Effective Development Cooperation*, available at www.busanhlf4.org Accessed March 2012

OECD (2010), *PISA 2009 Results: Ireland* OECD.

OECD (2010), *Revenue Statistics,* Paris, OECD.

OECD (2010), *Labour Force Statistics 1989-2009*, Paris, OECD.

OECD (2009), *Ireland: Development Assistance Committee (DAC) Peer Review*, Paris, OECD Publishing

OECD (2008), *Economic Survey of Ireland,* Paris, OECD Publishing.

OECD (2005), *Society at a Glance*, Paris, OECD Publishing.

OECD (2004), *OECD Factbook,* Paris, OECD Publishing.

Office of Minister for Children and Youth Affairs, (2010) *State of the Nation's Children Ireland 2010,* Government Publications, Dublin.

Office of the Refugee Applications Commissioner (2012), *Monthly Statistical Report January 2012* available at http://www.orac.ie/pdf/PDFStats/Monthly%20Statistics/2012/2012%2001%20 January%20ORAC%20monthly%20report.pdf Accessed March 2012

Office for Social Inclusion (2007), *National Action Plan for Social Inclusion 2007-2016.* Dublin; Stationery Office.

O'Siochru, E. (2004), "Land Value Tax: unfinished business" in B. Reynolds, and S. Healy (eds.) *A Fairer Tax System for a Fairer Ireland,* Dublin, CORI Justice Commission.

O'Sullivan, E. (2008) *Researching Homelessness in Ireland Explanations, Themes and Approaches* in, Downey, D. (eds.), *Perspectives on Irish Homelessness, Past Present and Future* The Homeless Agency, Dublin.

O'Toole, F. and N. Cahill (2006), "Taxation Policy and Reform", in Healy, S., B. Reynolds and M.L. Collins, *Social Policy in Ireland: Principles, Practice and Problems,* Dublin, Liffey Press.

Oxfam (2002), *Make Trade Fair Campaign,* available at www.maketradefair.com Accessed March 2012

Pavee Point, (2011) *Irish Travellers and Roma, Shadow Report, A response to Ireland's Third and Fourth Report on the International Convention on the Elimination of all Forms of Racial Discrimination (CERD),* Pavee Point Travellers Centre, Dublin.

Pope John Paul II, (1981), *Laborum Exercens, Encyclical Letter on Human Work,* Catholic Truth Society, London.

Pope Paul VI, (1967), *Populorum Progressio,*Vatican City, Rome

Private Residential Tenancies Board (2010), *Annual Report and Accounts 2010.* Dublin

Public Health Alliance for the Island of Ireland (2007), *Health Inequalities on the Island of Ireland – the facts, the causes, the remedies,* Dublin, PHAI.

Public Health Alliance for the Island of Ireland (2004), *Health in Ireland – An Unequal State,* Dublin, PHAI.

Rapple, C. (2004), "Refundable Tax Credits" in B. Reynolds, and S. Healy (eds.) *A Fairer Tax System for a Fairer Ireland,* Dublin, CORI Justice Commission.

Reception and Integration Agency (2011), *Annual Report 2010* available at http://www.ria.gov.ie/en/RIA/RIA%20Annual%20Report%202010.pdf/Files/RIA%20Annual%20Report%202010.pdf Accessed March 2012

Revenue Commissioners (2011), *Analysis of High Income Individual's Restriction 2009,* Dublin, Stationery Office.

Revenue Commissioners (2011), *Statistical Report 2010,* Dublin, Stationery Office.

Revenue Commissioners (various), *Effective Tax Rates for High Earning Individuals,* Dublin, Stationery Office.

Reynolds, B. and S. Healy (eds.) (2009), *Beyond GDP: what is progress and how should it be measured,* Dublin.

Robertson, J (2007), *The New Economics of Sustainable Development* report to the European Commission, Brussels.

Russell, H., B. Maitre & N. Donnelly (2011), *Financial Exclusion and Over-indebtedness in Irish Households* Dublin, Department of Community, Equality and Gaeltacht Affairs.

Safefood (2011), *Food on a Low Income,* Safefood.

Scarpetta, S, Sonnett, A & Manfredi, T (2010), *Rising Youth Unemployment during the Crisis: How to Prevent Negative Long Term Consequences on a Generation?* Paris; OECD Social, Employment and Migration Working Papers.

Scott S. and Eakins, J. (2002), *Distributive effects of carbon taxes,* paper presented to ESRI conference entitled "The sky's the limit: efficient and fair policies on global warming" December, Dublin.

Social Justice Ireland (2011), *Analysis and Critique of Budget 2012.* Dublin, Social Justice Ireland.

Social Justice Ireland (2011), *Policy Briefing: Budget Choices a fairer future is possible.* Dublin, Social Justice Ireland.

Social Justice Ireland (2010), *Building a Fairer Taxation System: The Working Poor and the Cost of Refundable Tax Credits.* Dublin, Social Justice Ireland.

Society of St. Vincent de Paul, Combat Poverty Agency and Crosscare (2004), *Food Poverty and Policy.* Dublin, Combat Poverty Agency.

Steering Group on Financial Inclusion (2011), *Strategy for Financial Inclusion Final Report* available at http://www.finance.gov.ie/documents/publications/reports/2011/Fininclusrepo rt2011.pdf Accessed February 2012

Stiglitz Commission (2008), *Report by the Commission on the Measurement of Economic Performance and Social Progress*: Paris available at http://www.stiglitz-sen-fitoussi.fr/documents/rapport_anglais.pdf Accessed February 2012

Sweeney, P. (2004), "Corporation Tax: leading the race to the bottom" in B. Reynolds, and S. Healy (eds.) *A Fairer Tax System for a Fairer Ireland*, Dublin, CORI Justice Commission.

Teagasc (2012), *Outlook 2012 Economic Prospects for Agriculture* http://www.teagasc.ie/publications/2012/1069/Outlook_2012.pdf Accessed February 2012

Tegasc (2011), *National Farm Survey 2010* Teagasc available at http://www.teagasc.ie/publications/2011/1016/NFS10.pdf Accessed March 2012

The Irish Sports Council, (2009), *Building Sport for Life: The Next Phase The Irish Sports Council's Strategy 2009-2011*
http://www.irishsportscouncil.ie/About_Us/Strategy/ISC_Strategy_2009-2011.pdf Accessed February 2012

UNAIDS (2011), *Data Tables*, United Nations Publications.

UNEP (2011), *Decoupling natural resource use and environmental impacts from economic growth, A Report of the Working Group on Decoupling to the International Resource Panel*; UNEP Paris available at
http://www.unep.org/resourcepanel/decoupling/files/pdf/decoupling_report_english.pdf Accessed February 2012

UNEP (2011), *Keeping track of our changing environment from RIO to RIO +20 1992-2012;* UNEP Nairobi.

United Nations High Commission on Refugees (2011), *UNHCR Statistical Yearbook 2010* United Nations.

United Nations Human Rights Council (2011), *Report of the independent expert on human rights and extreme poverty, Magdalena Sepulveda Carmona: Mission to Ireland* United Nations.

United Nations Development Programme (2011), *Millennium Development Goals Report 2011*, New York: United Nations Publications.

United Nations Development Programme (2011), *Human Development Report 2011*, New York: United Nations Publications.

United Nations Development Programme (2003), *Human Development Report*, New York: United Nations Publications.

UK Statistics Authority and Department of Work and Pensions (2011), *Statistics on National Insurance Number Allocations to Adult Overseas Nationals Entering the UK* London, UK Statistics Authority.

Vatican Council II, (1966), *Gaudium et Spes*, Orbis, New York.

Vincentian Partnership for Social Justice (2010), *Minimum Essential Budgets for Households in Rural Areas*, Dublin, VPSJ.

Vincentian Partnership for Social Justice (2006), *Minimum Essential Budgets for Six Households*, Dublin, VPSJ.

Wackernagel, M., Shulz N.B., Deumling D., Linares A.C., Jenkins M., Kapos V., Monfreda C., Loh J., Myers N., Norgaard R. and Randers J. (2002), Tracking the ecological overshoot of the human economy in *Proceedings of the National Academy of Sciences,* Vol. 99, Issue 14, 9266-9271

Weir, S & Archer P (2011), *A Report on the First Phase of the Evaluation of DEIS* Dublin, Educational Research Centre.

Whelan, C.T., R. Layte, B. Maitre, B. Gannon, B. Nolan, W. Watson, J. Williams (2003) *Monitoring Poverty Trends in Ireland: Results from the 2001 Living in Ireland Survey.* ESRI Dublin, Policy Research Series No. 51, December.

WHO (2011), *World Conference on the Social Determinants of Health, Rio Political Declaration on Social Determinants of Health,* WHO.

WHO (2001), *Mental Health: New Understanding, New Hope,* Geneva, Switzerland

Wilkinson, R. & M. Mormot, (eds) (2003), *Social Determinants of Health, The Solid facts (2nd ed),* World Health Organisation, Denmark.

Woods, C.B., Tannehill D. Quinlan, A., Moyna, N., and Walsh, J., (2010), *The Children's Sport Participation and Physical Activity Study (CSPPA).* Research Report No 1. School of Health and Human Performance, Dublin City University and The Irish Sports Council, Dublin, Ireland.

World Commission on Environment and Development (1987), *Our Common Future (the Bruntland Report),* Oxford University Press.

World Economic Forum (2011), *Global Competitiveness Report 2011-12.* www.weforum.org.

World Economic Forum (2008), *Global Competitiveness Report 2008-09.* www.weforum.org.

World Economic Forum (2003), *Global Competitiveness Report 2002-03.* www.weforum.org.

ONLINE DATABASES [accessed March 2012]

CSO QNHS online database, web address: http://www.cso.ie/px

CSO Live Register online database, web address: http://www.cso.ie/px

CSO Statistical Data Bank, web address
http://www.cso.ie/px/pxeirestat/statire/SelectTable/Omrade0.asp?Planguage=0

Eurostat Income and Living Conditions online database, web address:
http://epp.eurostat.ec.europa.eu

OECD, Government revenue, expenditure and main aggregates:
http://stats.oecd.org/Index.aspx?DatasetCode=SNA_TABLE11